Social Tagging in a Linked Data Environment

Social Tagging in a Linked Data Environment

Edited by

Diane Rasmussen Pennington and Louise F. Spiteri

© This compilation: Diane Rasmussen Pennington and Louise F. Spiteri 2019
The chapters: the contributors 2019

Published by Facet Publishing,
7 Ridgmount Street, London WC1E 7AE
www.facetpublishing.co.uk

Facet Publishing is wholly owned by CILIP: the Library and Information Association.

British Library Cataloguing in Publication Data
A catalogue record for this book is available from the British Library.

ISBN 978-1-78330-338-0 (paperback)
ISBN 978-1-78330-339-7 (hardback)
ISBN 978-1-78330-340-3 (e-book)

First published 2019

Text printed on FSC accredited material.

Typeset from editors' files in 11/14 pt Elegant Garamond and Myriad Pro by Flagholme Publishing Services
Printed and made in Great Britain by CPI Group (UK) Ltd, Croydon, CR0 4YY

Contents

List of figures and tables

Figures

Tables

Contributors

Laurie Bonnici

Dr Laurie Bonnici's interests lie in the construction and use of knowledge by members in specialised social media groups. Laurie researches the adoption of second-hand knowledge as information source in critical decision contexts specifically related to health and personal welfare. The broad aim of her research is to provide tools and strategies to evaluate information constructed in social media contexts and to understand how second-hand knowledge facilitates decisions, particularly in contexts of formal knowledge deficits. Laurie is Associate Professor at the University of Alabama and currently a visiting faculty scholar at the Social Media Lab at Ryerson University, Toronto.

Laura Cagnazzo

Laura Francesca Cagnazzo received her BA degree in Conservation of Cultural Heritage in 2008, from the Universita' D'Annunzio in Chieti (Italy) and her MA in History of Arts from the same institution in 2010. After spending some time travelling, in 2015 Laura obtained a role as Library Assistant at the Royal Society of Chemistry in London. Laura received her MSc in Information and Library Studies (with Distinction) from the University of Strathclyde in Glasgow in 2017. Laura's MSc project focused on the investigation of current use and implementation of linked data across European national libraries.

Ryan Deschamps

Dr Ryan Deschamps is a postdoctoral scholar in the Department of History at the University of Waterloo, Ontario (Canada). Ryan's research interests include digital history, data analytics and the influence of technology on public policy agenda setting. Along with policy research using Twitter and web data for analysis, Ryan has participated in the development of the Archives Unleashed Toolkit (AUT), Graphpass, Archives Unleashed Cloud (AUK) and a number of software projects to support the use of computational methods in the humanities and social sciences.

Max Dobson

Max Dobson is an information professional working with the Scottish Maritime Museum's archive. Max's academic work focuses on the development of online folksonomies and the history of transformative works. Max prefers to research new topics in the familiar surroundings of a local library.

Kishor John

Dr Kishor John is an Officer on Special Duty at the Department of Higher Education, Government of Madhya Pradesh, Bhopal (India). Kishor is also an Associate Professor of Library and Information Science at the Government TRS College, Centre of Excellence, Rewa MP, with 24 years' experience of teaching and administrative experience and seven years' experience as a librarian. Kishor's key areas of research interests are information literacy, Web 2.0 and information technology applications. Kishor has authored several research articles, has presented at over twenty national and international conferences and has edited three books.

Sanjay Khanna

Sanjay Khanna, MBA, CMC and CKM (Certified Knowledge Manager) has worked with multiple organizations in creating and implementing enterprise information management (EIM) frameworks and strategies. Sanjay taught an Information Systems course (MBA) at St Mary's University in Halifax, Nova Scotia (Canada), focusing on the importance of aligning information technology to the overall strategic objectives of the organization. Sanjay volunteers his time as a member of the Board of Trustees for the IWK Foundation based in Halifax, Nova Scotia. In his spare time, Sanjay enjoys basketball, exploring new foods and supporting his daughter on her quest of becoming an accomplished swimmer.

Jinxuan Ma

Dr Jinxuan Ma is an Assistant Professor in the School of Library and Information Management at Emporia State University, United States. She is interested in examining how people's personal variables shape their health information-seeking behaviours and what contextual factors or tools can bridge users' barriers in seeking, sharing and assessing information for informed health decision making. Her broad research subjects include anti-vaccination information on Facebook, curriculum development of health science librarianship, public library community health engagement, dementia caregivers during cognitive-behavioural therapy for depression and information technology education across high school and colleges.

Diane Rasmussen Pennington

Dr Diane Rasmussen Pennington is a Lecturer in Information Science at the University of Strathclyde (Scotland). Diane worked as a corporate IT professional and then a systems librarian before becoming a full-time academic in 2005. Diane's PhD dissertation focused on social-tagging practices of photojournalism professionals and tagging has remained a central focus of her research. Diane served as the Association for Information Science & Technology's Social Media Manager from 2014 to 2016. Diane teaches in the areas of social media for libraries, library technology systems, organization of information and cataloguing and classification.

Louise F. Spiteri

Dr Louise Spiteri is Associate Professor at the School of Information Management, Dalhousie University, Halifax, Nova Scotia (Canada). Louise's areas of research interest focus on social tagging, user-generated metadata, discovery systems, classification systems and taxonomies. Louise's most recent research has focused on the creation of taxonomies for affect, based on an analysis of user-generated reviews and content in public library catalogue records. Louise teaches in the areas of metadata, cataloguing, knowledge management, information management and records management.

Sue Yeon Syn

Dr Sue Yeon Syn is an Associate Professor in the Department of Library and Information Science at the Catholic University of America, Washington, D. C. (United States). Sue's research focuses on user information behaviour in the aspect of users' involvement in information creation and sharing on the social web. Sue applies various methods to make the best use of user-generated information for different purposes such as information organization, including resource descriptions, information seeking and information sharing. Sue's recent publications address understanding user-generated tags for digital humanities collections, personal information management and social tags for linked data and analysing users' information behaviours for health information seeking and sharing.

Chapter 1

Introduction: the continuing evolution of social tagging

Diane Rasmussen Pennington and Louise F. Spiteri

The genesis of an idea: Louise's perspective

I was introduced to the concept of social tagging when I was asked by Library and Archives Canada to speak about folksonomies at a metadata conference in Ottawa in 2005. Although I had heard the term, which was coined by Thomas Vander Wal (2007) in 2004, I did not know much about it, but I was certainly interested in the opportunity to learn more about this concept. As with most scholars in this field, my first in-depth exposure to the concept of social tagging was Adam Mathes' now classic article on folksonomies (2004). My area of expertise was in the areas of cataloguing, classification and thesaurus construction, all areas where language and descriptors are carefully chosen and controlled by professional information managers. I became intrigued at the possibilities that social tagging could provide to our carefully curated metadata records in libraries, which was the basis for my first article on the topic on social tagging (Spiteri, 2006) and which opened a new area of research interest that has continued to grow over the years.

For several years, I have studied the contributions of social tagging to library discovery systems (Spiteri, 2006; 2007; 2009); my interest in this particular topic was inspired by courses I teach in the areas of the organization of information, cataloguing and classification, as well as my involvement in social reading sites such as LibraryThing and Goodreads. I was struck by the dynamic and interactive nature of these reading sites: readers voluntarily edited metadata records for books, added social tags to describe content, created and shared reading lists, engaged in discussions with other readers, wrote reviews of items they had read and responded to reviews written by others. I was struck also by the difference between these dynamic sites and the static nature of the public library catalogues that I used, and used as exemplars for my students. These catalogues contained carefully constructed metadata records, using established and standardised metadata standards such as Anglo-American Cataloguing Rules and, more recently, Resource Description and Access, codified via the MARC (MAchine Readable Cataloging) framework and standard Library of Congress Subject Headings to describe the content and genre of a work. These practices are what I taught – and continue to teach – my students. I have never questioned the importance of these standardised records to describe the collection of a library; in fact, I continue to promote them actively to my students and colleagues. In comparison to the social reading sites, however, the library catalogues I used, both personally and professionally, struck me as somewhat sterile: To use social media language, they *pushed* information, but did not allow for any interaction with the users of the catalogue. From this observation emerged my interest in using social tagging as a means to help library discovery systems become social spaces – a concept I explored closely with another colleague, Laurel Tarulli (Spiteri and Tarulli, 2012; Tarulli and Spiteri, 2012) – where users could input and interact with content, in much the same way as they can in social reading sites.

In Spiteri (2006) I suggested a research agenda for social tagging in the following areas: what is the tagging behaviour of people who use folksonomies? Why do people choose the tags they use; what motivates them to modify these tags; how often do they modify them? How are folksonomies used communally? How do folksonomies foster consensus in the use of tags? How does the community affect which tags are used and how? To my delight, these questions have been explored comprehensively over the years and have produced a rich corpus of knowledge in the field of social tagging. The internet is moving rapidly from the social web embodied in Web 2.0, to the semantic web (Web 3.0), where information resources are linked in such a way as to make them comprehensible to both machines and humans. The Web 3.0 environment provides us with the opportunity to explore the evolving role of social tagging (including hashtags, geotags and the like) in the semantic web. Hashtags, for example, have expanded beyond the scope of Twitter to include many other platforms, such as Facebook, Instagram, Pinterest, WordPress, Tumblr, YouTube and so forth; one single hashtag can thus link information resources from a variety of platforms, as will be discussed later in this chapter. This book is an exploration of the role that social tagging can play in helping to link people and information resources in a linked data environment. I am pleased to share this journey with my co-editor, Dr Diane Rasmussen Pennington, whose research focuses on information engagement and includes social media, digital consumer health information, digital photograph representation and online education pedagogies.

The genesis of an idea: Diane's perspective

I was thrilled when Dr Louise Spiteri invited me to co-edit this book with her. As we both teach information organization and cataloguing and we overlap in certain areas of research such as social tagging and linked data, it has been the perfect opportunity to assemble a group of authors together who are also thinking in similar terms towards this emerging area of research and practice in LIS and on the internet more generally.

I was first exposed to the concept of social tagging when I read my PhD co-advisor's book *Explorations in Indexing and Abstracting: Pointing, Virtue and Power* (O'Connor, 1996). At this time, social tagging as a term did not exist, but he explained his vision of a 'community memory interface' that would address the difficulty of searching for and describing the aboutness of pictures using words (O'Connor, 1996, 151). It would allow library patrons to contribute their own 'functional or adjectival descriptors' to a digital collection of pictures and the system would develop user profiles over time through these descriptors, both of which would lead to relevant searching and browsing results based on similar user profiles. His empirical research into this idea, in which he elicited descriptors about a set of images from a group of people, found that people struggled with assigning Library of Congress Subject Heading types of terms to the pictures. Instead, they enjoyed assigning non-restricted captions, such as 'That's what friends are for!', many of which moved beyond basic topicality, including emotions, metaphors and so on.

This research, as well as Brian O'Connor's follow-up related work (Greisdorf and O'Connor, 2002; O'Connor and Wyatt, 2004), inspired me to write my PhD dissertation on photojournalism professionals' preferences for description and representation within their online photograph archives, published under my former name, Diane Rasmussen Neal (Neal, 2006; Neal, 2008). Among other interesting results, I found that they needed and wanted control over the descriptors used to index and search for their images, but this control was not readily available in their systems. I wrote my dissertation around the time when social tagging was becoming a phenomenon, as Louise mentioned above (Mathes, 2004; Vander Wal, 2007), but was not yet widespread. Therefore, I used the term 'user-assigned descriptors' (UADs) in my dissertation research, rather than 'social tagging', to label photojournalism professionals' assignment of their own terms to their own pictures. I argued for the need to combine UADs and vocabulary control, such as automatic suggestions of UADs, to allow for the best possible mix of freedom and reliability.

My further research in this area has continued to explore the use of social tagging for non-textual documents – not only for images, but also music and video – especially the potential for describing, searching and browsing by users' emotions (Neal et al., 2009; Lee and Neal, 2010; Knautz et al., 2011; Neal, 2012, Pennington, 2016). Through these studies, I am finding that social tagging needs to be collective as well as individual; if a user wants to find a song that makes them feel happy on a Friday afternoon, some elements may be somewhat universal within a Western context (major key, fast tempo, uplifting lyrics) but may also be personal (individual tastes in and associations with, music differ among individuals).

I had first heard the terms linked data and semantic web discussed generally at the 2004 Association for Information Science & Technology conference, when Sir Tim Berners-Lee described his vision for the semantic web in his remarkable plenary session. My deeper explorations into it began when I was asked to present about linked data to Library and Archives Canada, when I was still working at Western University in London, Ontario, Canada, just like Louise's early introductions to social tagging. Developing a substantial understanding of linked data required considerable effort, but eventually I realised the similar goals of social tagging and linked data: while the practices and approaches are different, each one has the power to establish meaningfully unique connections between online documents, whether that document is an image, a social media post, a written text or anything else we might find online (Neal, 2010). When used together, their socio-technological power will be even stronger.

I have been working in collaboration with my students to explore the barriers and opportunities associated with implementing linked data in library and information settings. I introduced this in my 2016 *CILIP Update* article (Pennington, 2016) and I am actively writing and presenting in this area (Pennington and Cagnazzo, 2018). Some obstacles are institutional in nature, such as lack of staff and funding. Other issues involve a mismatch in technical implementations at different sites, which makes the semantic sharing of data envisioned difficult. I am, however, optimistic about the ability of social tagging within linked data, based on my own reflections as well as the work presented in this book. This is because the true power inherent in social tagging lies within the multitude of users and they therefore control the rich semantic connections made possible through the technology of linked data. This is ultimately Brian O'Connor's 'community memory interface becoming alive', although in a much different implementation than he could have imagined in the mid-1990s. I am privileged to have trained under his vision and to be a researcher in the area now during this rapid evolution.

Related works

Other excellent books have been published about social tagging. Gene Smith's 2007 publication, *Tagging: people-powered metadata for the social web*, introduces the concept of social tagging, how it could be used to improve the user experience and its role in information architecture and online communities. *Folksonomies, Indexing and Retrieval in Web 2.0* (Peters and Becker, 2009) discusses the applications, strengths and weaknesses of social tagging in collaborative information services and examines how established methods of knowledge representation and models of information retrieval could be translated to this new format. *Recommender Systems for Social Tagging Systems* by Marinho et al. (2012) examines the three recommendation modes in social tagging systems: users, resources or tags and surveys recommender systems built to serve social tagging systems. *Recommender Systems and the Social Web: leveraging tagging data for recommender systems* (Gedikli, 2013) looks more broadly at recommender systems designed to provide personalised recommendations of products or services to users and how social tagging data can be used to improve these systems. *Folksonomies Social Tagging: a clear and comprehensive guide* (Blokdyk, 2017) provides practical suggestions for how to make the best and most efficient use of social tagging to organise business and project activities and processes.

Themes covered in this book

The books discussed above have provided valuable insight into the role of social tagging in information discovery. The emphasis of social tagging has often tended to focus on discrete applications, such as social bookmarking sites, library discovery systems, blogs and so forth. This book extends the scope of social tagging to examine its contribution to the semantic web as a form of linked data. 'The Web has evolved from a global information space of linked documents to one where both documents and data are linked. Underpinning this evolution is a set of best practices for publishing and connecting structured data on the Web known as Linked Data' (Bizer, Heath and Berners-Lee, 2009, 1–2). Web documents often contain data that cannot be understood easily by machines. The semantic web is about facilitating access to web data by making it available in machine-readable formats that allow both people and machines to collect this data. Linked data is a way of creating links between data from different sources across different platforms. Berners-Lee (2006) proposed the following linked data principles for publishing web data to enable a single global data space:

1   Use uniform resource identifiers (URIs) as names for things.
2   Use URIs so that people can look up those names.
3   When someone looks up a URI, provide useful information, using standards such as Resource Description Framework (RDF) and SPARQL.
4   Include links to other URIs so that they can discover more things.

There are several examples of linked data repositories, such as DBpedia (https://en.wikipedia.org/wiki/DBpedia), which extracts structured content from the Wikipedia site; the FOAF (Friend Of A Friend) ontology (www.foaf-project.org), which describes persons, their activities and their relations to other people and objects; and GeoNames (www.geonames.org), which contains over 10,000,000 geographical names. These datasets contain discrete units of information such as names, locations, music albums, film titles and so forth. This book explores social tagging as a potential form of linked data; hashtags, for example, can already link content across a variety of platforms, such as Twitter, Facebook, Tumblr, WordPress, Instagram, YouTube and Pinterest. So, for example, a hashtag on a specific topic such as #PreventingType2 (preventing Type 2 diabetes) can link us to information from the following resources:

- Twitter (http://bit.ly/2jfWsJZ)
- YouTube playlist (http://bit.ly/2jk6Osz)
- Instagram (http://bit.ly/2rbfllC)
- Google Image results (http://bit.ly/2jfWRMv), which lead to several other results
- individual articles (e.g. http://bit.ly/2r5XEEf and http://bit.ly/2jfXGVB)
- a variety of Facebook pages (http://bit.ly/2jht9H9)
- Storify (http://bit.ly/2rbKl52).

In the next two chapters, Laura Cagnazzo and Sue Yeon Syn look more broadly at the role of social tagging in a linked data environment. These chapters examine the main features of the semantic web and linked data and on the relationship between the semantic web and Web 2.0. Cagnazzo examines a series of frameworks designed to enhance social tagging and to overcome some of its limitations through linked data. Syn explores efforts to format social tags as RDF triples and to define the semantic meanings and relationships of tags. Although these efforts are still limited, they successfully demonstrate that formatting tags with RDF-based models can allow tags to contribute to linked data in the semantic web environment.

Ryan Deschamps examines the connection between public policy and hashtags via three Canadian case studies. Deschamps shows the close connection between social tagging and Canada's political and social context and highlights the need for a more comprehensive framework for inclusion of online interactions to social change.

Louise Spiteri explores the potential contributions of hashtags to library discovery systems via an examination of three hashtags and their equivalent Library of Congress Subject Headings. Spiteri suggests that hashtags can serve as an important way to link library resource discovery systems to information resources in a variety of social media services, such as Twitter, Facebook, Instagram, Pinterest and YouTube.

Laurie Bonnici and Jinxuan Ma analyse how effectively hashtags have been used within two special information-based interest groups on Facebook and develop user instruction and intervention strategies for use in Facebook. Bonnici and Ma suggest that linking works is an important way to consolidate information relevance and currency in the process of contextualising discoverability of information across social dimensions.

Max Dobson examines the use of tagging as a form of linked data in an online fan community. Fandoms have created functioning online communities and relationships around particular tags and use searchable tags and descriptive tags to make the content in fandom spaces more easily searchable.

Diane Rasmussen Pennington uses dementia as a case study to demonstrate how user-generated hashtags, or other forms of surrogate representation, could be applied in a linked data environment in order to improve access to care, resources, people and other needs. This could enable people to make more informed decisions about treatment and lifestyle options.

Sanjay Khanna explores how social tags can serve to link content within enterprises. Social tags can contribute to greater information discovery in the workplace and can be an important way to link employees through shared expertise and interests. Khanna examines also the role of social tagging in linking communities of practice within an enterprise.

Given the continued importance of recommender systems in the creation of tagged content, Kishor John discusses social tagging recommender systems. As information resources on the web continue to grow and particularly those that involve collaborative – or social – input, recommender systems can play an increasingly important role in helping people to tag resources by reducing the cognitive burden that this task may involve. Further, by suggesting tags based on the analysis of user input, recommender systems can help create more structured tagging vocabularies that reduce the drawbacks with which tags are often associated, such as polysemy, synonymy and homonymy. John examines the different types of recommender systems, highlighting their strengths and weaknesses:

- collaborative filtering recommender systems
- content-based recommender systems
- context-based recommender systems
- demographic recommender systems
- knowledge-based recommender systems
- hybrid recommender systems.

This book examines the themes above through the lens of academic researchers and practitioners. The authors reflect different geographic perspectives from the United Kingdom, India, Canada, and the United States. Intended readers include practicing library and information professionals who implement electronic access to collections, such as cataloguers and systems developers, as well as information architects and web developers. Of value to researchers and practitioners is the potential to link social tags, hashtags, or geotags to the RDF data model. So, for example, social tags could form an ontology that could be used in semantic web applications, which would allow different web-based resources to be linked to a stable URI for the social tags. This use could have practical implications as well to practitioners who wish to link resources from different platforms via social tags or hashtags. The chapters could lead to an increased understanding of user behaviour about how social tags, hashtags, or geotags could assist in the design of better and more intuitive user interfaces. Instructors and students in different academic disciplines, such as library and information science, computer science, informatics, and information management, could apply the themes of this book to courses, particularly in the areas of metadata, taxonomies, ontologies, information architecture, records and information management and bibliographic description.

Since its genesis as a concept in 2004, social tagging continues to provide a wealth and variety of exciting research avenues. With the continued growth of the Web 3.0 semantic web, social tagging can provide an increasingly important way to categorise and store information resources to make them understandable to both humans and computers.

References

Berners-Lee, T. (2006) *Linked Data – Design Issues*, www.w3.org/DesignIssues/LinkedData.html.

Bizer, C., Heath, T. and Berners-Lee, T. (2009) Linked Data – The Story So Far, *International Journal on Semantic Web and Information Systems*, 5, 1–22.

Blokdyk, G. (2017) *Folksonomies Social Tagging: a clear and comprehensive guide*, CreateSpace Independent Publishing Platform.

Gedikli, F. (2013) *Recommender Systems and the Social Web: leveraging tagging data for recommender systems*, Springer.

Greisdorf, H. and O'Connor, B. (2002) Modelling What Users See When They Look at Images: a cognitive viewpoint, *Journal of Documentation*, 58, 6–29.

Knautz, K., Neal, D. R., Schmidt, S., Siebenlist, T. and Stock, W. G. (2011) Finding Emotional-laden Resources on the World Wide Web, *Information*, 2, 217–46.

Lee, H-J. and Neal, D. (2010) A New Model for Semantic Photograph Description, *Journal of Information Science*, 36, 547–65.

Marinho, L. B., Hotho, A., Jäschke, R., Nanopoulos, A., Rendle, S., Schmidt-Thieme, L., Stumme, G. and Symeonidis, P. (2012) *Recommender Systems for Social Tagging Systems*, Springer.

Mathes, A. (2004) *Folksonomies – Cooperative Classification and Communication Through Shared Metadata*, http://adammathes.com/academic/computer-mediated-communication/folksonomies.html.

Neal, D. R. (2006) *News Photography Image Retrieval Practices: locus of control in two contexts*, University of North Texas.

Neal, D. R. (2008) News Photographers, Librarians, Tags and Controlled Vocabularies: balancing the forces, *Journal of Library Metadata*, 8, 199–219.

Neal, D. R., Campbell, A., Neal, J., Little, C., Stroud-Mathews, A., Hill, S. and Bouknight-Lyons, C. (2009) 'Musical Facets, Tags and Emotion: Can We Agree?' In *Proceedings of the 2009 iConference, Chapel Hill, NC*.

Neal, D. R. (2010) Emotion-Based Tags in Photographic Documents: the interplay of text, image and social influence, *Canadian Journal of Information and Library Science*, 34, 329–53.

Neal, D. R. (ed.) (2012) *Indexing and Retrieval of Non-Text Information*, De Gruyter Saur.

O'Connor, B. C. (1996) *Explorations in Indexing and Abstracting: Pointing, Virtue and Power*, Libraries Unlimited.

O'Connor, B. C. and Wyatt, R. B. (2004) *Photo Provocations: thinking in, with and about photographs*, Scarecrow Press.

Pennington, D. R. (2016, July/August). Demystifying linked data: are you ready for what's next?, *CILIP Update*, 34-6.

Pennington, D. R. (2016) 'The most passionate cover I've seen': emotional information in fan-created U2 music videos, *Journal of Documentation*, **72**, 569–90.

Pennington, D. R. and Cagnazzo, L. (2018) Relationship Status: libraries and linked data in Europe. In *Proceedings of the 15th International ISKO Conference, Porto, Portugal*, ISKO.

Peters, I. and Becker, P. (2009) *Folksonomies, Indexing and Retrieval in Web 2.0*, De Gruyter Saur.

Smith, G. (2007) *Tagging: people-powered metadata for the social web*, New Riders.

Spiteri, L. F. (2006) The Use of Folksonomies in Public Library Catalogues, *The Serials Librarian*, **51**, 75–89.

Spiteri, L. F. (2007) The Structure and Form of Folksonomy Tags: the road to the public library catalog, *Information Technology and Libraries*, **27**, 13–25.

Spiteri, L. F. (2009) The Impact of Social Cataloguing Sites on the Construction of Bibliographic Records in the Public Library Catalogue, *Cataloging & Classification Quarterly*, **47**, 52–73.

Spiteri, L. F. and Tarulli, L. (2012) Social Discovery Systems in Public Libraries: if we build them, will they come?, *Library Trends*, **61**, 132–47.

Tarulli, L. and Spiteri, L. F. (2012) 'Library Catalogues of the Future: a social space and collaborative tool?, *Library Trends*, **61**, 107–181.

Vander Wal, T. (2007) *Folksonomy Coinage and Definition*, www.vanderwal.net/folksonomy.html.

Chapter 2

Tagging the semantic web: combining Web 2.0 and Web 3.0

Laura Cagnazzo

Introduction

As Sir Tim Berners-Lee states in his TED talk *The Next Web of Open, Linked Data* (TED, 2009), the topic of linked data does not exclusively pertain to expert information technology (IT) developers, but to all of us. Data are a substantial part of our everyday lives more than we may realise: all the actions we carry out on social networking sites produce data, which are then reused for various purposes by major organizations. At present, an authentic data exchange across social networks has not been achieved, as data are still locked in silos, preventing interoperability. Berners-Lee offers an example of the potential of combining social tagging with linked data requirements, explaining how he could add information about the location where the TED talk was occurring on the OpenStreetMap, a wiki resource (www.openstreetmap.org/#map=5/54.910/-3.432). People add content to the wiki and contribute to the creation of new information in a linked environment: this is the concept underlying linked data expressed at its simplest level.

The aim of this chapter is to illustrate examples of applications in which social tagging is combined with linked data and semantic web principles, in order to demonstrate how social tagging can benefit from linked data and vice versa. The chapter begins with a brief explanation of the main features of the semantic web and linked data. After an outline of the key principles characterising Web 2.0, attention will focus on the relationship, tested and potential, between the semantic web and Web 2.0, through the outline of frameworks and applications used to investigate and attempt such integration. All the frameworks presented aim to enhance social tagging, overcoming its main flaws through linked data imple-mentation. On the other hand, the popularity and the collaborative character of social tagging help the expansion of the semantic web. Reflections on future directions and recommendations for best practice will conclude this chapter.

The semantic web and linked data

When Tim Berners-Lee invented the web, his intention was to create a virtual environment where anyone could add and share documents. He soon realised, however, that his idea had not developed in the way he had hoped and he decided to work on a new project, with the aim of having data on the web, rather than only documents: 'I want to think about a world where everybody has put data on the web . . . and I'm calling that "linked data"' (TED, 2009). The primary concept that underlies linked data is building relationships. The ultimate goal of linked data is to provide a seamless experience of navigating a 'web of trust', where users can make their own contribution (Library of Congress, 2012). The broader idea to which linked data relates is the semantic web (also known as Web 3.0), whose purpose is to communicate the content of web resources in a way that is understandable by computers (Pennington, 2016). If machines are enabled to comprehend the meaning of web content, they can build relationships between resources, enrich users' experience and improve discoverability. The semantic web was first presented as an extension of the existing world wide web, in which information is provided with well defined meaning, with the benefit of a better co-operation between humans and machines (Berners-Lee, Hendler and Lassila, 2001; Baker et al., 2011).

Beyond a slight ambiguity and uncertainty generated by the use of these terms, a common interpretation is that while the semantic web reflects the overall, high-level vision, the term linked data, used for the first time by Berners-Lee in 2006, conveys the practice and methods to concretise this vision (Heath, 2009; Tallerås, 2013; Calaresu and Shiri, 2015).

The key requirements for linked data to be classified as such were clearly stated by Berners-Lee (2006) in his four rules, known as the linked data principles:

1 Use uniform resource identifiers (URIs) as names for things.
2 Use hypertext transfer protocol (HTTP) URIs so that people can look up those names.
3 When someone looks up a URI, provide useful information, using the standards Resource Description Framework (RDF) and SPARQL.
4 Include links to other URIs, so that users can discover more things.

To summarise, linked data is a way of connecting related data across the web using URIs, HTTP and RDF (Heath, 2009).

The semantic web idea has been spreading unceasingly over the last decade. Started in 2007 and supported by the W3C (World Wide Web Consortium) Semantic Web Education and Outreach Group, the Linking Open Data Project was generated with the goal of identifying existing datasets available under open licences, converting them into RDF and publishing them on the web, with links to other data sources (Bizer, 2009).

The Linking Open Data (LOD) cloud diagram in Figure 2.1 shows datasets published as linked data by the Linking Open Data community project. The metadata published in the LOD cloud is collected and curated by contributors to the DataHub (https://datahub.io), a free data management platform by Open Knowledge International, where organizations can publish and manage collections of their data (http://lod-cloud.net). At the source of such initiatives is the Open Data Movement, whose aim is to make data freely available to everyone (W3C, 2017a). A comparison between earliest and latest versions of the diagram (Figures 2.1 and 2.2 on the next page) offers a graphic visualisation of the growth and application of the semantic web across different fields. Each node in the diagram represents a distinct dataset published as linked data. The arcs indicate links between items in two datasets. Heavier arcs correspond to a greater number of links and bidirectional arcs indicate that each dataset contains outward links to the other (Bizer, 2009).

One of the central interlinking hubs of the LOD diagram is DBpedia, an important resource in the linked data context, generated from community efforts to extract structured information from Wikipedia and make this information available on the web (DBpedia, 2017). At 2014, the DBpedia corpus consisted of 3 billion RDF triples. The overall count has recently reached 23 billion triples (Freudenberg, 2017). Linking to DBpedia enables connections to other datasets and enriched information, thanks to the network of resources gravitating around DBpedia (Choudhury, Breslin and Passant, 2009).

Multinational companies, such as Google and Facebook, have embraced the semantic web concept and have realised the benefits it conveys. In 2010, Facebook developed the Open Graph Protocol, a framework that allows any web page to have the same functionality as any other object on Facebook (Open Graph Protocol, 2017). This protocol is the mechanism behind the popular thumbs-up of the Facebook Like tab on various websites. Built on RDFa, a W3C recommendation that adds a set of attribute-level extensions for encoding structured data within web documents, the Open Graph Protocol enables site

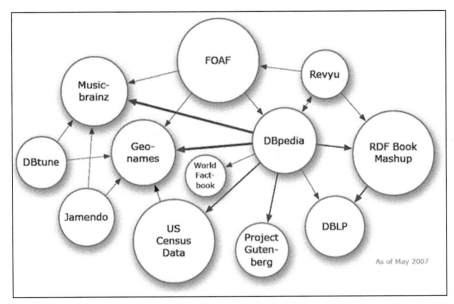

Figure 2.1 *First version of the LOD cloud diagram published in 2007* (Cyganiak and Jentzsch, 2007)

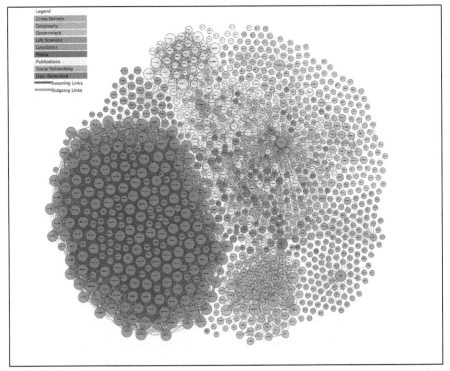

Figure 2.2 *Latest version of the LOD cloud diagram published in August 2017* (Abele et al., 2017)

owners to determine how entities are described on the social network (Heath and Bizer, 2011).

Google adopted linked data technologies to design the Google Knowledge Graph, which provides information drawn from various sources to millions of users every day (Pennington, 2016). It is visually represented by a panel appearing on the right side of the screen when searching for a popular topic or person (see Figure 2.3). The Knowledge Graph is presented by Google as a tool to make information search easier and quicker and to obtain more relevant results: this is

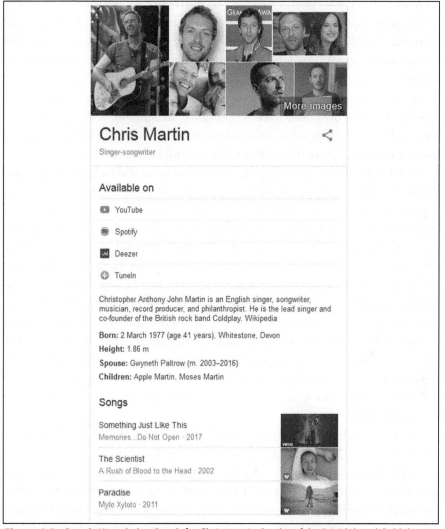

Figure 2.3 *Google Knowledge Graph for Chris Martin, leader of the British band Coldplay (https://goo.gl/ZL7feK)*

achieved thanks to the disambiguation ability of linked data and its capacity of 'understanding' information in a way that is closer to human comprehension than traditional search engines (Singhal, 2012).

Web 2.0

Prior to diving into the heart of the matter, an introduction to Web 2.0 principles is necessary. The term Web 2.0 was made popular by Tim O'Reilly in 2005 to indicate a collaborative platform where users can publish content and subscribe to news and other services. Compared to the traditional web, Web 2.0 is more social, more open and cheaper, since it is nourished by user-created content (Breslin, 2009). This second-generation web provides the space for communities to create knowledge and solve problems, through common efforts, towards the achievement of shared objectives (Singh and Shadbolt, 2013). In Web 2.0, users play the role of not only consumers, but also of creators of content, through blogs and wikis, for instance; in addition, with tagging, users can index any form of content they publish, such as images, videos, presentations and posts (Choudhury, Breslin and Passant, 2009).

Social network sites (SNS) are one of the most successful Web 2.0 applications. Inspired by the six degrees of separation theory, according to which each of us is separated from a perfect stranger by a chain of six other people (Milgram, 1967), SNS were designed to foster relations between individuals who share mutual interests (Downes, 2005). Under the label of SNS are gathered all those 'applications that foster collaborative and participative behaviour of profiled human users'; users can easily interact with each other toward a common goal (Maccioni, 2013, 207). Since their appearance, SNS such as Facebook and Twitter have become an integral part of everyday life for millions of users; their success is attributable to the ease of communication they allow (Papadakis et al., 2017). The main issue presented by applications driven by large communities, as is the case with SNS, is the challenge of organising content and finding relevant information across the wide amount of data continuously generated (Singh and Shadbolt, 2013).

Amongst the most interesting characteristic features of Web 2.0 and introduced by Delicious in 2003, is tagging: this tool enables users, who have already contributed to creating content, to also organise it and describe it, by selecting and adding metadata (Passant and Laublet, 2008). Tagging moves the focus from an object-centred to a user-centred approach, allowing the expression of multiple perspectives (Stuart, 2011). Its enormous success derives from the fact that it does not require any expertise from the users' side (Kim et al., 2008). Focusing their attention on video resources, which are increasingly created and uploaded to the web by users, Choudhury, Breslin and Passant (2009) identified different types of user-generated tags: functional tags (meaningful and mostly single keywords); noisy tags (words which are arbitrarily chosen and unrelated to the image); compound tags (tags consisting of more words without spacing); and emerging tags (of recent creation). An additional category is represented by subjective/ judgemental tags, which express users' opinions rather than reflect the video content.

This collaborative form of contribution in the form of social tagging is common to most of the Web 2.0 resources (Breslin, 2009), from social network sites, such as Flickr (www.flickr.com) and YouTube (www.youtube.com), which allow free selection of keywords, to social bookmarking sites, such as Diigo (www.diigo.com) and Delicious (now discontinued), which enable users to annotate web documents with URIs (Stuart, 2011). A discussion of the limitations of social tagging may be found below in the section on semantic annotation.

Web 2.0 meets the semantic web

Born approximately at the same time and united by the concept of sharing, Web 2.0 and Web 3.0 successively took two very different evolutionary paths, which saw Web 2.0 quickly proliferating through successful applications, such as wikis, blogs, tagging systems and social networks; in no way comparable to the slow and less clamorous development of the semantic web (Greaves, 2007).

Bizer (2009) highlights a key difference between the two web versions: while Web 2.0 resources are usually based on a fixed set of data sources, applications employing linked data allow the discovery of new data sources at runtime (by following links at data level) and therefore the retrieval of more relevant and comprehensive answers as new data sources are published on the web. Nevertheless, other web areas have seen a convergence of semantic web technologies and Web 2.0 applications (Breslin, 2009):

- semantic blogs: blogging is enhanced with semantic web tools and transformed from individuals' individual entries to rich information context (Cayzer, 2001)
- semantic wikis, such as Semantic MediaWiki, an extension of MediaWiki (the wiki application supporting Wikipedia), which allows the addition of semantic annotations to wiki content (www.semantic-mediawiki.org/wiki/Semantic_MediaWiki)
- semantic social networks: in this case, semantic web principles are applied

to social networks and online social media, e.g., FOAF (Friend Of A Friend, www.foaf-project.org)
- semantic desktop, a collective term gathering frameworks that aim to improve computers' user interface and data-handling abilities through semantic web technologies (Wikipedia, 2017a).

All these applications fall under the umbrella of the metaweb, or social semantic information space. Furthermore, Breslin indicates that folksonomies are the result of a step taken by Web 2.0 towards the semantic web. Folksonomies are internet-based information organization/classification systems developed collaboratively by a community of users that collects tags created and assigned by people to web content (Kruk et al., 2009). The term 'folksonomy' was created by Vander Wal in 2004 to describe a key feature of the social tagging phenomenon: 'the result of personal free tagging of information and objects (anything with a URL) for one's own retrieval. The tagging is done in a social environment (usually shared and open to others)' (García-Silva et al., 2012, 2). Unlike thesauri and taxonomies, which are controlled vocabularies created by experts, folksonomies are generated by users, with the advantage of rapidly adapting to changes in terminology. Users tend to stabilise the vocabulary adopted to tag a resource, thanks to several successive iterations and mechanisms of tag suggestion based on previously assigned tags. Problems arise, however, from the lack of uniform representation affecting folksonomies, which hinder the sharing and reuse of tags (García-Silva et al., 2012). To provide a solution to issues such as synonymy and polysemy, efforts have been directed to either the creation of ontologies to gather and organise tags used in folksonomies or to linking folksonomies to external resources that can explicate the meaning of tags (García-Silva et al., 2012). 'Semantic enrichment of folksonomies can bridge the gap between the uncontrolled and flat structures typically found in user-generated content and structures provided by the semantic web' (Choudhury, Breslin and Passant, 2009, 747).

In their forecast on the future of social networks Breslin and Decker (2007) identify a key issue related to SNS, namely, the lack of interoperability between different sites (data silos). According to the authors, the semantic web provides agreed-upon formats to describe content, people and their relationships, enabling a better interoperability across SNS. Steps in this direction have produced initiatives such as FOAF, SIOC (Semantically Interlinked Online Communities), http://rdfs.org/sioc/spec, and the previously mentioned Semantic Media Wiki, an example of an ontology-enhanced wiki (Breslin and Decker,

2007). Further details about these initiatives follow later in this chapter.

More predictions on possible future developments of SNS were advanced in 2008 by Yeung et al., including Sir Tim Berners-Lee. The authors start from the consideration that the way SNS were designed at the time raised privacy issues; for example, the fact that users had limited control of their data and the reuse by SNS for their financial advantage. The initial design of SNS as information silos hindered their interoperability and did not allow the exchange and sharing of information amongst different services. The proposed solution is a decentralised framework, based on open technologies such as linked data. A decentralised approach, argue Yeung et al., enables users to better control the way their data are presented and what information is shared, even with third parties. Furthermore, a decentralised approach allows better interoperability among various sites. The suggested framework implies that each user is assigned a Web ID in the form of a URI. Relationships with other people are established through the FOAF vocabulary (e.g. with the 'foaf:knows' property). All data are stored on a local server and can be accessed with the Web ID. The downside of this system, as well as other newly introduced frameworks, is the disruption and change of habits required from users (Yeung et al., 2008).

Social semantic web

Theories have been formulated along the path towards the potential integration of Web 2.0 applications and semantic web principles. The social semantic web envisions the outcome of the encounter between Web 2.0 and Web 3.0. The concept refers to a data space on the web where information produced by users is enriched and shaped through semantic web technologies (Maccioni, 2013). The social semantic web idea stemmed from the aim of formalising the meaning of the vast amount of data generated by SNS in order to make it machine-understandable. An interesting example of the steps taken towards the social semantic web realisation is represented by the Social Graph: promoted and implemented by Facebook through the Open Graph, it offers representations of social networks by depicting personal relations of internet users (Wikipedia, 2017b).

Although the benefits of applying semantic web principles to Web 2.0 sites are acknowledged, primarily via the identification of each user through a URI, there are still several challenges hindering the spread of the social semantic web. The fact that each social network provides a set of APIs (application programming interfaces) which, once queried, return data in different formats (e.g. JSON, XML), hampers the integration of data from various sources. The solution suggested by Maccioni (2013) implies that SNS players agree on adopting a framework able to produce data natively in RDF format and automatically integrate them. In this way, social data are able to feed the semantic web.

A related idea, more specifically focused on SNS, is the semantic social network, the product of the combination of semantic web and social networks (Downes, 2005). The two primary requirements for semantic social network are that:

- descriptions of people and possibly of their relationships, expressed in XML or RDF should be made publicly available on the web
- references to these descriptions should be gathered in XML or RDF files.

The foundations of such theories lie on the identification of the advantages offered by Web 3.0, which provides the means to overcome problems such as ambiguity, thanks to the unique identification of entities through URIs and allows the linkage of concepts of the same type, even if they are expressed in different languages. All these features contribute to highly enhanced information retrieval (Passant and Laublet, 2008). The requirements are far more complex than free tagging, however (Passant and Laublet, 2008; Miličić, 2008). Adding semantics to tagging data implies an agreed attribution of meaning across communities (Kim et al., 2008). The next section will focus on the concepts of semantic annotation and semantic tagging.

Semantic annotation

Under the label of semantic annotation are collected linguistic annotations (e.g. semantic classes) and user annotations (e.g. tags). With the aid of increasingly refined tools that enable automatic extraction of information from texts, semantic annotation can play a fundamental role in information retrieval. Alonso, Kamps and Karlgren argue that the full potential of semantic annotations can be fulfilled only if they are matched by more complex, articulate queries from the users' side. An interesting reflection offered by the authors is that improvements in information retrieval are increasingly harder to achieve, as they are more dependent on cognitive aspects, such as the need to understand content and query and the relation between the two, rather than computational. The debate remains between the aspiration towards better organised information and the need to facilitate the users' task at a given place and time (Alonso, Kamps and Karlgren, 2015).

The W3C Web Annotation Working Group, whose goal was to 'develop a set of specifications for an interoperable, sharable, distributed Web Annotation architecture' (W3C, 2017c), published its recommendations for web annotation, which include:

- web annotation data model: describes a structured model and format (expressed in JSON) that enables annotations to be reused and shared across various resources
- web annotation vocabulary: specifies RDF properties, classes and entities used in the web annotation data model
- web annotation protocol: describes the processes to create and manage annotations in a method consistent with further W3C standards.

As previously stated, tagging is one of the most successful phenomena generated by Web 2.0. Nonetheless, the ease of use offered by free tagging is counterbalanced by the several obstacles hindering the employment of tags as information organization and retrieval tools. The literature presents a thorough evaluation of the role, benefits and flaws of social tagging.

Stuart (2011) identifies the advantages and disadvantages of tagging: on the one hand, tagging offers the means to classify web content that would otherwise lack any classification or, alternatively, it can add new perspectives where a classification is already in place. On the other hand, tags have not been applied to all web documents and have been used mainly at the document level, rather than the data level. Furthermore, one of the risks connected to crowdsourced resources is the possibility of them being filled with malicious material, as was the case with the *Los Angeles Times'* wikitorial: the newly launched site was suspended after being vandalised with pornographic material (Stuart, 2011).

The unstructured nature of tags is the reason behind their usefulness, since terms can be freely selected or created, rather than picked from controlled vocabularies (Rattenbury, Good and Naaman, 2007). Nevertheless, the uncontrolled nature of tags negatively affects their potential role in information retrieval (Kim et al., 2008). Ambiguity, heterogeneity (the same concept is linked to more than one tag, often occurring when several users adopt different tags, (Passant, 2010)) and lack of relationships between tags (which hinders the identification of concepts related to a given entry point) are tags' primary flaws. While their meaning can be interpreted by humans, tags do not convey any semantics about the concepts they represent that can be understood by machines (Passant and Laublet, 2008). Furthermore, they do not provide information on the meaning of words, thus factors such as polysemy (the same word has different meanings, e.g.

'orange' for colour and fruit), misspelling variations (e.g. 'labour/labor') and synonymy (different words can express the same concept, e.g. 'movie/film') represent limitations to the use of tags to identify and retrieve information (Miličić, 2008).

A common solution suggested to enhance the potential of free tagging in the areas of knowledge organization and information retrieval is the application of semantic web principles to Web 2.0 sites. Semantic tagging, which consists of tagging content with URIs, offers several advantages: it solves the issue of ambiguity, as tags are linked to unambiguous URIs. Semantic tagging allows the reuse of tags across different applications, enabling the exchange and sharing of data. More importantly, semantic tagging enables data enrichment, through the linkage of tags with external resources, such as DBpedia and FOAF (Passant, 2008).

Focusing on the technical requirements of creating semantic tags, García-Silva et al. (2012) propose a three-step process to associate semantics to tags:

1 data selection and cleaning
2 identifying context of tagging activities, which will help associate tags with semantic concepts or related tags
3 disambiguation, such as grouping tags according to the resources they refer to, or to the users who created them.

According to García-Silva et al., different techniques can be applied to associate semantics to tags, such as: grouping tags with similar meaning (i.e. clustering); linking tags to ontologies, in order to disambiguate their meaning; and hybrid approaches combining ontologies and clustering. The next section presents several examples of the results that the application of semantic web technologies to Web 2.0 resources can deliver.

Applying semantic web principles to Web 2.0

Miličić (2008) identifies the key advantages that semantic technology has to offer to Web 2.0 resources:

- enabling a tag standardisation by adding a meaning
- connecting Web 2.0 and the semantic web with semantic tags
- connecting Wikipedia and social bookmarking
- reusing RDF data available on the web
- facilitating information integration and knowledge discovery

- facilitating communication between different services
- enabling auto-classification and multilingual semantic tagging.

Several approaches have been suggested to demonstrate how Web 2.0 applications could benefit from semantic web technologies. In this section some frameworks are outlined for integrating Web 2.0 and 3.0.

Hashtags are a particular type of tag, introduced by Twitter, to create and follow threads of discussion. They have been adopted by several social websites to categorise content and have emerged as one of the most common features of the social web (Papadakis et al., 2017). Twitter provides an API that allows users to identify and follow the most popular tags; thus, hashtags can be seen as tools to identify trending topics. In addition, hashtags are useful in organising, indexing and sharing tweets, as well as making them more discoverable. Hashtags are defined by users and employed to index tweets. Searchable through Twitter, Google and other services, hashtags represent a powerful classification tool for the social web: they form a particular type of vocabulary created by users of the SNS and are, to some extent, controlled, as the most popular tags are evaluated by users before being reused (Papadakis et al., 2017). The framework suggested by Papadakis et al. aims to build a digital library service that gathers popular Twitter hashtags in order to identify relevant resources. The steps taken to achieve this goal are:

1 collecting trending hashtags
2 checking spelling
3 funnelling hashtags to DBpedia to discover related terms
4 matching the enriched set of terms against the subject index of a digital library.

The authors affirmed their trust in the potential of semantic web technologies to bring a certain degree of control and organization to the noise of user-generated content in SNS, thus enabling the development of new services in the context of digital libraries, based on sourcing information from crowdsourcing websites.

The problems derived from the lack of space delimiters in hashtags, since words are combined to express compound concepts, encouraged Bansal, Bansal and Varma (2015) to propose a framework for the segmentation of hashtags into their component parts, the identification of semantics and the linkage of each element to related Wikipedia content. It is essential that the hashtag segmentation takes into account the context of the tweet to obtain meaningful results. To assist in this phase of the process, the system produces a ranked list of probable segmentations from which to select. The positive outcomes of the experiment show that this suggested method of extracting semantic content from hashtags can facilitate topic detection and search on social media.

LODr is an application, inspired by the Linking Open Data principles previously stated, that converts normal, free-text tags into semantically enriched tags, facilitating the transition between Web 2.0 and Web 3.0 (Passant, 2008). In this application, users are provided with personal profiles, with information expressed in RDF, where they can access and modify all their tagged data. Users contribute to the semantic enrichment of tags by assigning them either new URIs, or those from an existing list. According to Passant, the key advantage of LODr is the combination of Web 2.0 collaborative principles with semantic web modelling principles in a way that is hidden to users and which leads to easy tagging processes and highly improved discoverability. The heterogeneity of tagging systems can be problematic, as each SNS usually adopts different tagging processes. Flickr, for example, uses a media:category attribute, Bibsonomy uses dc:subject and Twitter tagging is expressed through hashtags in user posts (Passant, 2008).

Singh and Shadbolt (2013) examined StackOverflow (https://stackoverflow. com), a crowdsourcing social network, where users contribute to generate content. The authors discussed how the application of linked data and semantic web technologies in StackOverflow contributes to an improvement in topic recognition and disambiguation of concepts and allows for better categorisation, search and discovery of information across the website.

In his overview of linked data principles and their application to a wide range of resources, Bizer (2009) discussed the various categories of linked data applications that form the LOD cloud diagram and briefly reviewed cases of applications that make available, as linked data, metadata related to user-generated content from Web 2.0 sites. Amongst the applications mentioned, Flickr wrappr, Zemanta and Faviki will be considered in this section. There are several cases of applications that attempt to solve the problems of ambiguity deriving from the adoption of free-tagging with semantic web technologies. All these annotation tools aim to connect the traditional web with the semantic web, enriching users' experience.

Flickr wrappr, a project of the Freie Universität in Berlin (http://wifo5-03.informatik.uni-mannheim.de/flickrwrappr), was designed to extend DBpedia with RDF links to photographs posted on Flickr and to generate collections of

Flickr photographs to represent DBpedia concepts (Becker and Bizer, 2009). Flickr is one of the largest public photograph repositories, where users are free to apply a wide range of tags to the pictures they upload. Becker and Bizer focused on the analysis of geotags – tags that express geographical information – to demonstrate the potential benefits of applying Web 3.0 technologies to free-tagging. When users are able to assign any keyword to their pictures, they may adopt the same geotag for an entire album of photographs, even when the photographs depict various locations. Alternatively, users may use different languages or inaccurate terms to describe a photograph. In order to overcome these problems and obtain relevant results, search by geographic location is combined with search by topic: DBpedia can match geographical locations and topic and provide multilingual labels. Flickr wrappr enabled links connecting DBpedia concepts with photo collections (using 'dbpedia:hasPhotoCollection' RDF links) through semantic web browsers, such as Marbles (http://mes.github.io/marbles). Another option offered by Flickr wrappr allowed geographic queries; in this case, information was drawn from Flickr world map (www.flickr.com/map) rather than from DBpedia (Becker and Bizer, 2009).

Flickr has provided a field for several experiments based on the combination of semantic web principles and Web 2.0 sites. Rattenbury, Good and Naaman (2007) extracted event and place semantics from tags assigned to Flickr photographs to facilitate image search, tag suggestions and automated association between photos and place/event metadata. The study suggested that finding a way for mapping of tags to events and places may improve search and allow the realisation of various photography-related tasks (e.g. creating gazetteers).

Zemanta (www.zemanta.com) is a private company that provides content marketing strategies, whose initial focus was the adoption of semantic web technologies to help bloggers, publishers and content creators to make their publications easier to find, through a system of tags and links that would assist the identification of related material (Wikipedia, 2017c). This application provides tools for semi-automatic annotation of blog posts with links to DBpedia, MusicBrainz (https://musicbrainz.org) and other datasets. Zemanta is one of the services on which Faviki relied to link multilingual content to the English version of Wikipedia (Miličić, 2008).

Faviki was a social bookmarking tool that enabled users to adopt Wikipedia concepts to annotate web content. Social bookmarking services have become a popular way to share knowledge. They are usually designed according to one of these two models: sharing tagged information, allowing users to attribute tags to any resource they find interesting (this is the case of Delicious and Connotea);

or sharing folders with bookmarks, enabling users to filter information in a collaborative way (Grzonkowski et al., 2009). In Faviki, bookmarks could be easily added through a user-friendly interface by one of these methods:

- typing a word in the input field and selecting one of the Wikipedia concepts from the autocomplete list
- selecting one of the auto-suggested concepts
- searching for a Wikipedia concept on search engines
- browsing through users' tags already adopted for other web pages.

Helpful features of Faviki provided information on tags (e.g. abstracts, images and links to Wikipedia articles), which helped users to easily browse tags (e.g. tag clouds) and automatically showed related tags. Furthermore, the automatic classification of tags allowed the identification of broader topics (Miličić, 2008). Another advantage of this tool, which is generally recognised as a main benefit of the application of semantic web technologies, was the support of multilingual semantic tagging: even when web pages are tagged with words in different languages, semantic links still bring together related concepts (Miličić, 2008). What made Faviki more efficient than other bookmarking tools was that it granted all users access to the same collection of tags. Adopting concepts from Wikipedia means solving issues related to polysemy and synonymy, thanks to Wikipedia's disambiguating and redirecting functions. In order to keep the service up-to-date, Faviki was periodically synchronised with the latest DBpedia releases.

Another example of semantically enhanced tagging is offered by MOAT (Meaning Of A Tag), www.w3.org/2001/sw/wiki/MOAT, a framework designed to bridge the gap between free tagging and semantic annotations (Passant and Laublet, 2008) and to provide a semantic web model to define the meaning of tags in a machine-readable way (Kim et al, 2008). To reach this goal, MOAT defines the global (list of all meanings that can relate to a tag in a folksonomy) and local (meaning of a tag in a specific tagging context) meanings of tags. MOAT consists of two main elements:

1   an ontology representing the relationships between tag and resource URIs, extending the tag ontology; and
2   a collaborative, open-source framework that enables the sharing of tags and their meanings within a community (Passant, 2008; Kim et al., 2008).

Defining the meaning of tags remains a problem, however. To this end, Passant and Laublet designed an architecture to help users to choose the URIs to attribute to a specific tag, as well as to select a URI from an existing set in a given tagging context. In MOAT, users are not confronted with complex RDF structures, so they can still enjoy the simplicity of free-tagging; but since each tag is linked to a URI, problems such as ambiguity (a single tag can relate to more than one URI) and heterogeneity (various tags can be linked to a single URI) can be solved. By allowing linkages to reference datasets such as GeoNames (www.geonames.org) and DBpedia, MOAT enables tag enrichment and identification of relevant content (Kim et al., 2008).

Ontologies

Ontologies are one of the primary components of the semantic web, along with URIs and RDF. Defined as 'collections of information', ontologies can improve retrieval and enable search engines to find specific concepts, rather than ambiguous keywords (Berners-Lee, Hendler and Lassila, 2001). Ontologies provide a shared understanding of a domain, gathering together its important notions, expressed in RDF and establishing their relationships, including hierarchical (Bizer, 2009; Antoniou et al., 2012). The definition of properties and classes through the reference to widely adopted vocabularies offers the basis for meaning- and content-sharing across domains (Tallerås, 2013).

Goldbeck and Rothstein (2008) discussed how by using the FOAF (Friend Of A Friend) ontology and applying Web 3.0 principles, users' profiles from various SNS can be merged, thereby overcoming the problem of data fragmentation. Written in the OWL ontology (www.w3.org/OWL), FOAF is a very successful semantic web framework that provides a standard vocabulary for describing personal information, social connections and all the details needed in the social network context. Two of the mostly widely-used FOAF properties are: *foaf:Person*, to describe people and *foaf:knows*, to establish social connections between people.

Efforts have been directed to the development of vocabularies that could assist the integration between social tagging and semantic web requirements. TagOntology described the relation between an agent, a resource and tag(s). Each tag was assigned a URI, allowing for the establishment of connections and identification of similarities between tags. Properties were used from existing vocabularies FOAF, Dublin Core, (http://dublincore.org) and SKOS, (Simple Knowledge Organization System), www.w3.org/2004/02/skos, (Kim et al., 2008). Developed by Tom Gruber (2005), the TagOntology identified four key concepts:

1   term: a phrase that describes a document that is machine and human readable
2   document: an entity tagged and identified by a URI
3   tagger: person/agent carrying out the act of tagging
4   tagged: statement declaring that the document has been tagged with a term by a tagger (Grzonkowski et al., 2009).

In addition, Gruber proposed two properties:

1   polarity: enables users to filter and refuse bad tags
2   source: describes the application or site where the tagging occurred.

An initiative based on the adoption of the TagOntology was TagCommons, which aimed to develop mechanisms for facilitating the sharing of tagging data and improve interoperability, in order to make accessible various tagging sources across sites and applications (Grzonkowski et al., 2009). A similar project is the SIOC ontology: both initiatives defined minimal concepts to enable data interchange across different systems. Nevertheless, SIOC is a more abstract framework, which took into account community metadata, while TagCommons focused on the process of tagging (Grzonkowski et al., 2009). The SIOC project points to the benefits derived from users' collaboration to link together related online discussions, topics and people (Breslin and Decker, 2007).

Another initiative similar to TagCommons was int.ere.st, which allowed the 'aggregation of Social Semantic Cloud of Tags (SCOT) ontologies from tagging sites based on persons, objects or tags' (Grzonkowski et al., 2009, 135). Through int.ere.st, users could share SCOT ontologies and identify similar tagging patterns or persons based on their tags, through a tool for tag meta-searches (Grzonkowski et al., 2009). The SCOT ontology aims to describe the structure and semantics of tagging data, in order to facilitate data sharing across social applications (Kim et al., 2008).

In order to actually achieve interoperability, alignment between the various ontologies adopted is essential to allow the use of the same tags across different resources (Kim et al., 2008). The effort of unifying existing tagging ontologies, such as MOAT and TagOntology, has produced the Modular Unified Tagging Ontology (MUTO), http://muto.socialtagging.org/core/v1.html, an ontology for folksonomies and tags, supporting various forms of tagging – e.g. semantic, automatic, group, etc. (Lohmann, 2011). Aligned with vocabularies such as SIOC and SKOS, MUTO is based on the idea that anything can be tagged, provided that the entity has a URI. Tagging creators are identifiable through their user accounts.

Image tagging systems

This section outlines examples of applications aimed at the semantic enrichment of web videos and images. Image retrieval follows mainly two approaches: content-based, which focuses on the visual features of the image and annotation-based, which allows users to add metadata to content (Im and Park, 2015). Annotation approaches can imply the selection of tagging terms from ontologies, such as OWL and WordNet (https://wordnet.princeton.edu) or, alternatively, a collaborative tagging system, where many users can suggest concepts (Im and Park, 2015). In the content-based approach, low-level visual features, which can be automatically extracted, are used to represent images and to retrieve similar ones (Jeong, Hong and Lee, 2013). Although less time-consuming, this method suffers from a major problem, the semantic gap, which refers to the 'inconsistency between the high-level abstraction from images and the low-level visual features' (Jeong, Hong and Lee, 2013, 452). Attempts at improving the results of image search based on folksonomies have not proved satisfactory, due to the limitations of social tags identified previously. A solution to solve the problems related to tag-based image retrieval involves calculating the tag's rank, that is, the tag's position, according to the relatedness between each tag and an image (Jeong, Hong and Lee, 2013). Tag ranking reflects the tag's relevance with respect to the image: the higher the ranking value, the more relevant the tag is to the image (Im and Park, 2015).

To explain the benefits that semantic enrichment can bring to tagging spaces, Choudhury, Breslin and Passant (2009) offer the following example: if videos are tagged with *New York city*, *nyc* and *big apple*, using one of the tags will only retrieve resources tagged with the exact match. On the other hand, if all the tags are linked to the same concept, which is uniquely identified by a URI, the search will disambiguate the terms and retrieve related concepts.

The study conducted by Jeong, Hong and Lee considered Flickr samples in order to demonstrate the efficacy of the i-TagRanker, an image tag ranking system. The authors argued that the lack of order in assigning free tags to an image means a lack of information on the grade of relevance between a tag and the resource. The purpose of the i-TagRanker is, in fact, to establish an order that reflects the relevance of tags to an image. The system proposed consists of two main phases:

1 tag propagation: given an untagged image, collect most relevant tags for similar images in the database and attribute them to the untagged image
2 tag ranking: relevance of each tag to an image is measured and ranked using WordNet (https://wordnet.princeton.edu).

Choudhury, Breslin and Passant elaborated a framework based on the application of semantic web principles to YouTube tag spaces. The process of semantically enriching multimedia content has the potential to bridge the gap between uncontrolled and flat structures, typical of user-generated content and semantic web structures. The ease of creating and uploading videos on the web has contributed to an exponential increase in multimedia resources. The main problem identified by the authors, which reflects the key challenges of the various frameworks outlined in this chapter, is that the free selection of annotation terms implies ambiguous and subjective choices, which could hinder the identification of related information. Lack of structure and of control over the descriptions exclude the possibility of interoperability at the content level (Choudhury, Breslin and Passant, 2009). The three main phases for this framework are:

1 context analysis and tag expansion, that is, expanding the context where tags come from, adding social, temporal, geographical contexts
2 tag ranking
3 concept matching and integration with the LOD cloud, via DBpedia.

Tag ranking is necessary to assign an order to the various types of tags associated with each video. The next step consists of linking the enriched data to the LOD resources (Choudhury, Breslin and Passant, 2009). The study showed several benefits of applying semantic web principles to tag spaces. In particular, linking tags to external resources (e.g. DBpedia) improves their reliability as content descriptors. At the same time, the connection established with other datasets enables the discovery of related concepts, enriching users' experience. Furthermore, ambiguities due to subjective choices of keywords are highly reduced. Thanks to the association of related concepts, it is possible to determine a hierarchical structure of categories, which allows a more detailed description of the video content.

A similar framework was suggested by Im and Park (2015) with Linked Tag, a semi-automatic image annotation system that aims to enrich tags with semantic relationships. The starting point is, as for the framework suggested by Choudhury, Breslin and Passant, the consideration of the challenges that free-tagging poses to information retrieval. Linked Tag presents the advantage of eliminating the manual annotation efforts; in addition, relationships between tags are established, allowing a better representation of the semantics of images than tag-based annotations (Im and Park, 2015). What is common to the two frameworks is the adoption of RDF, the linkage to DBpedia concepts and the elaboration of tag ranking systems/algorithms. An extra service offered by Linked Tag is the SPARQL query processing available for image retrieval, which offers the advantage of identifying images on the basis of visual characteristics, as well as of semantic information (Im and Park, 2015). SPARQL is one of the W3C standards, a query language for RDF that allows manipulation and retrieval of data from the database of RDF triples (W3C, 2017b; Stuart, 2011).

Hildebrand and van Ossenbruggen proposed a semi-automatic process to attribute meaning to tags by linking them to concepts hosted in the LOD cloud. In this case, the starting point is Waisda? (https://github.com/beeldengeluid/waisda), a video labelling game initiated by the Netherlands Institute for Sound and Vision. The goal of the game is to enable users to add their own tags to video content, in order to facilitate access. Nonetheless, as mentioned for other applications, the uncontrolled nature of tags permitted by the game hinders long-term access to information (Hildebrand and van Ossenbruggen, 2012). A process called *reconciliation* helps solve the problems of free-tagging; it provides a unique interpretation of a concept by linking it to existing vocabularies. The Freebase (now Wikidata, www.wikidata.org) and Europeana (www.europeana.eu) reconciliation services were adopted by Hildebrand and van Ossenbruggen in their experiment. The authors attempted an integration of Waisda? with reconciliation services, with the goal of improving tagging quality and thus information retrieval. To achieve this target, they implemented an interface that allowed users to select from a list of the most relevant and appropriate tags to the content of the video. The inspiration for this framework came from Google Refine (now OpenRefine, http://openrefine.org), a tool for enhancing data quality, that reconciles data values to concepts from external sources. This framework is intended to be a semi-automatic service, where users are asked to select the most appropriate term from a list of candidate concepts. Although it is feasible to reach an automatic linkage of tags to LOD cloud concepts, as happens for YouTube videos and Flickr photographs, Hildebrand and van Ossenbruggen argued that no algorithm will ever be so precise as to satisfy the high-quality standards of long term archival preservation. Therefore, human assessment will always be needed. The authors formulated recommendations to achieve better results in the semi-automatic linkage of tags to LOD concepts:

- Reconcile tags against multiple sources at the same time, in order to obtain best coverage.
- To better use combined results, merge duplicates into a single suggestion.
- Present results of reconciliation divided into different categories, such as people, locations, subjects, so that users focus on the correct type.
- Use a pre-processing phase, which merges similar tags, to deal with mistakes and spelling variations.
- Present higher-precision results at the top of the list of choices, to facilitate the selection of the most appropriate concept.

Recommendations and conclusion

It is interesting to note how a decade ago there were doubts about the further development of SNS and a high trust in the potential of semantic web as the perfect solution to solve problems related to information retrieval and to unlock the full potential of Web 2.0. The forecast by Breslin and Decker (2007) of the development of SNS toward object-centred networks, thus embracing semantic web technologies to assist information discoverability and retrieval, could have not been further from reality.

Questioning the contribution of semantic web technologies to Web 2.0 applications, Greaves (2007) highlighted that, to foster the growth of Web 2.0, designers have allowed the use of natural-language tags, thus sacrificing the formality and precision required by the semantic web. The author argued that the complex nature of Web 3.0, together with the challenges of co-ordinating meaning between large amounts of constantly changing information, has hindered the adoption of semantic web technologies within Web 2.0 applications. At the time when Greaves wrote his article, the situation was such that, even if Web 2.0 tools were needed to create or use machine-readable content, software developers would have opted for easier semantic representation, such as XML, rather than OWL and RDF. The situation today has not really changed. One of the key reasons behind the success of Web 2.0 over the semantic web derives from financial considerations: Web 2.0 sites are relatively more affordable to maintain, since they are fed by users' contributions and use open sources for software development (Greaves, 2007). The economic proliferation of Web 2.0 could be further boosted by the semantic web, which offers the means to gather and manage users' content and, above all, a 'powerful query and reasoning capability' (Greaves, 2007, 96).

Most of the semantic tagging applications described in this chapter are no longer functional. Rather than interpreting this as a sign of the failure of semantic web technologies to enhance Web 2.0 sites, it should be instead taken as a call for further research in the area. Although it is evident that web resources such as social networks represent a considerable source of business opportunities and income in a time where the amount of data grows at an exponential rate, problems such as long-term conservation and accessibility of information should not be ignored. Tags can be a powerful instrument to organise and retrieve the rich data spread across Web 2.0; this potential can be realised if tags are linked to ontologies or other semantic resources that can disambiguate their meaning. To avoid discouraging user contributions, as semantic web requirements can certainly be intimidating, more user-friendly interfaces are needed. Furthermore, some of the frameworks outlined in this chapter have demonstrated that semantic tagging systems benefit greatly from automatic/semi-automatic mechanisms to alleviate users' contributions.

Zambonini (2005) affirmed that while Web 2.0 is about empowering people, letting them create and share content in a collaborative manner, prioritising ease and speed of use over standards and long-term solutions, Web 3.0 gravitates around structured data and standardised ways to publish and share data. The author argued that, although appealing and pleasant to use, Web 2.0 applications are not the way forward, as they tend to satisfy users' needs in the here and now. It is the semantic web that should instead lead the advancement of the web, since it provides the tools to take full advantage of the potential of data. Nonetheless, Zambonini acknowledged that the progress of Web 2.0 cannot be arrested and suggested its integration with Web 3.0, so that they can benefit from each other's strengths.

While a complete semantic understanding of tags is hard to achieve, partially assigning semantics to tags will enhance the usefulness of tagging, improving search and enabling disambiguating systems (Rattenbury, Good and Naaman, 2007). Breslin (2009) proposes a hypothetical framework, combining semantic web principles and Web 2.0 sites, that he defines as a 'semantic social collaborative resource aggregator'. Its main characteristics are listed below:

1   Social network members select their favourite content sources.
2   Users specify any topic of interest.
3   Users indicate friends whose topic lists they value.
4   The metadata aggregator gathers content from sites that users like, which may be human-tagged or auto-tagged.
5   Content that may be of interest to individual users and their friends is highlighted.

6 If nothing of interest is available, semantically related sources in other communities may be identified.

7 Users bookmark, tag and share content of interest.

There is no denying the fact that Web 2.0 has outshone Web 3.0, achieving a primary position in the life of millions of users. However, this chapter has shown how the adoption of Web 3.0 technologies to tagging systems has the potential to solve problems affecting free-tagging, support multilingualism and enrich users' experience by delivering related information. The semantic web could benefit from the popularity of Web 2.0 to achieve further development; it is a mutually beneficial relationship worth exploring.

References

Abele, A., McCrae, J. P., Buitelaar, P., Jentzsch, A. and Cyganiak, R. (2017) *Linking Open Data Cloud Diagram 2017*, http://lod-cloud.net.

Alonso, O., Kamps, J. and Karlgren, J. (2015) Report on the Seventh Workshop on Exploiting Semantic Annotations in Information Retrieval (ESAIR'14), *ACM SIGIR Forum*, **49**, 27–34.

Antoniou, G., Groth, P., van Harmelen, F. and Hoekstra, R. (2012) *A Semantic Web Primer*, 3rd edn, MIT Press.

Baker, T., Bermès, E., Coyle, K., Dunsire, G., Isaac, A., Murray, P., Panzer, P., Schneider, J., Singer, R., Summers, E., Waiters, W., Young, J. and Zheng, M. (2011) *Library Linked Data Incubator Group Final Report*, W3C, www.w3.org/2005/Incubator/lld/XGR-lld-20111025.

Bansal, P., Bansal, R. and Varma, V. (2015) *Towards Deep Semantic Analysis of Hashtags*, https://arxiv.org/pdf/1501.03210.pdf.

Becker, C. and Bizer, C. (2009) *Flickr Wrappr*, http://wifo5-03.informatik.uni-mannheim.de/flickrwrappr.

Berners-Lee, T. (2006) *Linked Data*, www.w3.org/DesignIssues/LinkedData.html.

Berners-Lee, T., Hendler, J. and Lassila, O. (2001) The Semantic Web, *Scientific American*, **284**, 29–37, https://www-sop.inria.fr/acacia/cours/essi2006/Scientific%20American_%20Feature%20Article_%20The%20Semantic%20Web_%20May%202001.pdf

Bizer, C. (2009) The Emerging Web of Linked Data, *The Semantic Web*, September–October, 87–92.

Breslin, J. G. (2009) Social Semantic Information Spaces. In Kruk, S. R. and McDaniel, B. (eds), *Semantic Digital Libraries*, Springer, 55–68.

Breslin, J. and Decker, S. (2007) The Future of Social Networks on the Internet: the need for semantics', *IEEE Internet Computing*, 11, 86–90.

Calaresu, M. and Shiri, A. (2015) Understanding Semantic Web: a conceptual model, *Library Review*, 64, 82–100.

Cayzer, S. (2001) *SWAD-Europe deliverable 12.1.4: Semantic Blogging – Lessons Learnt*, www.w3.org/2001/sw/Europe/reports/demo_1_report.

Choudhury, S., Breslin, J. G. and Passant, A. (2009) Enrichment and Ranking of the YouTube Tag Space and Integration with the Linked Data Cloud. In Bernstein, A., Karger, D. R., Heath, T., Feigenbaum, L., Maynard, D., Motta, E. and Thirunarayan, K. (eds), *The Semantic Web – ISWC 2009*, Springer, 747–62.

Cyganiak, R. and Jentzsch, A. (2007) *The Linked Open Data Cloud*, https://lod-cloud.net/.

DBpedia (2017) http://wiki.dbpedia.org/about.

Downes, S. (2005) Semantic Networks and Social Networks, *The Learning Organization*, 12, 411–17.

Freudenberg, M. (2017) *ANN: DBpedia Version 2016-10 Released, listhub.w3.org, 4 July*, available via e-mail: public-lod@w3.org.

García-Silva, A., Corcho, O., Alani, H. and Gómez-Pérez, A. (2012) Review of the State of the Art: discovering and associating semantics to tags in folksonomies, *The Knowledge Engineering Review*, 27, http://oa.upm.es/6376/1/Review_of_the_state.pdf.

Goldbeck, J. and Rothstein, M. (2008) Linking Social Networks on the Web with FOAF. In *AAAI'08 Proceedings of the 23rd National Conference on Artificial Intelligence*, http://hcil2.cs.umd.edu/trs/2008-40/2008-40.pdf.

Greaves, M. (2007) Semantic Web 2.0, *The Semantic Web*, March–April, 94–6.

Gruber, T. (2005) *TagOntology: a way to agree on the semantics of tagging data*, http://tomgruber.org/writing/tagontology-tagcamp-talk.pdf.

Grzonkowski, S., Kruk, S. R., Gzella, A., Demczuk, J. and McDaniel, B. (2009) Community-Aware Ontologies. In Kruk, S. R. and McDaniel, B. (eds), *Semantic Digital Libraries*, Springer, 123–35.

Heath, T. (2009) Linked Data? Web of Data? Semantic Web? WTF?, *Tom Heath's Displacement Activities*, 2 March, http://tomheath.com/blog/2009/03/linked-data-web-of-data-semantic-web-wtf.

Heath, T. and Bizer, C. (2011) Linked Data: evolving the web into a global data space, *Synthesis Lectures on The Semantic Web: Theory and Technology*, 1, www.morganclaypool.com/doi/pdf/10.2200/S00334ED1V01Y201102WBE001.

Hildebrand, M. and van Ossenbruggen, J. (2012) Linking User Generated Video Annotations to the Web of Data. In Schoeffmann, K., Merialdo, B., Hauptmann,

A. G., Ngo, C. W. Andreopoulos, Y. and Breiteneder, C. (eds), *Advances in Multimedia Modeling,* Springer, 693–704.

Im, D. H. and Park, G. D. (2015) Linked Tag: image annotation using semantic relationships between image tags, *Multimedia Tools and Applications*, **74**, 2273–87.

Jeong, J. W., Hong, H. K. and Lee, D. H. (2013) i-TagRanker: an efficient tag ranking system for image sharing and retrieval using the semantic relationships between tags, *Multimedia Tools and Applications*, **62**, 451–78.

Kim, H. L., Passant, A., Breslin, J. G., Scerri, S. and Decker, S. (2008) Review and Alignment of Tag Ontologies for Semantically-Linked Data in Collaborative Tagging Spaces. In *Second IEEE International Conference on Semantic Computing (ICSC),* IEEE, 315–22.

Kruk, S. R., Cygan, M., Gzella, A., Woroniecki, T. and Dabrowski, M. (2009) JeromeDL: the social semantic digital library'. In Kruk, S. R. and McDaniel, B. (eds), *Semantic Digital Libraries*, Springer, 140–50.

Library of Congress (2012) *Bibliographic Framework as a Web of Data: linked data model and supporting services*, www.loc.gov/bibframe/pdf/marcld-report-11-21-2012.pdf.

Lohmann, S. (2011) *Modular Unified Tagging Ontology (MUTO)*, http://muto.socialtagging.org/core/v1.html.

Maccioni, A. (2013) Towards an Integrated Social Semantic Web. In Sheng, Q. Z. and Kjeldskov, J. (eds), *ICWE 2013 Workshops, LNCS 8295*, Springer, 207–14.

Miličić, V. (2008) *W3C Semantic Web Use Cases and Case Studies. Case Study: Semantic Tags*, www.w3.org/2001/sw/sweo/public/UseCases/Faviki.

Milgram, S. (1967) The Small World Problem, *Psychology Today*, May, 60–7.

Open Graph Protocol (2017) http://ogp.me.

O'Reilly, T. (2005) *What is Web 2.0?*, www.oreilly.com/pub/a/web2/archive/what-is-web-20.html.

Papadakis I., Kyprianos K., Karalis A. and Douligeris C. (2017) Employing Twitter Hashtags and Linked Data to Suggest Trending Resources in a Digital Library. In Kamps, J., Tsakonas G., Manolopoulos Y., Iliadis L. and Karydis I. (eds), *Research and Advanced Technology for Digital Libraries*, Springer, 407–18.

Passant, A. (2008) *Linked Data Tagging with LODr*, https://pdfs.semanticscholar.org/52b2/84efdb60d13e25bfd5acaed731f8c4d3906b.pdf.

Passant, A. (2010) *Semantic Web Technologies for Enterprise 2.0*, IOS Press.

Passant, A. and Laublet, P. (2008) Meaning of a Tag: a collaborative approach to bridge the gap between tagging and linked data. In *Proceedings of the Linked Data on the Web Workshop (LDOW 2008) at the 17th International Conference on the World Wide Web (WWW 2008), Beijing, China*, ACM.

Pennington, D. R. (2016) Demystifying Linked Data: are you ready for what's next?, *CILIP Update*, July–August, 34–6.

Rattenbury, T., Good, N. and Naaman, M. (2007) Towards Automatic Extraction of Event and Place Semantics from Flickr Tags. In *SIGIR '07 Proceedings of the 30th Annual International ACM SIGIR Conference on Research and Development in Information Retrieval*, ACM, 103–10.

Singh, P. and Shadbolt, N. (2013) Linked Data in Crowdsourcing Purposive Social Network. In *Proceedings of the 22nd International Conference on World Wide Web held in Rio de Janeiro, Brazil, May 13–17, 2013*, ACM, 913–18.

Singhal, A. (2012) Introducing the Knowledge Graph: things, not strings, *Google: official blog*, 16 May, https://googleblog.blogspot.co.uk/2012/05/introducing-knowledge-graph-things-not.html.

Stuart, D. (2011) *Facilitating Access to the Web of Data: a guide for librarians*, Facet Publishing.

Tallerås, K. (2013) From Many Records to One Graph: heterogeneity conflicts in the linked data restructuring cycle, *Information Research*, **18**, www.informationr.net/ir/18-3/colis/paperC18.html#.WUEwnZB95dg.

TED (2009) Tim Berners-Lee: The Next Web of Open, Linked Data, www.youtube.com/watch?v=OM6XIICm_qo&t=6s.

W3C (2017a) *Linking Open Data*, www.w3.org/wiki/SweoIG/TaskForces/CommunityProjects/LinkingOpenData.

W3C (2017b) *SPARQL*, www.w3.org/2001/sw/wiki.

W3C (2017c) *Three Recommendations to Enable Annotations on the Web*, www.w3.org/blog/news/archives/6156.

Wikipedia (2017a) *Semantic Desktop*, https://en.wikipedia.org/wiki/Semantic_desktop.

Wikipedia (2017b) *Social Graph*, https://en.wikipedia.org/wiki/Social_graph.

Wikipedia (2017c) *Zemanta*, https://en.wikipedia.org/wiki/Zemanta.

Yeung, C., Liccardi, I., Lu, K., Seneviratne, O. and Berners-Lee, T. (2008) Decentralization: the future of online social networking. In *W3C Workshop on the Future of Social Networking Position Papers*, W3C, www.w3.org/2008/09/msnws/papers/decentralization.pdf.

Zambonini, D. (2005) *Is Web 2.0 Killing the Semantic Web?*, http://archive.oreilly.com/pub/post/is_web_20_killing_the_semantic.html.

Chapter 3

Social tags for linked data with Resource Description Framework (RDF)

Sue Yeon Syn

Introduction

Social tags are often considered as another type of metadata, since they provide information about the resources for users' needs (Kim et al., 2010; Passant et al., 2009). In addition, its social aspect allows tags to become a form of collective knowledge. The term *folksonomy*, a term created by combining 'folk' and 'taxonomy' to indicate a user-driven collective taxonomy generated from tags (Vander Wal, 2007), also reflects such perspectives.

As simple keywords assigned to a resource, tags have some limitations as resource descriptions. First, simple keyword tags without any context encounter problems with ambiguity in their semantic meanings (Guy and Tonkin, 2006; Passant et al., 2009). A good example of this limitation is homograph terms such as *apple*, which can mean a fruit or a company. Second, because the tagging systems allow users to input free form text as tags, the tag terms may vary in their forms and selections. This could be related to the use of synonymous terms such as *car* and *automobile,* where users can select one or the other for the same concept. Another example could be related to different tag term forms. For instance, user-generated compound tag forms such as *semantic web*, *SemanticWeb*, *Semweb*, *semantic-web* and so forth, are considered heterogeneous in tagging systems and when computers process tags (Guy and Tonkin, 2006; Passant et al., 2009; Syn, 2014). In addition to these cases, there can be additional problems of tag variations that occur due to human errors such as misspelling. Third, a folksonomy does not have a concrete structure; unlike the hierarchical structure of controlled vocabularies, a folksonomy is considered to be a flat organization (Shirky, 2005). In addition, depending on users' contributions, a tag set may change over time, making a folksonomy dynamic (Lin et al., 2012; Mika, 2007).

Finally, there is an issue with the use of tag sets, as user tags are dependent on tagging systems (Gruber, 2007; Kim et al., 2010; Mika, 2007). Various types of systems and applications offer tagging features, including bookmarking systems, such as CiteULike (www.citeulike.org), photo-sharing systems, such as Flickr (www.flickr.com) and Instagram (www.instagram.com), microblogging systems, such as Twitter (https://twitter.com) and library online public access catalogue (OPAC) systems, such as BiblioCommons (www.bibliocommons.com). In most cases, user-generated tags stay in the system or application and they are not shared across systems and applications. Therefore, although a user tags various resources, it is impossible to search bookmarks from CiteULike and photos from Flickr together. In some cases, user-generated tags are shared among organizations using the same application platform; for example, hashtags are now searchable through online search engines and library tags with features from LibraryThing for Libraries (www.librarything.com/forlibraries) or BiblioCommons are shared across libraries using the same services, but it is still limited to a few platforms and services.

Researchers have used user-generated tags mainly in information organization and discovery for indexing, ranking and potentially supplementing controlled vocabularies. With the recognition of the problems of social tags, much research has focused on minimising tag noise by, for example, filtering tags according to frequency (e.g. Bao et al., 2007) or developing means for reducing the long tail (e.g. Guy and Tonkin, 2006; Syn, 2014). The tag distribution presents a power law graph with a small number of tags assigned by many users and a large number of tags assigned by a small number of users. The power law graph visually presents a long tail where most of the tags in a tag set lack mass agreement and which could potentially be considered as tag noise. Thus, the effort to reduce tag noise and the long tail focuses on the part of a tag set that draws mass agreement from taggers. Other researchers have suggested ways to try to shape folksonomies into controlled vocabularies (e.g. Golub, Lykke and Tudhope, 2014). A group of researchers focused their discussions on the flatness of social tags (e.g. Shirky, 2005) and that tags are linked rather than hierarchically structured. In considering the usefulness of folksonomies, the lack of hierarchical structure in folksonomies has led to the debate about how hierarchical organization systems have worked well in information organization and how social tags can be used within existing hierarchical organization systems such as controlled vocabularies. Some researchers tried to find ways to use social tags for existing well-structured controlled vocabularies. Lu, Park and Hu (2010) and Yi and Chan (2009) examined the similarity of social tags to controlled vocabularies such as Library of Congress Subject Headings and discussed the potential of social tags to supplement controlled vocabularies. Others have favoured the flat structure, arguing that the linked network of tags works well in digital environments (e.g. Shirky, 2005).

Some researchers have recognised a potentially synergistic relationship between folksonomy and developments toward the semantic web. Different applications of social tags in the semantic web environment have been examined, such as formatting tags as Resource Description Framework (RDF) triples and defining the semantic meanings and relationships of tags (e.g. Huang, Lin and Chang, 2012; Jabeen et al., 2016; Mika, 2007; Weller, 2007). This chapter will introduce the use of social tags as linked data in the development of the semantic web, focusing on the design of tag data models based on the RDF and efforts to apply tag data models for implementing folksonomy as linked data.

Social tags as linked data: a case scenario

To demonstrate how social tags can be used in a linked data environment, let us think about a case scenario of using tags in information discovery. When a user searches with the keyword *Shakespeare,* or tags a resource with the term *Shakespeare*, the user could be referring to the person Shakespeare, works written by Shakespeare, objects representing Shakespeare, such as his statue, books discussing Shakespeare, his life or his works, or other works related to Shakespeare, such as films. Types of information resources would vary and the term *Shakespeare* may describe different elements of a resource; for example, Shakespeare could be an author, an object, or a subject (Figure 3.1, left, on the next page). We can also think about this scenario in relation to primary and secondary sources. For example, if a resource is tagged with *Romeo and Juliet*, the tag could represent the title of the work or a subject of a critic, a performance, or a drawing (Figure 3.1, right). In information retrieval systems, all these resources could be retrieved if the resource descriptions or metadata contain *Shakespeare* in the title, author, or subject and *Romeo and Juliet* in the title or subject. The user still needs to go through all retrieved results to identify the types of resources that meet their information needs.

NINES (Networked Infrastructure for Nineteenth-Century Electronic Scholarship, www.nines.org) aggregates 19th-century digitised materials for research and education purposes. The system includes a tagging feature that allows researchers, educators and students to contribute to organising and describing information resources. It is expected that the NINES tags will represent the needs and uses of tags for humanities and social science researchers as well as include less tag noise, as the platform is designed for targeted user groups and purposes.

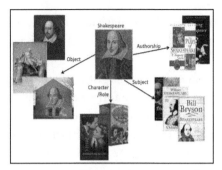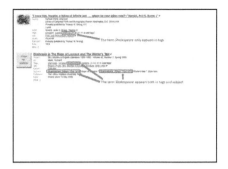

Figure 3.1 *Different representations of resources with a tag term (left: an example of Shakespeare; right: an example of Romeo and Juliet)*

A search for the tag *Shakespeare* in NINES produced 13 results: ten were visual materials, two were text materials and one was citation information. From the resource descriptions provided by NINES, only six items included the term *Shakespeare* in subject (1 item), title (5 items), or exhibits (2 items) with some overlaps (Figure 3.2, bottom). For the remaining seven items retrieved, the tag *Shakespeare* was the only descriptor to show the items' relevance to William Shakespeare (Figure 3.2, top). In fact, Choi and Syn (2016) found that about 42% of NINES tags were not found in the metadata descriptions of the NINES resources, meaning they could potentially be used as additional descriptors. This example demonstrates how tags could enhance information discovery and supplement existing resource descriptions, which aligns well with discussion from prior studies (Choi and Syn, 2016; Golub, Lykke and Tudhope, 2014; Lu, Park and Hu, 2010; Yi and Chan, 2009).

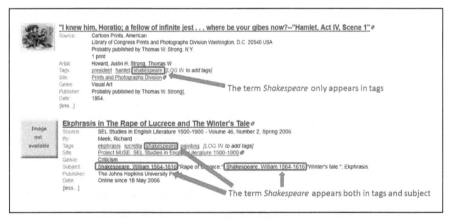

Figure 3.2 *Examples of search results from NINES (www.nines.org) with tag term Shakespeare (top: resource without Shakespeare in description; bottom: resource that includes Shakespeare as subject)*

Further analysis of NINES tags revealed that user-generated tags actually describe resources and their contents in more detail. User tags described objects, persons, organizations, concepts, events, locations and periods of information resource contents (Choi and Syn, 2014). This is additional information to what can be described in the subject field of the resource description. The study further found that of the 8310 tags reviewed, 20.75% represented person, 16.29% concept, 8.01% place, 7.35% object, 4.54% event, 2.07% period and 1.30% organization. Only 2.73% of the tags were taken from the title of the work. Identifying the attributes of the tags could enhance information discovery. This demonstrates how tags can be used efficiently as a part of linked data; for example, the tags can be used to indicate that *this book is about a person.* Such tag relationships could help a user searching with a keyword *Shakespeare* to identify resources *written by* Shakespeare and resources *about* Shakespeare. Tag relationships would also allow users to perform a semantic search. For example, a user can search with a query *find all images that represent works by Shakespeare* and the search results can include items that are relevant to Shakespeare, such as a sketch of the story of Romeo and Juliet, even though the resource description does not include the term Shakespeare (Figure 3.2). The Resource Description Framework is considered to be one of the major semantic web technologies that supports implementation of the relationships between tags and tagged resources.

Resource Description Framework and tag triple

The Resource Description Framework (RDF) is a data model to describe resources in the form of subject–predicate–object expressions, also known as RDF triples. The subject denotes the resource and the object is the description or annotation of the resource. The predicate denotes aspects of the resource that express a relationship between the subject and the object. For example, the statement 'Romeo and Juliet is written by William Shakespeare' can be represented with an RDF triple (Figure 3.3 on the next page). The RDF triples describe an information resource with a set of descriptive properties and relationships and are an efficient data model for the semantic web. RDF is expressed with RDF Schema and RDF Vocabulary in XML encoding and can employ SPARQL (SPARQL Protocol and RDF Query Language) for retrieving functions. As all semantic web applications tend to be, the RDF statement is indicated with URIs (Uniform Resource Identifiers). Schreiber and Raimond (2014) pointed out that RDF:

● adds machine-readable information to web resources

- enriches datasets by linking various datasets, including APIs and existing linked data datasets
- builds social networks among people and communities
- supports standard data exchanges between databases
- enables performing cross-dataset queries using SPARQL.

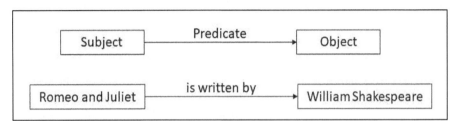

Figure 3.3   *RDF triple*

Figure 3.4 presents an example of how RDF triples can be used to describe resources or concepts. The left diagram in Figure 3.4 represents the following descriptions: 'Leonardo da Vinci is the creator of the Mona Lisa and the video *La Joconde à Washington* is about the Mona Lisa'. Additional information to describe the resource such as 'the artwork is titled the Mona Lisa' could be added. These RDF triples can be expressed with URIs from existing knowledge bases or vocabularies. For example, Table 3.1 and the right diagram in Figure

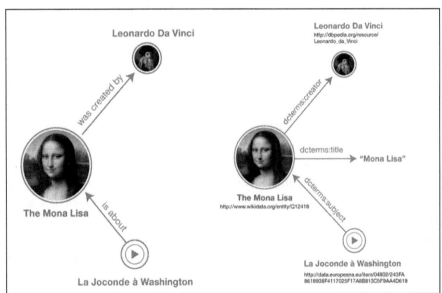

Figure 3.4   *Example of RDF triples* (modified from Schreiber and Raimond, 2014)

3.4 present how URIs are adopted from schemas such as Dublin Core (http://dublincore.org/documents/dcmi-terms/), Wikidata (www.wikidata.org/wiki/Wikidata:Main_Page) and DBpedia (http://wiki.dbpedia.org/).

Table 3.1   *Example of RDF triples with URIs*

Subject	Predicate	Object
The Mona Lisa www.wikidata.org/entity/ Q12418	Creator http://purl.org/dc/terms/ creator	Leonardo Da Vinci http://dbpedia.org/resource /Leonardo_da_Vinci
La Joconde à Washington http://data.europeana.eu/ item/04802/	Subject http://purl.org/dc/terms/ subject	The Mona Lisa www.wikidata.org/entity/ Q12418
The Mona Lisa www.wikidata.org/entity/ Q12418	Title http://purl.org/dc/terms/ title	"Mona Lisa"

The RDF triples can be easily applied to tag sets in a tagging system; the typical design is that a tag is associated with a resource. In general, social tagging systems are based on a collection of 3-tuples consisting of users, tags and resources (Mika, 2007; Smith, 2008). The tag triple represents relationships among users, tags and resources, that is, a *User* assigns a *Tag* to a *Resource* within a tagging *System* (Figure 3.5). Some consider that the tag triple model is to represent tagging behaviours with an actor involved (tagger) (Gruber, 2007; Kim et al., 2010).

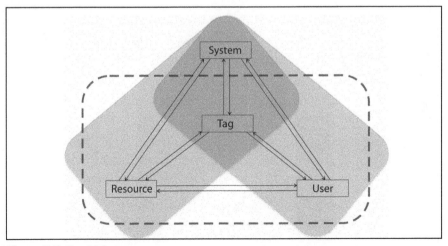

Figure 3.5 *Tag triples*

Previous studies tend to consider the tag triples in different levels, depending on the purpose of tag use, as shown in Figure 3.5. For example, when tags are used for information retrieval, tags assigned to resources are given emphasis for tag processing (the left-hand, light grey part in Figure 3.5), using tags as one type of index or description for resources. Although using tags as an index does not fully solve the linguistic problems of full-text indexing, tags are expected to provide more precise semantic information with shared agreement and can be used to index or rank web resources (Golder and Huberman, 2006; Mika, 2007; Shirky, 2005). On the other hand, other studies focus on the network of users associated with tags (the right-hand, darker part in Figure 3.5). They emphasise the social and collaborative aspects of tagging systems and examine the community networks formed through tagging activities (Mika, 2007; Ohmukai, Hamasaki and Takeda, 2005). Since tags are assigned to a resource by different users collaboratively, the triple association and networks can be formed from linking entities in the triple model. While the tag-resource sets are more critical in retrieval purposes, the user element of the triple becomes significant in network analysis (Figure 3.5).

Mika (2007) explained that the tripartite model of folksonomies, that is, the *Actor-Concept-Instance* model, has different layers of RDFs. Simply put, in the *Actor-Concept-Instance* model, the *actor* denotes taggers, the *concept* denotes user tags and the *instance* denotes various types of resources in the folksonomy. Mika indicated that different layers consist of communities and their relations, semantics (ontologies and their relations) and content items and their relations (the hypertext web) (Figure 3.6). Each of these layers is represented with RDF

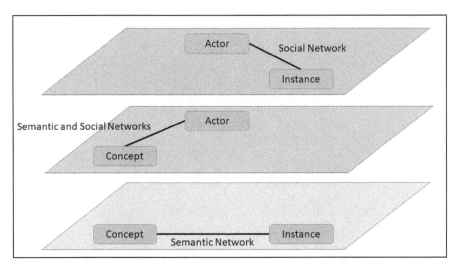

Figure 3.6 *The tripartite model in three layers*

triples of different entities, that is, actor, concept and instance. The RDF triples are the Actor-Concept link (a social network of users) and concepts (a semantic network), the Concept-Instance link (a semantic network) and the Actor-Instance link (another social network of persons). When these layers are combined, they are linked together with relationships, or predicates of RDF, and form linked data collectively (Figure 3.7). It can be easily imagined that when there are many actors, concepts and instances, the linked data will grow large and complicated quickly.

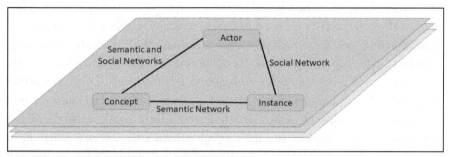

Figure 3.7 *The tripartite model as linked data*

Tags to linked data: application of RDF for bibliographic description and semantic vocabulary

In the library community, the discussion relating to social tags and folksonomy has focused on the potential use of tags for bibliographic description and as a supplement to controlled vocabulary. As the initial purpose of tags is to provide a user-based method for organising web resources, it is natural to consider the possible use of tags for bibliographic descriptions in library catalogues. Initial efforts include comparing tags with controlled vocabularies such as Library of Congress Subject Headings (LCSH) (e.g. Lu, Park and Hu, 2010; Thomas, Caudle and Schmitz, 2009; Yi and Chan, 2009) and categorising tags for description or metadata categories (Cantador, Konstas and Jose, 2011; Choi and Syn, 2016). When LibraryThing tags were compared to LCSH and multiple OPACs, only 14% of tags were found to overlap with LCSH (Thomas, Caudle and Schmitz, 2009) and Delicious tags were identified to be either more general or specific than LCSH terms (Yi and Chan, 2009). Researchers generally agreed that user-generated tags may bridge the gap between professional descriptions and user terminologies (Lu, Park and Hu, 2010; Trant, 2006).

Further to the NINES study mentioned previously, Choi and Syn (2016) categorised social tags into four main categories: (a) content-related, which characterises the subject aspects of a resource; (b) document-related, which presents document attributes; (c) user-context-related, which focuses on personal context, tasks or self-reference; and (d) not applicable. Choi and Syn found that 95.28% of the NINES tags were categorised as content- and document-related tags, which are closely relevant to bibliographic description. In comparison with metadata descriptions, 58.11% of the NINES tags were classified to be the same as keywords in metadata descriptions. In their study of Flickr, Cantador, Konstas and Jose (2011) demonstrated how folksonomies can be automatically processed to identify the types of tags based on their purpose-oriented categories. They defined the categories as (a) content-based, which describes the content of the item; (b) context-based, which provides contextual information about the item; (c) subject, which describes the content of the item; and (d) organizational, which defines personal usage and tasks, or indicates self-reference. They argued that they could identify about 45.9% of Flickr tag sets to content- and context-based categories. In comparing Choi and Syn and Cantador, Konstas and Jose, although the tag categories and the tagging systems analysed were different in these two studies, they have demonstrated the possibility of processing and utilising tags with associated semantic entities from existing resource descriptions or external knowledge bases such as WordNet (https://wordnet.princeton.edu) and Wikipedia (www.wikipedia.org).

Although user tags can be used to supplement controlled vocabularies or bibliographic descriptions, the lack of structure and dynamic characteristics of folksonomies make it challenging to adopt user-generated tags for controlled vocabularies. Even given the differences in tagging behaviours of different groups of users using different sets of information resources (Lin et al., 2012), folksonomies still serve as collective knowledge. Tags are useful as subject access points because they collectively represent and describe the information resources and objects with variations in the selection of terms (Bates and Rowley, 2011; Gaffney and Rafferty, 2009).

Considering tags as data sets for linked data to support users' information discovery and browsing seems to have more practical potential than trying to adopt social tags for standardised bibliographic descriptions and as supplements to controlled vocabularies. The effort that the semantic web community has made to design and organise tags into ontologies as a part of the semantic web makes sense (Mika, 2007; Ohmukai, Hamasaki and Takeda, 2005), since tags provide semantic information about resources or objects. The limitations identified for the use of tags for strictly standardised bibliographic descriptions or to supplement controlled vocabularies get resolved to some extent with the spectrum that ontologies cover in terms of their design and use. In discussing whether folksonomies could be used as ontologies, Mika (2007) explained folksonomies in comparison to ontologies based on Elst and Abecker's (2002) three-dimensional characterisation of ontologies: that is, stability, sharing scope and degree of formality. Stability indicates different levels of information stability, sharing scope indicates the level of sharing of information within groups and degree of formality indicates whether information is formalised or informal. Mika characterised folksonomies as lightweight in terms of stability, as they are not structured, limited in terms of sharing scope, as the use of folksonomy is often limited within a tagging system, and dynamic in terms of degree of formality, as they change over time depending on users' tagging actions. Folksonomies as lightweight, dynamic and limited in scope support the semantic web as one type of vocabulary. Similarly, Coyle (2015) discussed how library and information science-based models and standards, such as the Functional Requirements for Bibliographic Records (FRBR) and Resource Description and Access (RDA), are aligned with technologies related to the semantic web, such as RDF and ontologies. Coyle also discussed how semantic web technologies have been used as the foundation for many bibliographic data models in the development of the semantic web. Specifically, in using social tags as semantics or knowledge descriptions in the semantic web, the RDF triple of subject–predicate–object can be considered as the basis of the linked data structure.

RDF triples in social tag models

Some research projects have demonstrated the use of tags for the linked data environment, expanding the tag triples to different perspectives based on the limitations of social tags addressed earlier in this chapter, namely, ambiguity of semantic meaning, various forms of tag terms and dependency on tagging systems. Efforts to expand tag triples focus on suggesting social tag models that represent the design of tagging systems and tagging behaviours and resolve the limitations of tags to better utilise folksonomies for linked data and the semantic web.

Gruber's TagOntology was an early attempt to conceptualise tagging activity, based on discussions in the tagging and the semantic web communities. TagOntology, 'is about identifying and formalizing a conceptualization of the activity of tagging and building technology that commits to the ontology the semantic level' (Gruber, 2007, 6) and provides a way to represent tagging in the semantic web. The entities for TagOntology are explained carefully with the consideration of the tagging system environment and how users actually tag. Starting with the application of the basic RDF triple model, the tagging behaviour in a closed environment can be defined as *Tagging(object, tag)*, where the tagging activity in a tagging system is to associate a *tag* to an information resource or *object*. Taking the social aspect of tagging systems into consideration, the model expands with tagger entity as *Tagging(object, tag, tagger)*, where a *tagger* assigns a *tag* to an information resource or *object*. Of course, in real practice, a tagger may perform multiple tagging activities for the same resource or multiple resources; this is what the tag triples represent (the dashed area in Figure 3.5). Gruber further extends the tag triples with the notion of *source* to indicate either a community or application where the tagging activity occurs. This now makes the tag triples into a four-place relation as *Tagging(object, tag, tagger, source)*, where *object* is the resource item tagged, *tag* is the tag term assigned, *tagger* is a user who tags and *source* is either a tagging community or tagging system. This four-place relation allows us to share the tag sets across platforms, as it can differentiate tagging activities performed in different systems. For example, *Tagging*(mypicture, apple, Jane, Instagram) and *Tagging*(mypicture, apple, Jane, Flickr) can be distinguished by the source indication even if the same object, tag and tagger were involved in the tagging activity. Gruber further explained that the TagOntology model can be extended with information about metatagging, such as relating the meaning of tags to resources, or filtering tags based on votes for or against the insertion of a tag. He also stressed that the use of these entities with the RDF framework, particularly the use of identifiers, makes the design of TagOntology realisable.

Another example of a social tag model is the MOAT (Meaning Of A Tag) framework to bridge the gap between free-tagging and semantic annotation for the semantic web (Passant and Laublet, 2008). The main purpose of the MOAT framework is to provide a way to deal with problems inherent to tagging, particularly ambiguity and heterogeneity. If the semantic meanings of tags are clearly identified, these problems will be resolved not only for human users but for software agents. With MOAT, for example, one should be able to identify that the tag *paris* could be a city, a person and so forth and use it differently. In order to represent the meaning of a tag, MOAT extends the TagOntology with an addition of meaning: *Tagging(users, resources, tag, meaning)*. It recognises the social aspect of tagging systems and differentiates the *local meaning* of a tag from the *global meaning* of the tag term. The *local meaning* is the meaning of a tag for a particular tagging activity. The *global meaning* is to represent the list of all different meanings of a tag with *Meanings(Tag)* = {*(Meaning, {User})*}. It suggests using existing external knowledge bases such as GeoNames (www.geonames.org) and DBpedia to associate the meanings of tags through URIs. For example, the tag *paris* for the city will have <http://dbpedia.org/resource/Paris> assigned as its URI, while the person *paris* will have <http://dbpedia.org/resource/Paris_Hilton> as its URI. For a tag term, a list of available meanings will be provided for clarification. MOAT offers an RDF model to define the meanings of tags and provides a way to allow tagged resources to be included in the linked data through tags and their URIs.

The Semantic Social Cloud of Tags (SCOT) is a semantic model to represent the structure and the semantics of tag sets (Kim et al., 2008; 2010). Unlike TagOntology and MOAT, SCOT is designed to provide a folksonomy model – rather than a tagging model – that represents the folksonomy as a collection of instances of the tagging behaviours and as a way to share tag clouds between social tagging systems. The uniqueness of the folksonomy model compared to other tagging models is that it focuses on the collective tags by a set of users for a set of resources, presented as *Folksonomy (user group, tag set, source, occurrence, Tagging)*. The SCOT ontology is designed on the folksonomy model to provide semantic links of tagging data across heterogeneous sources or systems. It is suggested that through SCOT, the merged folksonomy from individual users' tag clouds, which they call *personomies*, would be a *platform-independent folksonomy* placed on heterogeneous platforms without boundaries (Kim, Decker and Breslin, 2010).

These models are examples of some efforts to represent tagging systems as well as tagging behaviours. They may have slightly different emphases, depending on their purposes, such as tagging behaviours, meanings of tags and collective and social features of tagging systems. However, regardless of their foci, they all attempt to express folksonomies with a semantic model to utilise tags for linked data. The next section will introduce some examples of the implementation of social tags as linked data using a social tag model.

Social tags as linked data: examples of implementations

This section introduces examples of applications that employ folksonomy-based linked data including Revyu.com, int.ere.st, LODr and Linked Tag. They all apply one or the other social tag model using RDF to realise the tag data into the semantic web environment.

Revyu.com is a reviewing and rating website that is one of the early applications developed with semantic web technologies and linked data principles (Heath and Motta, 2007). It implements users' reviews data and tags of various information resources such as books and films along with external data sources such as DBpedia, Open Guides (http://openguides.org) and FOAF (www.foaf-project.org). Revyu.com is designed to be data-oriented and human-oriented mashups for reuse of integrated data with RDF and SPARQL. The application allows users to search by information resources, by users and by their tags. The design and search results present what is similar to Google's Knowledge Graph, that is, a curated result from multiple data sources.

An extended case of implementation of Revyu.com is int.ere.st., a prototype tag-sharing platform for reusing tagged resources across heterogeneous platforms based on the SCOT ontology (Kim et al., 2008; Kim, Decker and Breslin, 2010). int.ere.st used machine-readable RDF that solves the common problems of tags, including tag ambiguity and lack of organization. Most importantly, int.ere.st realised the problem of silos created by various tagging systems, such as bookmarking systems or photo-sharing systems, and provided a platform to aggregate tags and tagged items from multiple systems to share them as linked data (Figure 3.8). This is possible with the conceptualisation of tags from tag model, the *Folksonomy Model* and with RDF vocabularies such as the SCOT ontology. In int.ere.st, tag search is implemented with SPARQL-based query search, which allows users to look for similar tags, tagging behaviours, or tagged items. It is possible to search across tagging systems with queries like 'find all tweets and photos tagged with a tag term Apple from Twitter and Instagram' or 'find all users who tagged Apple in Flickr'.

Passant and colleagues employed a linked data platform using the MOAT framework to provide an intuitive and lightweight way to relate tagging to linked data (Passant et al., 2009). Their extended so-called quadripartite model is used to associate clear and unambiguous meaning to a tag. To do so, existing linked data knowledge bases such as DBpedia, GeoNames and DBTune

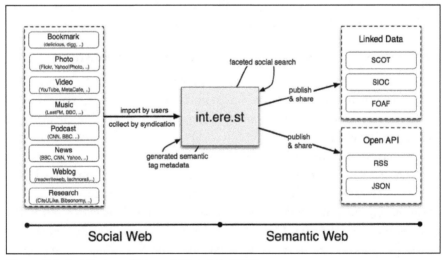

Figure 3.8 *Architecture of int.ere.st* (Kim et al., 2010)

(http://dbtune.org) were used for MOAT (Figure 3.9). Figure 3.9 presents how the term *apple* can be associated with different meanings, resolving the issues of homograph terms in tags. Meaning 1 of the term *apple* indicates Apple Inc., the company, defined with a URI from DBpedia as <http://dbpedia.org/resource/ Apple_Inc> associated with *moat:meaning* relationship. On the other hand, meaning 2 of the term *apple* indicates a fruit, as it is associated to a DBpedia URI <http://dbpedia.org/resource/Apple>. Passant and colleagues claimed that this method would also solve both the ambiguity and heterogeneity issues of tagging. With the meanings assigned, synonyms and various forms of tag terms are associated with their concepts, thus reducing their ambiguity. For example, tag terms *car* and *automobile* can be related as synonymous terms to represent a concept of transportation method; and *semantic web*, *SemanticWeb*, *Semweb* and *semantic-web* can all be associated with the concept semantic web and be realised as terms indicating the same meaning. The use of RDF allows the tags from various tagging systems to be *linked* through the concepts represented with unique unifiers (URIs). Passant et al. (2009) demonstrated the implementation of the MOAT framework with LODr, which aggregates tag data from Flickr, formatted with RDF and stored in Drupal to interlink with concepts in DBpedia. LODr supports SPARQL query search.

Im and Park (2015) proposed a framework called Linked Tag, which semi-automatically employed semantic relationships between tags in an image annotation system. The semantic relationships were facilitated with linked data such as DBpedia (Figure 3.10 on the next page). The data was represented with RDF, making image retrieval with SPARQL-based query processing possible. Im

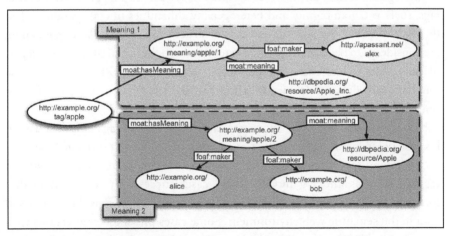

Figure 3.9 *Representation of different meanings in linked data using MOAT ontology* (Passant et al., 2009)

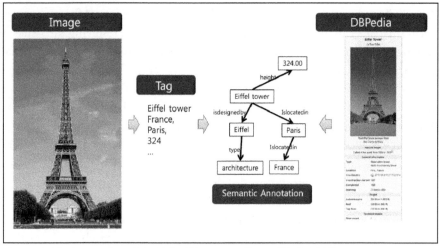

Figure 3.10 *An overview of the Linked Tag system* (Im and Park, 2015)

and Park argued that this approach leveraged tag-based keyword annotation to ontology annotation, as the semantic links would be inserted between tags and resources. Linked Tag also demonstrated how semantic retrieval can be possible with semantically related tag sets, for example, searching for 'find images of the plant whose colour is green and which tastes spicy'.

Conclusion

This chapter discussed how social tags can contribute to creating a linked data environment, focusing on their characteristics and explaining conceptually how technological foundations will facilitate this environment. The problems of social tags, such as tag ambiguity and heterogeneity, difficulties in aggregation of data due to silos of tagging systems and lack of structure caused by flat organization, are considered to be resolved to some extent through the use of social tags as a part of linked data. The main key for this process is using RDF triples as the foundation of data modelling, which is also used for various data sets for the semantic web and linked data. Along with RDF, the use of URIs for indicating subject, predicate and object allows the implementation of tags as linked data to become possible through the adoption of other linked data knowledge bases.

Although the examples of implementations may be limited to a few types of tagging systems and tag models, these cases successfully demonstrate that formatting tags with RDF-based tag models allows tags to contribute to linked data in the semantic web environment. Some cases presented connections with other knowledge bases and ontologies and others showcased retrieval functions using SPARQL.

Going back to our case scenario of Shakespeare, considering these examples of implementations, searching for a query 'find all images that represent works by Shakespeare' would be clearly possible when images are tagged with Shakespeare and a linked data knowledge base identifies Shakespeare as a person and relates Shakespeare with a set of his works. A retrieval system can traverse through the linked data to discover image items that are about works by Shakespeare. The representation of the relationships among the concepts and object becomes critical. They can be represented with multiple RDF triples; for example, this image is about Romeo and Juliet, Romeo and Juliet is the title of a work, Romeo and Juliet is written by Shakespeare, William Shakespeare wrote Hamlet and it can go on to find more relevant information.

As Mika (2007) described with the *Actor-Concept-Instance model* (Figures 3.6 and 3.7) and Berners-Lee (2009) emphasised, when all data elements become available and are *linked*, they will form linked and rich data points that support better information retrieval and discovery for users. This only becomes possible with more data becoming available in the right format with the right linkages to other data points. As Mika (2007) stated, 'the clues to the different qualities of these networks lie in the difference in the way associations are created between the concepts'.

References

Bao, S., Wu, X., Fei, B., Xue, G., Su, Z. and Yu, Y. (2007) Optimizing Web Search Using Social Annotations. In *Proceedings of the 16th International World Wide Web Conference (WWW '07), Banff, Alberta, Canada, May 8–12, 2007*, ACM, 501–10.

Bates, J. and Rowley, J. (2011) Social Reproduction and Exclusion in Subject Indexing, *Journal of Documentation*, **67**, 431–48.

Berners-Lee, T. (2009) *Linked Data*, www.w3.org/DesignIssues/LinkedData.html.

Cantador, I., Konstas, I. and Jose, J. M. (2011) Categorising Social Tags to Improve Folksonomy-Based Recommendations, *Journal of Web Semantics: science, services and agents on the world wide web*, **9**, 1–15.

Choi, Y. and Syn, S. Y. (2016) Characteristics of Tagging Behavior in a Digitized Humanities Online Collection, *Journal of the Association for Information Science and Technology*, **67**, 1089–104.

Coyle, K. (2015) Bibliographic Description and the Semantic Web. In Coyle, K. (ed.) *FRBR, Before and After: a look at our bibliographic models,* American Library Association Editions, 137–56.

Elst, L. and Abecker, A. (2002) Ontologies for Information Management: balancing formality, stability and sharing scope, *Expert Systems with Applications*, **23**, 357–66.

Gaffney, M. and Rafferty, P. (2009) Making the Long Tail Visible: social networking sites and independent music discovery, *Program*, **43**, 375–91.

Golder, S. A. and Huberman, B. A. (2006) Usage Patterns of Collaborative Tagging Systems, *Journal of Information Science*, **32**, 198–208.

Golub, K., Lykke, M. and Tudhope, D. (2014) Enhancing Social Tagging with Automated Keywords from the Dewey Decimal Classification, *Journal of Documentation*, **70**, 801–28.

Gruber, T. (2007) Ontology of Folksonomy: a mash-up of apples and oranges, *International Journal on Semantic Web & Information Systems*, **3**, 1–11.

Guy, M. and Tonkin, E. (2006) Folksonomies – Tidying up Tags?, *D-Lib Magazine*, **12**, www.dlib.org/dlib/january06/guy/01guy.html.

Heath, T. and Motta, E. (2007) Revyu.com: a reviewing and rating site for the web of data. In Aberer, K. et al. (eds), *The Semantic Web,* Lecture Notes in Computer Science 4825, Springer, 895–902.

Huang, S.-L., Lin, S.-C. and Chang, Y.-C. (2012) Investigating Effectiveness and User Acceptance of Semantic Social Tagging for Knowledge Sharing, *Information Processing and Management*, **48**, 599–617.

Im, D.-H. and Park, G.-D. (2015) Linked Tag: image annotation using semantic relationships between image tags, *Multimedia Tools and Applications*, **74**, 2273–87.

Jabeen, F., Khusro, S., Majid, A. and Rauf, A. (2016) Semantic Discovery in Social Tagging Systems: a review, *Multimedia Tools and Applications*, **75**, 573–605.

Kim, H. L., Breslin, J., Kim, H.-G. and Choi, J.-H. (2010) Social Semantic Cloud of Tags: semantic model for folksonomies, *Knowledge Management Research & Practice*, **8**, 193–202.

Kim, H. L., Breslin, J. G., Yang, S. K., Song, S. J. and Kim, H. G. (2008) int.ere.st: building a tag sharing service with the SCOT ontology. In *Proceedings of Association for the Advancement of Artificial Intelligence 2008 Spring Symposium (AAAI 2008) on Social Information Processing, Technical Report SS-08-06*, 42–7.

Kim, H. L., Decker, S. and Breslin, J. G. (2010) 'Representing and Sharing Folksonomies with Semantics', *Journal of Information Science*, **36**, 57–72.

Lin, N., Li, D., Ding, Y., He, B., Qin, Z., Tang, J., Li, J. and Dong, T. (2012) The Dynamic Features of Delicious, Flickr and YouTube, *Journal of the American Society for Information Science and Technology*, **63**, 139–62.

Lu, C., Park, J. and Hu, X. (2010) User Tags Versus Expert-Assigned Subject Terms: a comparison of LibraryThing tags and Library of Congress Subject Headings, *Journal of Information Science*, **36**, 763–79.

Mika, P. (2007) Ontologies are Us: a unified model of social networks and semantics, *Journal of Web Semantics: science, services and agents on the world wide web*, **5**, 5–15.

Ohmukai, I., Hamasaki, M. and Takeda, H. (2005) A Proposal of Community-Based Folksonomy with RDF Metadata. In *Proceedings of the ISWC 2005 Workshop on End User Semantic Web Interaction, Galway, Ireland, 7 November 2005.*

Passant, A. and Laublet, P. (2008) Meaning of A Tag: a collaborative approach to bridge the gap between tagging and linked data. In *The 17th International World Wide Web Conference (WWW 2008) Workshop on Linked Data on the Web (LDOW2008)*, Beijing, China, 22 April 2008, http://events.linkeddata.org/ldow2008/papers/22-passant-laublet-meaning-of-a-tag.pdf.

Passant, A., Laublet, P., Breslin, J. G. and Decker, S. (2009) A URI is Worth a Thousand Tags: from tagging to linked data with MOAT, *International Journal on Semantic Web and Information Systems*, **5**, 71–94.

Schreiber, G. and Raimond, Y. (2014) *W3C RDF 1.1 Primer*, www.w3.org/TR/rdf11-primer.

Shirky, C. (2005) *Ontology is Overrated: categories, links and tags*, www.shirky.com/writings/ontology_overrated.html.

Smith, G. (2008) *Tagging: people-powered metadata for the social web,* New Riders.

Syn, S. Y. (2014) Dealing with the Long Tail: providing uniformity to compound tags. In *Proceedings of the ASIS&T 2014 Annual Meeting, Seattle, WA, 31 October–4 November 2014.*

Thomas, M., Caudle, D. M. and Schmitz, C. M. (2009) To Tag or not to Tag?, *Library Hi Tech*, **27**, 411–34.

Trant, J. (2006) Social Classification and Folksonomy in Art Museums: early data from the steve.museum Tagger prototype, *Advances in Classification Research Online*, **17**, 1–30.

Vander Wal, T. (2007) *Folksonomy Coinage and Definition*, www.vanderwal.net/folksonomy.html.

Weller, K. (2007) Folksonomies and Ontologies: two new players in indexing and knowledge representation. In *Proceedings of the Online Information 2007, London, UK,* 108–15.

Yi, K. and Chan, L. M. (2009) Linking Folksonomy to Library of Congress Subject Headings: an exploratory study, *Journal of Documentation*, **65**, 872–900.

Chapter 4

Social tagging and public policy

Ryan Deschamps

Introduction

Recognising the importance of the diffusion of ideas and learning to policy change, policymakers have utilised social tagging to pressure governments to propose new legislation or forestall existing bills (Ems, 2014; Jeffares, 2014; Saxton et al., 2015). Among the many examples seen in the last decade include the use of Twitter by the Chicago Health Departments to discourage electronic cigarettes (Harris et al., 2014), by politicians to frame healthcare (e.g. #Obamacare) (Hemphill, Culotta and Heston, 2013) or to protest a lack of action on climate change (Segerberg and Bennett, 2011). This chapter will focus on the connection between social tagging as it is understood in the online environment and its connection to the apparatus of the state. Research on the use of social tags for identifying important legislation, promoting scientific knowledge or consulting the public is a growing yet uncertain area of study (Harris et al., 2014; Jeffares, 2014; Kapp, Hensel and Schnoring, 2015; Shapiro and Hemphill, 2014, 2017). Still, the potential of the internet to help bridge the gap between citizens and the state continues to be both an aspiration and a disappointment for the field of internet governance.

Social tagging in information science refers to 'the practice of publicly labeling or categorising resources in a shared, on-line environment' (Trant, 2009, 1). For sociologists, the novelty of social tagging lies in its public nature compared to more private forms of coding in sociological field work (see Postill and Pink, 2012), but for political scientists the public naming of resources is not new at all. Removing the term online from this definition does not erase a wide array of social organization that occurs on a daily basis. The rather arbitrary naming of items in the budgeting process of a government (e.g. for clean technology), in particular, involves public labelling and categorising of resources, conducted by members of affected organizations, political leaders, policy-makers and, in some cases, individuals with unique interest or power in the particular policy area.

Social tagging itself is not a new process and is closely connected to the role of institutions in public life. In policy theory, institutions refer to systems of formal and informal rules and routines in a society that have accumulated over time. The conventions around the naming of various significant objects are part of this process. Marking territory, assigning social roles and following rituals all require some demarcation of objects based not only on social convention, but also on the reinforcement of concepts over time. Online tagging adds a new dimension to these institutions and is worth examining not only on its own, but within the context of existing policy theory.

Online social tags are a highly versatile way of organising both ideas and people (Page, 2012). One of the most popular examples occurs on Twitter with the hashtag, an informal approach to tagging by placing an octothorpe in front of a keyword or phrase such as #exciting. According to Couldry (2012, 41), the hashtag on Twitter presents itself as a way for groups to cohere as a form of 'presencing for groups without previous identity or symbolic capital'. In theory, online social tagging separates the practical challenges of co-ordinating people around ideas from the historical institutions that formalise political behaviour. One does not get to influence a government budget without significant authority, but one can influence an online community with an appropriate or timely use of language. Symbolic capital – a tacit understanding in a society that one represents a particular cause due to honour or prestige – typically accumulates over time through social interaction and public events. The capacity to present a public movement potentially without this process does indicate something unique about social tagging in political life. Online tags are more accessible to the general public, making them less formal than the apparatus of the state, and they provide a wider scope for framing and interpreting issues. For example, instead of working through the formal language of agriculture, activists can evoke more emotional responses by framing issues with hashtags like #gmos, #food, #nutrition, #animalrights or #farmerrights.

The introduction of online environments to the development of institutions has been revolutionary to a limited extent. Historical examples of political changes occurring due to the marking and distribution of internet messages are numerous. The mass online presentation of secret government documents by Wikileaks, for instance, is often considered the impetus for mass online protests during the #ArabSpring, #kony2012 and the Occupy Wall Street (#ows) movements (Beckett and Ballho, 2012; Saleh, 2013). However, online activity often spreads a message to a wide audience, but often with short-lived or precarious effects. If the use of social tags online to identify, label and produce meaning for social problems effects social change, it does so with seemingly unpredictable results. Practitioners of historical method in policy theory have shown that most policy has a long institutional pedigree (Kingdon and Thurber, 1984; Skocpol and Amenta, 1986; Skocpol, Ganz and Munson, 2000). Policy change appears sudden and surprising to those who only pay attention to the latest news; policy-makers have simply been waiting for appropriate windows to introduce them to the public.

That the internet is an influential characteristic of life in the 21st century is hardly up for debate; nearly half of the world population uses the internet in some way. Facebook, the most popular social platform, has over 2 billion active users. Google conducts over 3.4 billion searches per day or 1.2 trillion searches per year. YouTube has over 1.3 billion users with over 5 billion video views per day. Seen as a single entity, the internet is a nation-state unto itself with global influence and enormous capacity to diffuse information and form virtual policy networks around policy ideas (Castells, 2010; McNutt, 2006, 2010). The risk of such macroanalysis is that it favours interpretations that are more proverbial than they are evidence-based. It is true that online social tagging is influential in an internal sense; it can raise attention to an online audience very quickly, for example. The extension of this online attention to the apparatus of the state is a very different matter. While the influence of online activity on the state is uncertain, the influence of state institutions on online activity is very apparent under empirical examination.

This chapter will examine the connection between public policy and social tagging in a number of ways. First, it will review the current literature on policy agenda setting and identify existing research agendas that connect to the use of social tagging in policy advocacy. Then it will provide some samples of Twitter hashtag use in Canadian political life, namely:

- established hashtags for Canadian provincial politics
- the example of Idle No More, a large political protest related to First Nations Treaty Rights
- the case of Amanda Todd and Rehtaeh Parsons, two victims of cyberbullying, whose stories became the impetus for new legislation by the Canadian federal government.

Through these examples, the chapter will show that social tagging is not disconnected from Canada's political and social context, although there is some evidence to suggest that global involvement can influence the distribution of ideas. The conclusion will discuss the importance of the institutional context on social tagging, calling for more inclusion of policy theory to solidify existing research into a more comprehensive framework for inclusion of online interactions to social change.

Defining policy agendas in the public organization of knowledge

In policy theory, the interface between public attention and government decision making usually occurs during a period of policy agenda setting. The term *agenda setting* has differing but connected meanings in communications, sociology and public administration (Wolfe, Jones and Baumgartner, 2013). Formally, a *policy agenda* refers to the policy items that reach the boardroom meetings of top political officials who govern over the particular policy area (Blakeney and Borins, 1998; Lasswell, 1956). However, public policy research usually extends its analysis to include the role of the bureaucracy, media and the wider public in identifying, framing and defining public policy problems. In some research programmes, agenda setting is defined as the 'organizational analogue to attention allocation at the individual level' (Jones and Baumgartner, 2005, 38). The human capacity to parallelise, that is, to focus on two or more things at the same time, is limited to short-term memory, meaning that many potential solutions to a problem can be missed. Organizations help improve parallelisation through the division of labour, but ultimately the parallel thinking across organizations must be brought to leaders for a decision (Simon, 1990). The formal naming of policy problems, through mission statements, recommendations or goal setting, for example, is a traditional strategy to communicate the complex data gathering and evaluation that occurs in a policy environment. Failure to categorise and describe research to leaders can result in criticism that one is stuck in the weeds and thus unable to lead the appropriate change across the organization (Burt, 2004).

Communication studies tend to focus on policies that have media attention, with the assumption that the media acts as an essential stakeholder in the process of bringing social problems to the attention of the state (McCombs and Shaw, 1972). The naive view of this process suggests that as someone recognises a social problem, the media provides a frame for the narrative that increases public attention and the shift in public attention encourages politicians to act in order to attract support from a voting public. The apex of this process is the focusing event – a natural disaster, accident or heinous crime – that captures the public imagination and results in an impetus to act in a way that will prevent the event from happening in the future (Birkland, 2004, 2006; Kingdon and Thurber, 1984). However, empirical evidence suggests that governments are more likely to use media as an index for policy issues for public consumption rather than the other way around (Jones and Wolfe, 2010). At various times, journalists rely on government or opposition experts to identify the key issues of upcoming debate and thus can be complicit in increasing attention for government agendas rather than public interests. Popular accounts of citizen journalism on social media are sometimes related to the challenges of consuming media that does not have some form of government influence (Bednar, 2012; Das et al., 2013; Goode, 2009; Qian and Yangagizawa, 2010; Whitten-Woodring, 2009).

For the sociologist, the focus in agenda setting research is the process between the recognition of a focusing event and a decision by government to act. The way that social movements form, co-ordinate and organise is often the unit of analysis as they operate in policy fields or policy domains – arenas of common interest or understanding based on an area of policy (Burstein, 1991). The language of a field is important for social tagging, because it is the way that groups form around policy ideas through coalitions (Sabatier, 1987, 1988, 2006), organizational networks (Knoke, 1986, 1993; Laumann and Knoke, 1987; Rhodes, 1997, 2006) or policy communities (Atkinson and Coleman, 1992). Nascent studies have suggested that a hybrid form of agenda setting occurs inside the social media environment, with interaction effects among traditional media sources, citizen journalists, bloggers and commenters showing considerable alignment in some cases (Chadwick, 2011, 2013; Toepfl and Piwoni, 2017).

For the public administrator, agenda setting involves actions of the bureaucracy – experts in a policy area, often with unique awareness of the intricacies of public policies and how they influence other areas of government concern. Collectively, public administrators are often aware of potential policy concerns before the public is, since governments wish to identify and resolve public policy problems before disastrous consequences occur. However, even large, well-organised bureaucracies cannot maintain awareness of all social problems at all times. Knowing this, they create routines and structures that help prioritise policy problems and allot resources accordingly. Among the structures that define government information are geographic borders, defined by legislature or government treaties. In turn, a great amount of government information is defined by jurisdiction first and then function. In contrast to beliefs of 'from the ground up' democratic discourse, think tanks, political organizations and interest groups find themselves forming around the geographic and cultural boundaries determined by government rather than imposing their own (Campbell and Pedersen, 2014; Milakovich, 2012; Skocpol, Ganz and Munson, 2000). In policy theory, ideas are an important, but subordinate element compared to established institutions. For the most part, established ideas trump novelty, constraining options for transformative policy change (Béland, 2009; Campbell, 2004; Hall, 1993).

Nascent research has shown that governments are interested in using tools like social tagging for government services, but the focus has been on one-way distribution of information and little testing as to the return on investment that such services provide (Criado, Sandoval-Almazan and Gil-Garcia, 2013; Deschamps, 2012; Mergel, 2013). The three goals for social media interaction by government tend to be related to increased transparency, greater citizen participation and increased collaboration among government departments (Mergel, 2013). This has included sharing of documents and source code for web platforms, research data, databases and documents via GitHub, a code repository service (Mergel, 2015). However, government organizations can face severe public criticism in their online activities. For example, the New York Police Department naively predicted that the public would treat their online campaign #myNYPD favourably, but instead faced a response that featured a global campaign showing photography of police brutality (Jackson and Foucault Welles, 2016; Mergel, 2017). While the goal of government use of social techniques like tagging to greater engage the population remains an aspiration for democratic theorists, the reality is that many governments are constrained by the risk of being exposed or defamed by media-savvy political activists.

Common approaches to classification of policy have included analysis of budget data, party manifestos and functional analysis of networks (John, 2006). Budget analysis typically applies a time-based causality analysis of one or more variables such as media attention or parliamentary debate against budgetary changes to test whether changes in the saliency of an issue reflect changes in government action (Hofferbert and Budge, 1992; Jones and Baumgartner, 2005; Soroka, 2002a, 2002b). Unfortunately, the design of budgets tends to be unique to national jurisdictions, making it difficult to compare across groupings.

While institutions structure policy development, ideas are increasingly observed as a catalyst for policy change. The heightened awareness of an issue in the public eye has long been of interest to policy theorists and researchers. The Policy Agendas Project has emerged as an indispensable tool in the measurement of policy agendas across nations (Baumgartner, Green-Pedersen and Jones, 2013;

Dowding et al., 2010; John, 2006; John and Margetts, 2003). Based on the Topics Codebook, a detailed thesaurus for coding major policy issues in news media, debates in congress, television and so on, the Policy Agendas Project hopes to provide a resource for consistent comparisons of policy agendas in research that compares government responses to similar policy problems.

Using the codebook, punctuated equilibrium theory has proposed that policy follows an incremental path, punctuated by moments of rapid change due to exogenous shocks in a policy system (Baumgartner, Jones and Mortensen, 2014; John and Margetts, 2003; Jones and Baumgartner, 2012). According to this theory, actors in political circumstances do not act solely according to a rational understanding of political preferences; instead, political preferences are 'multidimensional and . . . attentiveness to preferences can shift abruptly as the decisional context changes' (Jones, 1994, 5). Due to these attention shifts, governments respond with occasional punctuations shown through sudden changes to government budgets or shifts in political debate. With this constant shifting of attention, policies can either be constrained through negative feedback loops or amplified as public attention results in increased government responses, which in turn result in increased public attention. Such positive feedback loops can create situations where governments increase budgets to prevent crime even while crime is declining (Jones and Baumgartner, 2005).

Twitter as a political index

Since the 2016 US election, the use of Twitter as a governance tool by the President of the United States has been a source of incredulity by media. To Donald Trump, for example, Twitter has been a way of being 'modern day presidential' and a way of bypassing the media as a broker between the public and the state (Wootson, 2017). Predictions about the internet as a facilitator of expanded democratic involvement and disrupter of traditional institutions were well under way in the 1990s (Budge, 1996; Castells, 2010; Effing, Hillegersberg and Huibers, 2011), but forming research into an accepted comprehensive theory has eluded the policy research community thus far.

Beyond political uses, there is increased interest by the intelligence community in the use of colloquial language in social media to identify potential threats, properly characterise political events or predict trends in health risks, crime or political upheaval (Orman, Miller and Barlett, 2014). While standard terms provide a level of reliability in analysis, informal terms in large data sets can provide a highly flexible means to detect social problems in real time, cross-validated against other metadata such as the actors involved, the time of day the terms were used, the speed and spread of diffusion of its use across a population, and so on. The constant attempt to renew, redefine, exchange, endorse, criticise and discard policy ideas online is an important feature of social tagging data. According to Jeffares (2014, 13), 'policy ideas need to be understood as much for their ideational qualities as their visionary, brand-like, instrumental and absorptive qualities'. As such, they do not always operate on an incremental plane but instead can co-occur among different 'streams' focused on the nature of the problem, possible solutions or strategic relationships for resource gathering (Howlett, 1998; Kingdon and Thurber, 1984). Extant research has attempted to categorise political tags according to function. For example, Daer, Hoffman and Goodman (2014) suggest five categories of functional activities for a hashtag: *emphasising, critiquing, identifying, iterating* and *rallying*. They suggest (2014, 2–3) that 'user-generated ideas can help generate new functions for old forms' as they 'move across platforms, audiences and affordances, which communication designers must take into account as part of their development process'. Such a view is too optimistic in the case of policy development because it fails to take power and authority into account. Despite the interactivity of policy discussion that occurs both online and off, it is not a primary goal of most political leaders to interact with the public online, because risk associated with losing control of messaging is high compared to more formal communication approaches (Small, 2012; Stromer-Galley and Jamieson, 2001).

Exploration of political hashtags

To illustrate patterns in the connection between online tagging and policy behaviour, this section will provide some exploratory examples of policy-related social tagging. As discussed, political discussion is rife with multiplicities, that is, terms that take on different meanings depending on the social context, which can shift quite rapidly as information transports from social network to social network, to media reports, to political debates. According to policy theory, however, national institutions remain the most influential factor in social tagging activity. While this research focuses on Canadian tags, similar patterns can be shown elsewhere (Conover et al., 2013; Wang, Liu and Gao, 2016).

Exploratory analysis of political information on Twitter can be done in two ways. First, one can extract a sample of a general topic over a period (a month or a series of months) and explore general trends in the data, or specific events in the course of policy change can be observed. This chapter will provide an example of both types. In the first case, tweets containing the hashtags for Canadian provincial politics – #abpoli (Alberta), #bcpoli (British Columbia), #mbpoli

(Manitoba), #nbpoli (New Brunswick), #nspoli (Nova Scotia), #onpoli (Ontario) and #skpoli (Saskatchewan) – have been sampled across multiple months with no specific intention regarding events or context. This method is to focus on the general use of political hashtags for a given population. They were collected from September to November 2014 and then again in March and April of 2015 using the Twitter API and a custom Python script. Unfortunately, due to limitations of the Twitter API, only 5000 of the past tweets can be captured per search; the API provides a sample of the data, rather than the full 'firehose' output (Morstatter et al., 2013). In general, most of the listed hashtags only rarely extend beyond these rate limits.

For each sample, usernames were extracted for further exploration and stored in a table with each hashtag containing a list of *actors* (Twitter users) who have, at one time, used the hashtag in one or more of their tweets. The data frame is then converted to a table containing all the actors as rows, all the hashtags as columns and each cell contains a value of 1 or 0 to indicate whether the actor has or has not used the hashtag in question. This data was applied to the correspondence analysis which will be described in the Provincial politics section below. An additional table was created by collecting a random sample of 1000 users and marking each actor as a member of a profession based on content analysis of their Twitter profile. Based on user profiles, each of the thousand users selected were given a profession title as *media* (journalists or media organizations), *professionals* (lawyers, physicians, nurses, librarians etc.), government (public servants or government organizations), *politicians* (people in or running for political office), *business* (business owners or executives), *students* (academics or students), *activists* (people who declare themselves an activist or advocate for a social cause), or *citizen* (no declared professional status). In cases where individuals meet more than one of these categories, whichever item is listed first on their profile was accepted.

To observe patterns of policy events over time in the cases of policy related to the Idle No More movement and cyberbullying, tweets were collected manually, as the Twitter API does not provide free access to historical data. For the former, the hashtag #idlenomore was used almost exclusively, as this was the main pattern of use by the social movement. In the latter case, the advocates primarily used the names of two well publicised victims of cyberbullying, Amanda Todd and Rehtaeh Parsons, respectively. Key events were identified using media reports of events and then tweets that applied the associated hashtags were found using the Twitter search interface. Actor data was coded manually, ignoring those who did not reply or retweet another user to reduce the impact of spam, trolls or users posting irrelevant information. First the actors were identified as belonging either to Canada or the USA or as International users, to determine the impact of the policy on the global community. Users with no location information were coded as of *anonymous location*. Then the Canadian actors were coded for their participation as regional actors, using their provincial location. Some actors identified themselves as *Canadian* with no regional affiliation and these were coded as *Canada*.

These two samples of political tweets found among various hashtags provides a basis to explore the role of jurisdiction and region on political tweeting. Using this data, we will examine the role that national, provincial or regional identity plays on the spreading of policy-related messages and how it changes over time. This perspective follows the fundamental policy belief that knowledge communities form according to institutional rather than globally recognised patterns of identity (Campbell and Pedersen, 2014).

Provincial politics

When Canadians mark their tweets as having political content, one of the most important elements of their tagging is the jurisdiction of the issue, whether related to a province, municipality, a particular political leader or to a lesser extent a government department. In Canada, there are three levels of government, federal, provincial and aboriginal self-government, and two official languages, for which English Canada will be the focus here. British Columbia has a mountainous terrain that sets the western boundary for the Prairie Provinces, Alberta, Saskatchewan and Manitoba. Ontario, Canada's most populous province, containing nearly 40% of all Canadians, surrounds the Great Lakes, while the Atlantic Provinces New Brunswick, Nova Scotia, Prince Edward Island and Newfoundland, each contain between 500,000 and a million citizens.

In order to observe the relationships among Twitter users and political hashtags, the tweets and actors will be visualised using correspondence analysis, a technique for visualising the interrelation of categorical information in two-dimensional space (Faust, 2005; Wasserman and Faust, 1994). While a detailed description of correspondence analysis is beyond the scope of this chapter, the premise is that co-ordinates for the visualisation are created based on cross-relationships of categorical items. Graphs and analysis were conducted using the R programming language with the FactoMineR library (Lê, Josse and Husson, 2008). The relationships, either weighted or unweighted, are placed on a two-way matrix, normalised and then transformed using singular value decomposition (svd), which provides co-ordinate scores for the rows and columns plus eigenvalues, representing the overall contribution scores for each dimension of analysis. While the total number of dimensions is equal to the number of columns or rows, whichever is smaller, typically the two most influential dimensions are shown on a graph. In the case of this chapter, the columns (triangle points) represent different hashtags and the rows (circles) will represent different Twitter users, set individually, or in categories such as location or profession.

Some examples can help bring correspondence analysis into relief. Visualisations produced by a correspondence analysis can be analysed in a number of ways. First, items with similar memberships, for example, two or more hashtags that have a large number of similar users or users that tend to use the same hashtags, will tend to cluster together. Second, observations that are closer to the origin of the graph will tend to represent items with more mainstream appeal. For example, a hashtag that is used commonly with other hashtags will tend towards the centre of the graph, while a hashtag used with fewer other hashtags will tend towards the outside. Third, observations can be examined across the two dimensions – horizontal and vertical – of the graph. Thus, a separation of two hashtags on the horizontal axis will tend to suggest a way that some relationships are distinguished from one another. For example, if hashtags for #prochoice and #prolife appeared on opposite ends of the horizontal axis, this may suggest that the population of hashtag users was divided on the topic of abortion.

Five correspondence analysis visualisations are provided to show the cross-relationships of Twitter users of provincially coded English Canadian political hashtags: #abpoli (Alberta), #bcpoli (British Columbia), #mbpoli (Manitoba), #nbpoli (New Brunswick), #nspoli (Nova Scotia), #onpoli (Ontario) and #skpoli (Saskatchewan). Data for Quebec and Prince Edward Island have been removed due to differences in language and population size. The predominant language in Quebec is French and therefore likely to have different naming conventions. In some cases, the data for Newfoundland tweets was too small to include in the analysis, so it was excluded. Prince Edward Island's population is a fraction of the other provinces and so is not included in the analysis.

While the collection of Twitter hashtags in this section was conducted without a specific purpose, some political events may have had an influence on the patterns that emerged. For example, the correspondence analysis of provincial political tags shows generally that users conform to the dynamics of geopolitics in most cases, but occasionally one political region – usually Ontario, Alberta or British Columbia – will have additional concern from across the country. For example, in Figure 4.1 (September 2014) on the next page, a high-profile election of Jim Prentice to the leadership of the Conservative party in Alberta may have sparked increased interest in Alberta from different provinces. The clustering of the graph is according to region, with Prairie Provinces in the centre, New Brunswick and Nova Scotia top left, Ontario bottom left and BC (British Columbia) on the right.

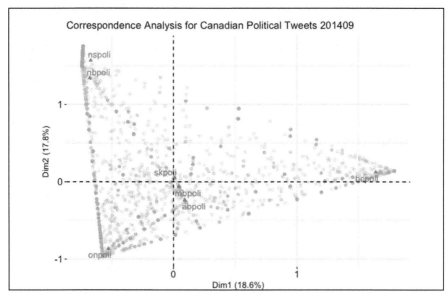

Figure 4.1 *Correspondence graph showing cross-use of hashtag by Twitter users, September 2014*

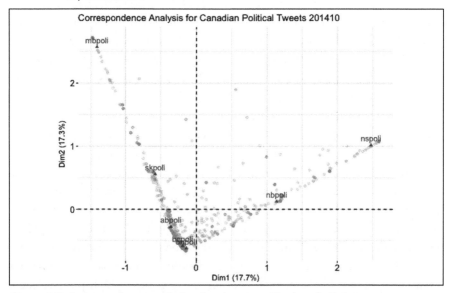

Figure 4.2 *Correspondence graph showing cross-use of hashtag by Twitter users, October 2014*

Similar patterns appear in Figures 4.2 and 4.3 (October and November 2014), as a terrorist shooting in Ottawa drew increased attention to Ontario, while a New Democratic Party (NDP) leadership convention created greater interest in Alberta, drawing #onpoli and #abpoli closer to the origin of the graph. In other words, Twitter users who used hashtags belonging to other provinces also tended to use #onpoli and #abpoli. This is probably because the Ottawa shooting brought greater attention to Ontario. Nonetheless, the regional character of the formation of the hashtags remains intact, with the Prairie Provinces in the top left quadrant, Nova Scotia and New Brunswick in the top right and the remainder mainstream political issues featured near the centre.

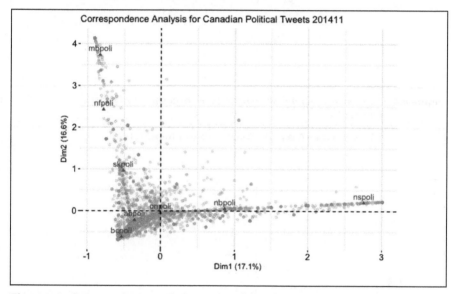

Figure 4.3 *Correspondence graph showing cross-use of hashtag by Twitter users, November 2014*

Again, while the tweets collected were generated without particular notice of news events, Figures 4.4 and 4.5 (March and April 2015) on the next page show a period when an election campaign in Alberta was the prominent news item; yet again the regional character of political tweeting remains stable across the board. Similar to patterns described by punctuated equilibrium and network theories, the relationship of political tweeting follows primarily long-lasting institutional trends based on regions punctuated by various streams of cross-regional events – usually in heavier populated areas – that attract greater mainstream interest. While the data follow general Canadian geopolitical patterns (people from Nova Scotia are more likely to tweet about New

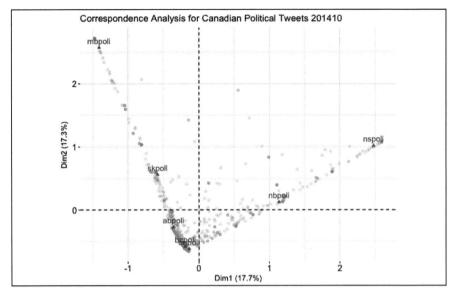

Figure 4.4 *Correspondence graph showing cross-use of hashtag by Twitter users, March 2015*

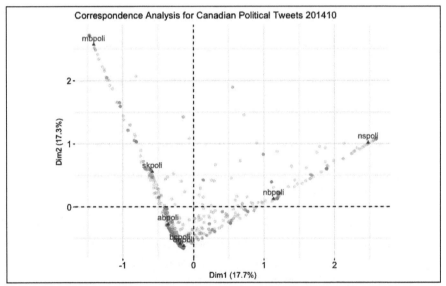

Figure 4.5 *Correspondence graph showing cross-use of hashtag by Twitter users, April 2015*

Brunswick than they are about British Columbia), we cannot rely upon these patterns to make useful predictions, as both predictable and unpredictable events can influence the way people come to notice hashtags on the service.

A further analysis was provided for a random sample of 1000 tweets in November 2014. These tweets were coded manually for provincial or national location and a similar analysis was conducted. In Figure 4.6, the visualisation shows that locale plays a strong role in the choice to tweet about one province or another. The location of the Twitter user (in triangles) closely matches the use of the hashtag (in circles). While intuitive, this result affirms the theoretical position that knowledge communities usually form national issues (or in this case, a regional issue) first and then traverse to more international discourse (Campbell and Pedersen, 2014). Interest from user accounts in the USA and international users from Europe or South America tends to follow the more populous provincial hashtags like #abpoli or #onpoli, rather than those of smaller regions like #skpoli and #nspoli. While the hashtag for Quebec politics was not included in the analysis, some people appeared to be from Quebec and tweeted about New Brunswick politics more than the other provinces. This result is likely due both to the proximity of New Brunswick to Quebec and the use of French language in both these provinces.

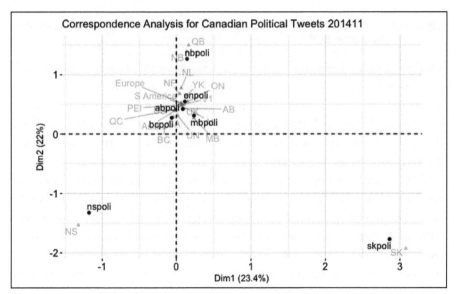

Figure 4.6 *Correspondence graph showing cross-use of hashtag by Twitter user location, November 2014*

The same sample was coded for user profile *profession* and is shown in Figure 4.7 on the following page. In this case, the horizontal axis, accounting for 39.1% of the total variance, separated media-oriented accounts (on the left side) from politicians and government organizations (on the right). On the vertical axis, politicians and governments were separated, potentially suggesting a separation between politically oriented actors and institutional ones. Activists were

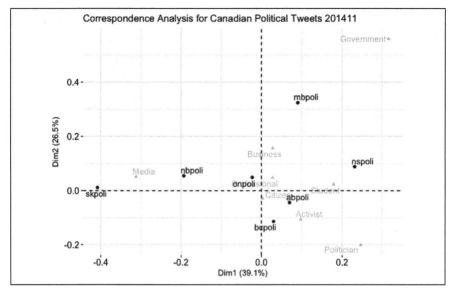

Figure 4.7 *Correspondence graph showing cross-use of hashtag by Twitter user profession, November 2014*

similarly separated from business actors, possibly for the same reasons. As might be expected, citizens were found close to the origin, with professionals and students. While a greater sample is necessary to determine a causal relationship between media and political hashtags, the separation of media-based users (on the left) from all other professions suggests that there is a distinction between the way the media interpret political events and other groups do.

Overall, the tweeting of the actors on these days suggests two fundamental patterns of behaviour. The first is time of participation, reflected in the geographic separation of east and west coast tweets, probably due to time zone differences. Time of participation probably explains the separation of Nova Scotia political tweets from other groups, for example. However, significant differences did not necessarily show for the case of Alberta and Ontario, where there is a two-hour difference in time zone. Second, geographic location, represented by the connection of regional political news to government agendas and voter interests, also appears to play a role in the separations of hashtag use. Due to the exploratory nature of the analysis at this stage, these two variables have not been controlled. However, Canadian political tweets do show a trend towards a pattern of interest in political topics based on regional interests, but are led by a flow of information coming from the economic centres of Ontario and Alberta, which in turn tend to attract more international interest than other regions. Discrepancies from these patterns occurred probably due to exogenous events such as an election or a dramatic instance such as the Ottawa shooting. Now that the general patterns of tweeting have been examined and analysed, it is worth examining specific cases of policy development over time and the use of hashtags.

Idle No More

In November 2012, First Nations peoples across Canada began to take notice of an omnibus budget bill C-45 thought to 'give oil and nuclear companies room to devastate the land and environment even further' (Tootoosis, 2012). It sparked the beginnings of an emerging battle between First Nations groups and the conservative Canadian government led by Stephen Harper after the passing of Bill C-45, believed to be hiding significant policy that had important impacts on First Nations treaty rights and environmental regulation of land and water. Idle No More was a cross-Canada movement developed with the partial goal of educating all Canadians on matters of the use of land resources and their potential effect on the environment (Coates, 2014; Tootoosis, 2012). Cross-Canada protests occurred, including circle dances and what Tanya Kappo called a constant community meeting over social media channels (Kappo and King, 2014). The term Idle No More was turned into a political tag #idlenomore to signal the frustration of First Nations peoples with government policy and a lack of awareness about both the treatment of First Nations peoples in Canada and the importance of long-lasting treaty relationships between First Nations peoples and the British Crown, which long preceded the birth of Canada through Confederation in 1867. Key to their concerns was the court-mandated *duty to consult* First Nations peoples prior to any policy that would affect their livelihood. Bill C-45 was seen by those in the movement as a breach of this duty.

Samples of tweets were taken from two separate hours during three events in the history of Idle No More, using a manual extraction method. In this case, it was important that not only actors mentioning #IdleNoMore but also the people replying to them would be captured in the analysis. Each event had particular relevance in the ultimate presentation of policy. The height of the Idle No More movement online was on 2 January 2013, with tens of thousands of tweets over the course of the evening, as well as a number of protests, including those in Vancouver, Ottawa, Toronto and Winnipeg, being reported by media. The date of 10 January 2013 saw meetings with First Nations leaders and Prime Minister Stephen Harper as a policy response to the month-long protests that had occurred. 7 October was the 250th anniversary of the 1763 Royal Proclamation, the first treaty agreement between the British Crown and First Nations peoples and an early model for the relationship between the Canadian Government and First Nations peoples.

As shown in Table 4.1, Canadians who used the #IdleNoMore hashtag on these days resemble the overall Canadian population in terms of provincial representation, with greater representation from the Prairie Provinces, where the proportion of First Nations peoples is higher. However, participation from Alberta was lower than from the other two Prairie Provinces. The predominantly French-speaking population of Quebec is also under-represented. Participation in B.C. was greater in the evening of 2 January, when the Vancouver protests occurred and in the evening of 7 October, where the increased participation by Atlantic Canadians predicts activity by fracking protesters ten days later (Deschamps, 2015).

Table 4.1 *Canadian national demographics for Idle No More networks*

		Canada	BC	AB	SK & MB	ON	QC	ATL	TERR
Idle No More Protests, 2 January 2013	AM	14.18%	12.26%	8.41%	10.57%	36.78%	12.5%	4.8%	0.48%
	PM	12.57%	24.96%	8.26%	9.51%	34.29%	4.67%	4.13%	0.75%
Meetings with Harper, 10 January 2013	AM	12.01%	10.21%	9.51%	11.42%	37.34%	10.71%	7.8%	1.00%
	PM	13.2%	15.9%	10.08%	10.39%	34.93%	9.15%	4.68%	1.25%
Demonstration for Royal Proclamation Act, 7 October	AM	19.61%	16.34%	10.46%	12.42%	30.72%	3.92%	6.54%	0.00%
	PM	13.77%	7.25%	6.52%	22.46%	34.06%	7.97%	7.96%	0.00%
Population		–	13.06%	11.62%	6.77%	38.49%	23.09%	6.65%	0.33%
First Nations population		–	16.6%	15.08%	25.3%	21.5%	10.1%	6.7%	4.5%

As shown in Table 4.2, while approximately 60% of users were Canadian, a sizable population did not cite their location in their profile and between 12% and 20% of the participating users came from the USA or other countries. The

Table 4.2 *Global demographics for Idle No More networks*

		Canada	USA	International	Unknown	N
Idle No More Protests, 2 January 2013	AM	62.18%	8.67%	4.04%	25.11%	669
	PM	58.05%	9.14%	3.89%	28.97%	962
Meetings with Harper, 10 January 2013	AM	53.25%	6.72%	5.22%	34.81%	1798
	PM	61.76%	9.12%	5.28%	23.84%	1611
Demonstration for Royal Proclamation Act, 7 October 2013	AM	52.04%	12.59%	6.46%	28.91%	294
	PM	52.67%	12.21%	8.40%	26.70%	262

international representation for Idle No More increased by 7 October, which is interesting because the Royal Proclamation is a fairly unique moment in Canadian jurisprudence and unlikely to have interest outside Canada. One reason is that the movement changed its focus to include broader environmental issues such as fracking and proposals to build the Keystone XL pipeline in the USA (Deschamps, 2014, 2015).

While the movement showed some continuity in terms of national and regional statistics, at the micro-level the movement was driven by a very small group of users with sustained interest in the movement, while a much larger percentage commented once and left the discussion. Figure 4.8 shows the relationship of users across the three days collected. According to traditional policy theory, the interest of actors within the policy field should contain a number of people sufficiently interested to participate across various notable policy events. In this case, the percentage of this interested group is less than 1%. Given that this group would include people who were mentioned (e.g. @stephenharper) during the events as well as people who participated, this appears like a very small number for such a large movement and implies a tendency for viral rather than substantive interest in the policy field. For this reason, it seems prudent to consider social tagging to have limited impact on policy development on its own. From observation of the tweets, the users who

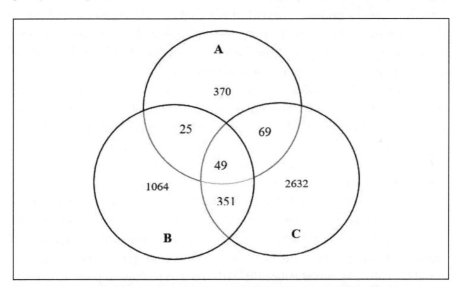

Figure 4.8 *Actor distribution for Idle No More Events. A: 2 January 2013* (Spence Hunger Strike and protests); B: 11 January 2013 (Meeting of the AFN Chiefs Council with PM Stephen Harper); C: 7 October 2013 (200th Anniversary of the Royal Proclamation Act).

participated in only one event tended to show emotive rather than substantive interest in the hashtag. For example, many simply called for Prime Minister Stephen Harper to acknowledge the Idle No More movement and meet with First Nations leaders. The influence of such tagging to co-ordinate real-life protests, on the other hand, may have had more impact. However, this connection is not visible through the observation of tweets.

Cyberbullying

In Canada the names Amanda Todd and Rehtaeh Parsons became international symbols for both cyberbullying and the apparent failure of police to prosecute people responsible for cybercrime. In November 2011 Rehtaeh Parsons was horrified to discover that intimate images were being distributed across her school without her consent. At the time, she alleged that the images recorded her being sexually assaulted (Segal, 2015). She attempted suicide multiple times, changed schools and faced weeks of hospitalisation as she struggled to deal with the implications of this prolonged cyberbullying and alleged assault. Not until after her death were two young men tried and convicted for distributing child pornography. A report by Segal (2015) found that the police did not follow proper protocol in the case, but the problems did not sit only with police. When police attempted to interview students at the high school Parsons attended, school authorities allegedly thwarted them. The report concluded that the prosecution made an error in advising police that the case for child pornography was unlikely to produce a conviction. Segal cited a lack of knowledge of the legal circumstances as the cause.

Amanda Todd, a native of British Columbia, was a victim of capping in 2012, which means convincing someone to share intimate photos, taking a screen capture and sharing it on the internet. She was blackmailed: repeatedly her pictures were shared with classmates in her school. Aydin Coban, a Dutch man, is charged in relation to the crimes but is not expected to appear in Canada until 2018, as Dutch authorities try him for 79 charges of sexual assault and extortion before they extradite him (White, 2014). Coban's capture was far too late for Amanda Todd. Her images were shared and Todd faced repeated bullying over the photos, forcing her to change schools multiple times. After a number of attempts, Todd committed suicide at the age of 15. Later reports showed that the Royal Canadian Mounted Police (RCMP) received multiple reports of Amanda Todd being victimised online, but no action was taken (CBC News, 2013).

After the death of Rehtaeh Parsons, Peter MacKay, then Justice Minister and a Nova Scotia Member of Parliament, introduced Rehtaeh's Law, Bill C-13

Protecting Canadians from Online Crime Act. The two most significant changes were an amendment to the criminal code to include the distribution of non-consensual intimate images and provisions to increase the capacity of police to retrieve information from internet service providers (ISPs). The latter policy was intended to address the challenges of cross-border exchange of police information in order to capture online perpetrators.

The names Amanda Todd and Rehtaeh Parsons became social tags to raise the awareness of cyberbullying and the unfair treatment of women online. Similar to the Idle No More case, three events were captured to examine the national characteristics of the Tweeters. On 19 October 2012 a vigil was organised across Canada by education departments in Ontario and British Columbia to raise awareness of cyberbullying and commemorate the death of Amanda Todd. On 6 April 2013, after Rehtaeh Parsons's parents wrote blog posts describing Rehtaeh's ordeal and ultimate death, two separate hashtags emerged. The first #rehtaeh decried the horrors of Rehtaeh's story. The second, organised by the online activist group Anonymous, was #OpJustice4Rehtaeh, which was organised to co-ordinate action against Rehtaeh's tormentors. Finally, #c13, referring to Bill C-13, tabled on 24 November 2013 in the Canadian federal parliament, was used to refer to the policy that would address public concerns about these two events.

As shown in Table 4.3, in contrast to the Idle No More scenario, cyberbullying as an issue had much greater interest and involvement by US and international users (between 25% and 32%) and a notable participation by users who chose not to disclose their location (between 30% and 45%). The high number of users was partially due to the involvement of Anonymous in the #OpJustice4Rehtaeh case; however, in the Amanda Todd case it was more likely individual citizens with no particular interest in developing an online profile. Many of these accounts could be online trolls (people engaging online to stir controversy) but

Table 4.3 Global demographics for Twitter population for cyberbullying networks

		Canada	US	International	Unknown	N
Amanda Todd Vigil, 19 October 2012		18.57%	13.85%	22.34%	45.24%	1061
Rehtaeh Parson, 6 April 2013	OpJustice4	35.62%	15.63%	10.31%	38.43%	320
	Rehtaeh	35.67%	22.23%	10.49%	31.61%	715
Bill C-13, 24 November 2013		71.23%	1.82%	0.91%	26.03%	219%

unfortunately there is no empirical way to delineate an online troll from a regular citizen with a controversial opinion. However, when the Bill was introduced to the House of Commons, the interest was primarily Canadian, with few international followers and 26% of users having no disclosed location.

Table 4.4 outlines that, within Canada, the distribution of users follows the regional nature of the problem with a greater proportion of the population from British Columbia tweeting about Amanda Todd and of Nova Scotians tweeting about both the Rehtaeh Parsons story and Peter Mackay's introduction of Bill C-13 to the House of Commons. It is also of note that Peter Mackay was a prominent politician from the province of Nova Scotia as well. It is worth restating here that the percentages in these cases are somewhat deceptive. While the number of British Columbians were more likely to tweet about Amanda Todd (for instance), their representation is less than five percent of all the people who tweeted on the subject.

Table 4.4 *Canadian national demographics for Twitter population for cyberbullying networks*

		Can	BC	AB	SK &	ON	QC	ATL	TERR
Amanda Todd Vigil, 19 October 2012		14.92%	26.37%	10.45%	4.98%	30.85%	4.48%	5.96%	0.%
Rehtaeh Parson, 6 April 2013	OpJustice	8.6%	6.03%	6.03%	0.86%	23.28%	1.72%	49.99%	0.%
	Rehtaeh	13.46%	7.69%	4.6%	0.76%	26.54%	7.69%	36.16%	0.38%
Bill C-13, 24 November 2013		19.87%	10.26%	3.84%	2.56%	42.95%	4.49%	16.02%	0.00%
Canadian population		–	13.06%	11.62%	6.77%	38.49%	23.09%	6.65%	0.33%

Figure 4.9 opposite shows the cross-connection of Twitter users referring to the events of Amanda Todd, Rehtaeh Parsons and policy development respectively. While the connection between Amanda Todd, Rehtaeh Parsons and the introduction of Rehtaeh's Law mentioning both victims as part of the tabling of the bill seems intuitive, the empirical connection among all three groups is so small as to be invisible. Only one individual Twitter user has been found to have tweeted on all three occasions out of thousands of potential users. There may be a number of reasons for this result. First, it is possible that the issue of cyberbullying may not have taken hold in Canada until after the introduction of Amanda Todd's story to the wider public on 19 October 2012. Second, it is possible that the different naming conventions for each event attracted different audiences. The evidence produced here points to a difference in regional interests in the policy and therefore possible differences in regional interpretation of the nature of the policy domain and its potential solutions.

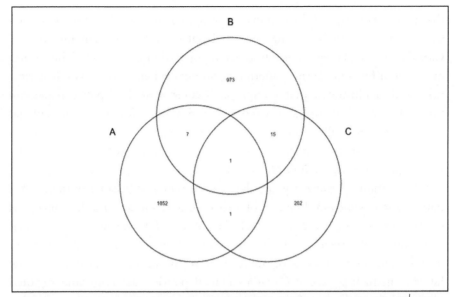

Figure 4.9 *Actor distribution for the three cyberbullying events.* A: Organised anti-bullying vigils in honour of Amanda Todd; B: Reaction to the death of Rehtaeh Parsons (including #OpJustice4Rehtaeh; C: Introduction of Bill C-13 'Rehtaeh's Law' to House of Commons

In the end, the examination of social tagging in the process of highlighting social problems and ultimately to influence public policy shows broad patterns of theoretical interest to both policy theory and information studies. The pattern of Tweet behaviour tends towards regional interest, reinforced by long-standing political and cultural institutions, tethered to more broadly interested audiences indicated by a smattering of accounts from a global scope. In one case, that of the Amanda Todd Vigil on 19 October 2012, we see a much larger international than national audience, although the real analysis is uncertain due to a large number of accounts with no disclosed location. Most importantly, while the two realities of public interest and the development of policy co-exist, the causal link between the two is very unclear. In both the examples of Idle No More and cyberbullying policy in Canada the continuity of the ideas that relate to the public policy is not met with a sizable continuity of actor participation. Whether this result is due to memes or abrupt shifts in policy attention must be left to further research.

Conclusion

This chapter focused on patterns of social tagging related to policy problems and political discourse. Canadian provincial use of Twitter hashtags showed that provincially tagged discussions are primarily conducted by people located in the province, while international and outside interests focus on areas of Canada with the largest concentrations of population and wealth. Time zones did account for some of this pattern but did not explain all of it. Two historical case studies illustrated that groups on Twitter related to policy issues are primarily formed along national characteristics, but with some international attention. Occasionally, international attention overtakes national attention, but the national character remains. Finally, there is very little sustained attention by individual actors across multiple events.

Observations of social tagging data capture interest because of their novel nature, such as the development of a social movement around the concept of treaty rights through the use of Idle No More. However, when such social behaviour is observed in real time, it is often shown to be bounded by more mundane features such as geographic proximity or institutional structures. The latter form in this case is Canada's federal political structure and regional identities. On a site like Twitter, the continuation of social activity occurs due primarily to the permanence of the tag itself, rather than through the formation of organizational structures and the presence of dedicated leaders. Where such continuity does occur, it is often due to symbolic interest, such as the case of Stephen Harper in the Idle No More case, rather than the accumulation and use of individual effort and influence.

The cases illustrated here merely point out that there is a great amount of research to do that identifies the connection between trends in online social tagging and the policy interest of a particular nation state. Policy theory suggests that, unlike many positions about the global nature of modern society, institutions indeed matter in the establishment of policy-related ideas. The diffusion of these ideas on Twitter hashtags presents an extension, not a refutation, of this basis. Further research may try to test such things as what traits cause certain social tags to gain international attention and why. While the case of Rehtaeh Parsons and Idle No More had media reports of international interest, it was, in fact, the Amanda Todd case that received more international attention, despite a lesser media profile. Like many scientific inquiries, the empirical evidence greatly confounds popular intuition about the role of online tagging in discussions of political interest.

References

Atkinson, M. M. and Coleman, W. D. (1992) Policy Networks, Policy Communities and the Problems of Governance, *Governance*, **5**, 154–80.

Baumgartner, F. R., Green-Pedersen, C. and Jones, B. D. (2013) Comparative Studies of Policy Agendas, *Journal of European Public Policy*, **13**, 959–74.

Baumgartner, F. R., Jones, B. D. and Mortensen, P. B. (2014) Punctuated Equilibrium Theory: explaining stability and change in public policymaking. In Sabatier, P. A. (ed.) *Theories of the Policy Process*, Basic Books, 59–103.

Beckett, C. and Ballho, J. (2012) *Wikileaks: news in the networked era*, Polity Press.

Bednar, M. K. (2012) Watchdog or Lapdog? A behavioral view of the media as a corporate governance mechanism, *Academy of Management Journal*, **55**, 131–50.

Béland, D. (2009) Ideas, Institutions and Policy Change, *Journal of European Public Policy*, **16**, 701–18.

Birkland, T. A. (2004) The World Changed Today: agenda-setting and policy change in the wake of the September 11 terrorist attacks, *Review of Policy Research*, **21**, 179–200.

Birkland, T. A. (2006) Agenda Setting in Public Policy. In Fischer, F. and Miller, G. J. (eds), *Handbook of Public Policy Analysis*, CRC Press, 63–78.

Blakeney, A. and Borins, S. (1998) *Political Management in Canada*, 2nd edn, University of Toronto Press, Scholarly Publishing Division.

Budge, I. (1996) *The New Challenge of Direct Democracy*, Polity Press.

Burstein, P. (1991) Policy Domains: organization, culture and policy outcomes, *Annual Review of Sociology*, **17**, 327–50.

Burt, R. S. (2004) Structural Holes and Good Ideas, *American Journal of Sociology*, **110**, 349–99.

Campbell, J. L. (2004) *Institutional Change and Globalization*, Princeton University Press.

Campbell, J. and Pedersen, O. (2014) *The National Origins of Policy Ideas: knowledge regimes in the United States, France, Germany and Denmark*, Princeton University Press.

Castells, M. (2010) *The Rise of the Network Society*, 2nd edn, Wiley-Blackwell.

CBC News (2013) Amanda Todd Suicide: RCMP repeatedly told of blackmailer's attempts, *CBC News Canada*, 15 November, www.cbc.ca/news/canada/amanda-todd-suicide-rcmp-repeatedly-told-of-blackmailer-s-attempts-1.2427097.

Chadwick, A. (2011) The Political Information Cycle in a Hybrid News System: the British Prime Minister and the Bullygate Affair, *The International Journal of Press/Politics*, **16**, 3–29.

Chadwick, A. (2013) *The Hybrid Media System: politics and power*, Oxford University Press.

Coates, K. (2014) *Idlenomore: and the remaking of Canada*, University of Regina Press.

Conover, M. D., Davis, C., Ferrara, E., McKelvey, K., Menczer, F. and Flammini, A.

(2013) The Geospatial Characteristics of a Social Movement Communication Network, *PloS One*, **8**, http://journals.plos.org/plosone/article?id=10.1371/journal.pone.0055957.

Couldry, N. (2012) *Media, Society, World: social theory and digital media practice*, Polity Press.

Criado, J. I., Sandoval-Almazan, R. and Gil-Garcia, J. R. (2013) Government Innovation Through Social Media, *Government Information Quarterly*, **30**, 319–26.

Daer, A. R., Hoffman, R. and Goodman, S. (2014) Rhetorical Functions of Hashtag Forms across Social Media Applications. In *Proceedings of the 32nd ACM International Conference on the Design of Communication CD-ROM,* ACM, 12–16.

Das, A., Gollapudi, S., Panigrahy, R. and Salek, M. (2013) Debiasing Social Wisdom. In *Proceedings of the 19th ACM SIGKDD International Conference on Knowledge Discovery and Data Mining,* ACM, 500–8.

Deschamps, R. (2012) Twitter User and the Governance of Social Media in Canadian Federal and Provincial Government Departments. In *Proceedings of the 2012 Prairie Political Science Association Conference*, Prairie Political Science Association, 21–2.

Deschamps, R. (2014) What Potential for YouTube as a Policy Deliberation Tool? Commenter reactions to videos about the Keystone XL oil pipeline, *Policy & Internet*, **6**, 341–59.

Deschamps, R. (2015) Social Learning and Online Discussion: is Twitter a wise crowd? In *Proceedings of the 16th Annual International Conference on Digital Government Research*, ACM, 1–9.

Dowding, K., Hindmoor, A., Iles, R. and John, P. (2010) Policy Agendas in Australian Politics: the Governor-Generals' speeches, 1945–2008, *Australian Journal of Political Science*, **45**, 533–57.

Effing, R., Hillegersberg, J. van and Huibers, T. (2011) Social Media and Political Participation: are Facebook, Twitter and YouTube democratizing our political systems? In Tambouris, E., Macintosh, A. and de Bruijn, H. (eds), *Electronic Participation,* Springer, 25–35.

Ems, L. (2014) Twitter's Place in the Tussle: how old power struggles play out on a new stage, *Media, Culture & Society*, **36**, 720–31.

Faust, K. (2005) Using Correspondence Analysis for Joint Displays of Affiliation Networks, *Models and Methods in Social Network Analysis*, **7**, 117–47.

Goode, L. (2009) Social News, Citizen Journalism and Democracy, *New Media & Society*, **11**, 1287–1305.

Hall, P. A. (1993) Policy Paradigms, Social Learning and the State: the case of economic policymaking in Britain, *Comparative Politics*, **25**, 275–96.

Harris, J. K., Moreland-Russell, S., Choucair, B., Mansour, R., Staub, M. and
Simmons, K. (2014) Tweeting for and Against Public Health Policy: response to
the Chicago Department of Public Health's electronic cigarette Twitter campaign,
Journal of Medical Internet Research, **16**,
www.ncbi.nlm.nih.gov/pmc/articles/PMC4210950.

Hemphill, L., Culotta, A. and Heston, M. (2013) *Framing in Social Media: how the US
Congress uses Twitter hashtags to frame political issues*,
https://papers.ssrn.com/sol3/papers.cfm?abstract_id=2317335.

Hofferbert, R. I. and Budge, I. (1992) The Party Mandate and the Westminster Model:
election programmes and government spending in Britain, 1948–85, *British
Journal of Political Science*, **22**, 151–182.

Howlett, M. (1998) Predictable and Unpredictable Policy Windows: institutional and
exogenous correlates of Canadian federal agenda-setting, *Canadian Journal of
Political Science*, **31**, 495–524.

Jackson, S. J. and Foucault Welles, B. (2016) # Ferguson is Everywhere: initiators in
emerging counterpublic networks, *Information, Communication & Society*, **19**,
397–418.

Jeffares, S. (2014) *Interpreting Hashtag Politics: policy ideas in an era of social media*,
Springer.

John, P. (2006) The Policy Agendas Project: a review, *Journal of European Public Policy*,
13, 975–86.

John, P. and Margetts, H. (2003) Policy Punctuations in the UK: fluctuations and
equilibria in central government expenditure since 1951, *Public Administration*, **81**,
411–32.

Jones, B. D. (1994) *Reconceiving Decision-Making in Democratic Politics*, University of
Chicago Press.

Jones, B. D. and Baumgartner, F. R. (2005) *The Politics of Attention: How government
prioritizes problems*, University of Chicago Press.

Jones, B. D. and Baumgartner, F. R. (2012) From There to Here: punctuated
equilibrium to the general punctuation thesis to a theory of government
information processing, *Policy Studies Journal*, **40**, 1–20.

Jones, B. D. and Wolfe, M. (2010) Public Policy and the Mass Media. In Voltmer, K.
and Koch-Baumgarten, S. (eds), *Public Policy and the Mass Media: the interplay of
mass communication and political decision making*, Routledge, 17–43.

Kapp, J. M., Hensel, B. and Schnoring, K. T. (2015) Is Twitter a Forum for
Disseminating Research to Health Policy Makers?, *Annals of Epidemiology*, **25**,
883–87.

Kappo, T. and King, H. (2014) Our People Were Glowing: an interview with Tanya

Kappo. In The Kino-nda-niimi Collective (ed.) *The Winter we Danced: voices from the past, the future and the Idle No More movement*, ARP Books, 67–70.

Kingdon, J. W. and Thurber, J. A. (1984) *Agendas, Alternatives and Public Policies*, Little, Brown.

Knoke, D. (1986) Associations and Interest Groups, *Annual Review of Sociology*, **12**, 1–21.

Knoke, D. (1993). Networks of Elite Structure and Decision Making, *Sociological Methods & Research*, **22**, 23–45.

Lasswell, H. D. (1956) *The Decision Process: seven categories of functional analysis*, University of Maryland.

Laumann, E. O. and Knoke, D. (1987) *The Organizational State: social choice in national policy domains*, University of Wisconsin Press.

Lê, S., Josse, J. and Husson, F. (2008) FactoMineR: a package for multivariate analysis, *Journal of Statistical Software*, **25**, 1–18.

McCombs, M. E. and Shaw, D. L. (1972) The Agenda-setting Function of Mass Media, *Public Opinion Quarterly*, **36**, 176–187.

McNutt, K. (2006) Research Note: Do Virtual Policy Networks Matter? Tracing network structure online, *Canadian Journal of Political Science/Revue Canadienne de Science Politique*, **39**, 391–405.

McNutt, K. (2010) Virtual Policy Networks: where all roads lead to Rome, *Canadian Journal of Political Science/Revue Canadienne de Science Politique*, **43**, 915–35.

Mergel, I. (2013) A Framework for Interpreting Social Media Interactions in the Public Sector, *Government Information Quarterly*, **30**, 327–34.

Mergel, I. (2015) Open Collaboration in the Public Sector: the case of social coding on GitHub, *Government Information Quarterly*, **32**, 464–72.

Mergel, I. (2017) Building Holistic Evidence for Social Media Impact, *Public Administration Review*, **77**, 489–95.

Milakovich, M. E. (2012) *Digital Governance: new technologies for improving public service and participation*, Routledge.

Morstatter, F., Pfeffer, J., Liu, H. and Carley, K. M. (2013) Is the Sample Good Enough? Comparing data from Twitter's Streaming API with Twitter's Firehose, https://arxiv.org/abs/1306.5204.

Orman, D., Miller, C. and Barlett, J. (2014) Towards the Discipline of Social Media Intelligence. In Hobbs, C., Moran, M. and Salisbury, D. (eds), *Open Source Intelligence in the Twenty-First Century: new approaches and opportunities*, Palgrave MacMillan, 24–43.

Page, R. (2012) The Linguistics of Self-Branding and Micro-Celebrity in Twitter: the role of hashtags, *Discourse & Communication*, **6**, 181–201.

Postill, J. and Pink, S. (2012) Social Media Ethnography: the digital researcher in a messy web, *Media International Australia*, **145**, 123–34.

Qian, N. and Yangagizawa, D. (2010) Watchdog or Lapdog? Media and the US Government, *CEPR Discussion Papers*, **7684**, https://ideas.repec.org/p/cpr/ceprdp/7684.html.

Rhodes, R. A. (1997) *Understanding Governance: policy networks, governance, reflexivity and accountability*, Open University Press.

Rhodes, R. A. (2006) Policy Network Analysis. In Goodin, R. E., Moran, M. and Rein, M. (eds), *The Oxford Handbook of Public Policy*, Oxford University Press, 423–45.

Sabatier, P. A. (1987) Knowledge, Policy-Oriented Learning and Policy Change: an advocacy coalition framework, *Science Communication*, **8**, 649–92.

Sabatier, P. A. (1988) An Advocacy Coalition Framework of Policy Change and the Role of Policy-Oriented Learning Therein, *Policy Sciences*, **21**, 129–68.

Sabatier, P. A. (2006) *Policy Change and Learning: an advocacy coalition approach*, Routledge.

Saleh, I. (2013) WikiLeaks and the Arab Spring: the twists and turns of media, culture and power. In Brevini, B., Hintz, A. and McCurdy, P. (eds), *Beyond Wikileaks: implications for the future of communications, journalism and society*, Palgrave MacMillan, 236–44.

Saxton, G. D., Niyirora, J. N., Guo, C. and Waters, R. D. (2015) #AdvocatingForChange: the strategic use of hashtags in social media advocacy, *Advances in Social Work*, **16**, 154–69.

Segal, M. D. (2015) *Independent Review of the Police and Prosecution Response to the Rehtaeh Parsons Case*, Murray D. Segal Professional Corporation.

Segerberg, A. and Bennett, W. L. (2011) Social Media and the Organization of Collective Action: using Twitter to explore the ecologies of two climate change protests, *The Communication Review*, **14**, 197–215.

Shapiro, M. A. and Hemphill, L. (2014) Policy-Related Communications and Agenda Setting: Twitter, New York Times and the Widening Soapbox., https://papers.ssrn.com/sol3/papers.cfm?abstract_id=2585126.

Shapiro, M. A. and Hemphill, L. (2017) Politicians and the Policy Agenda: does use of Twitter by the US Congress direct New York Times content?, *Policy & Internet*, **9**, 109–32.

Simon, H. (1990) *Reason in Human Affairs*, Stanford University Press.

Skocpol, T. and Amenta, E. (1986) States and Social Policies, *Annual Review of Sociology*, **12**, 131–57.

Skocpol, T., Ganz, M. and Munson, Z. (2000) A Nation of Organizers: the institutional origins of civic voluntarism in the United States, *American Political*

Science Review, **94**, 527–46.

Small, T. A. (2012) Are We Friends Yet? Online relationship marketing by political parties. In Marland, A., Giasson. T. and Lees-Marshment, J. (eds), *Political Marketing in Canada,* UBC Press, 193–208.

Soroka, S. N. (2002a) *Agenda-Setting Dynamics in Canada*, UBC Press.

Soroka, S. N. (2002b) Issue Attributes and Agenda-Setting by Media, the Public and Policymakers in Canada, *International Journal of Public Opinion Research*, **14**, 264–85.

Stromer-Galley, J. and Jamieson, K. H. (2001) The Transformation of Political Leadership? In Axford, B. and Huggins, R. (eds), *New Media and Politics,* Sage Publications, 172–90.

Toepfl, F. and Piwoni, E. (2017) Targeting Dominant Publics: how counterpublic commenters align their efforts with mainstream news, *New Media & Society*, https://doi.org/10.1177%2F1461444817712085.

Tootoosis, C. (2012) Idle No More North Battleford Teach in Event, www.facebook.com/events/112078182288731.

Trant, J. (2009) Studying Social Tagging and Folksonomy: a review and framework, *Journal of Digital Information*, **10**, https://journals.tdl.org/jodi/index.php/jodi/article/view/269.

Wang, R., Liu, W. and Gao, S. (2016). Hashtags and Information Virality in Networked Social Movement: examining hashtag co-occurrence patterns, *Online Information Review*, **40**, 850–66.

Wasserman, S. and Faust, K. (1994). *Social Network Analysis: methods and applications*, Cambridge University Press.

White, P. (2014). On the Trail of Amanda Todd's Alleged Tormentor, *The Globe and Mail*, 31 May, www.theglobeandmail.com/news/world/on-the-trail-of-amanda-todds-alleged-tormentor/article18935075/?page=all.

Whitten-Woodring, J. (2009) Watchdog or Lapdog? Media freedom, regime type and government respect for human rights, *International Studies Quarterly*, **53**, 595–625.

Wolfe, M., Jones, B. D. and Baumgartner, F. R. (2013) A Failure to Communicate: agenda setting in media and policy studies, *Political Communication*, **30**, 175–92.

Wootson, C. R. (2017) Trump Says his Tweets are 'Modern Day Presidential.' We Checked With Other Modern-Day Leaders, *Washington Post*, 2 July www.washingtonpost.com/news/worldviews/wp/2017/07/02/trump-says-his-tweets-are-modern-day-presidential-we-checked-with-other-modern-day-presidents/?utm_term.

Chapter 5

Hashtags and library discovery systems

Louise F. Spiteri

Introduction

Over the past several years, I have explored the role of user-generated metadata in library discovery systems, specifically social tagging and user reviews. In a previous monograph from Facet Publishing (Spiteri, 2016), I examined the specific contributions of user-generated metadata in the following areas:

- to enhance library subject analysis systems, such as the Library of Congress Subject Headings
- to provide *de facto* subject access to items in the catalogue to which few, or no, controlled subject headings have been assigned by library staff
- to enrich the content of bibliographic records through the expertise of the end users
- to enhance readers' advisory services through the provision of affective access points.

The purpose of this chapter is to examine the feasibility of expanding the scope of user-generated metadata in library discovery systems to include hashtags. Why would we want to do this? One of the possible limitations of library discovery systems is that, for the most part, they provide access only to items that the library system owns. There is nothing wrong with this, of course, as catalogues have traditionally been inventories of holdings. In a world of linked data and the semantic web, however, does this inward focus continue to work well? Can we provide an additional service to clients by linking them to related content that the library system does not own? Through an examination of relevant literature, as well as three specific case studies, this chapter will explore the potential contributions of hashtags to expanding the scope of resources available via library discovery systems.

Hashtags and resource discovery

According to Wikipedia a hashtag is:

> a type of metadata tag used on social networks such as Twitter and other microblogging services, allowing users to apply dynamic, user-generated tagging that makes it possible for others to easily find messages with a specific theme or content; it allows easy, informal markup of folk taxonomy without need of any formal taxonomy or markup language.
>
> (Wikipedia, 2018)

Hashtags are used in a variety of social media platforms, including Google+, WordPress, Tumblr, Pinterest, Instagram, Facebook and YouTube.

Chang and Iyer (2012) suggested that Twitter hashtag applications could provide users with the functionalities to organise, share, save, or publish the search results of information resources. The authors compared hashtag use over a two-month period among the Twitter accounts of library websites OCLC, WorldCat and the Library of Congress and social cataloguing websites Goodreads and LibraryThing. Their goal was to examine hashtag use through the lens of Taylor's value-added model, which posits that the following user requirements can add value to information systems: ease of use, noise reduction, quality, adaptability, time saving and cost saving (Taylor, 1986).

> These areas of user criteria define an effective interface for bridging the gap between user and system. The value-added processes in the system instantiate at the interface level. Thus, developing examples of value-added processes helps focus and deliver functional features to users.
>
> (Chang and Iyer, 2012, 250)

The authors' analysis of hashtag use revealed that the most consistently adopted type of hashtag relates to events or announcements, such as book festivals or online book clubs. More significantly, perhaps, the authors found that professional cataloguing organizations use Twitter and hashtags primarily to communicate the latest news and announcements, while social cataloguing sites actively engage followers in idea exchanges through adding hashtags to create and organise particular topics. The authors concluded that hashtag applications enable users to add value to the tweeted content by reorganising, publishing and distributing the content based on different criteria, ranging from hashtags to keywords to user names.

Chang and Iyer suggested that hashtags could assist in the information retrieval process:

> Imagine a reader following one hashtag connection to another and finding
> useful material. Such success might lead the reader to share and
> communicate their discoveries with others through hashtags, thus adding to
> the value-added processes. (Change and Iyer, 2012, 257)

Information professionals could use hashtags as a useful search strategy, following one hashtag connection to another. Further, Chang and Iyer suggested that linking library resources to popular or topical hashtags is another example of how hashtags can add value to information discovery. As an example, they used the following hashtags, which were popular after the death of Steve Jobs: #SteveJobs, #ThankYouSteve and #RIPSteveJobs. By linking these popular hashtags to library resources, users interested in learning more about Steve Jobs could find library materials of which they were previously unaware, rather than be directed to only internet-based resources. In this way, hashtags serve to expand the scope and depth of information available to searchers and also to promote library resources and services.

Marcia Bates (2013) suggested that social media sites are sources of useful content, generated not by the sites themselves, but by the users. Hashtags, in particular, are growing in popularity and they are ubiquitous in our society, appearing in many venues, advertisements, sports events and so forth. Hashtags allow users to self-catalogue content and also to filter which and whose content to see. Bates suggested that applications could be created for online service providers such as WestlawNext (www.westlawnextcanada.com) or ProQuest Dialog (www.proquest.com/products-services/ProQuest-Dialog.html) that would allow the addition of hashtags to content in order to allow users to better engage with that content. Bates commented, 'If Twitter has taught us nothing else, we know that a collection of information becomes more valuable when its users can engage with that information' (Bates, 2013, 80). Could we extend Bates' suggestion to library discovery systems?

Soergel (1985) discussed the concept of request-oriented indexing, in which indexers assign keywords to an information resource based on the anticipated request from users. Hjørland (1997) distinguished between content-oriented indexing, based on an analysis of the subject of the work at hand and need-oriented indexing, which is similar to Soergel's request-oriented indexing. Although both these works predate hashtags, they discuss concepts that are relevant to the hashtagging environment. Most indexing in library discovery systems is based on the subject or content of the work. User-generated content such as tags and, by extension, hashtags, reflects the contexts, language and interpretations of the users (Spiteri, 2012). Hashtags could thus be a form of needs-oriented indexing, with the added advantage of not requiring library professionals to anticipate user needs. User tags can contribute to library discovery systems by reflecting the perspectives and language of the users and by serving as access points to the content of the work, including its affect, for example readability, tone, mood and so forth (Pecoskie, Tarulli and Spiteri, 2014).

A characteristic of hashtags is their ability to highlight new and emerging topics. Naaman, Becker and Gravano (2011, 905) defined a Twitter trend – or a trending topic – as consisting 'of one or more terms and a time period, such that the volume of messages posted for the terms in the time period exceeds some expected level of activity'. Trends can be *exogenous*, in that they originate from outside Twitter, as, for example, hashtags pertaining to a particular event (e.g. #Canada150), or they could be *endogenous*, in that they originate from within Twitter as, for example, popular tweets posted by a public figure (e.g. #MAGA – Make America Great Again). Hashtag trends tie closely to the concept of the popularity of a given hashtag, as studied, for example, by Ma, Sun and Cong (2013), who defined the popularity of a hashtag as the number of users who post at least one tweet containing the hashtag within the given period (one day). A new hashtag can either be a newly created hashtag that has not appeared before, or a hashtag created earlier, which was popular, then unpopular for a predefined period (e.g. a week) and is now popular again. Users who have adopted a hashtag form a virtual community.

Sharma (2013) and Romero, Meeder and Kleinberg (2011) examined an important aspect of hashtag trends: the concepts of the *stickiness* and *persistence* of hashtags. Stickiness refers to the level of diffusion of a hashtag, that is, how many people will use the hashtag; the higher the stickiness, the greater the diffusion of information. Persistence refers to how long and widely a hashtag will continue to be used. With regard to library discovery systems, the stickiness and persistence of hashtags could be important factors to consider and, possibly, to measure. For example, hashtags that are sticky and persistent could result in greater long-term exposure to library resources. The hashtag #Canada150, for example, was both very sticky and persistent in Canada in 2017, as it related to the country's sesquicentennial celebrations that culminated on 1 July 2017. The popularity of this hashtag could have led a number of users to related resources in public and academic library catalogues, of which users would have otherwise been unaware. Further, although the persistence of this hashtag diminished by the end of that year, it could serve as an important archival record of the various conversations, events and information sources related to Canada's sesquicentennial celebrations.

Alfonzo (2014) examined the use of Twitter hashtags in information literacy instruction. Alfonzo noted the ubiquity of hashtags, which now appear in a number of platforms besides Twitter, such as Facebook, Pinterest, YouTube, Instagram, Google+ and Tumblr. Alfonzo described hashtags as a form of social classification, or folksonomy, similar to tags used in social bookmarking sites (e.g. Diigo) and blogging content management systems, such as WordPress:

> Hashtags are the love child of IT and social media brought about by Web 2.0. They combine the social and back-end functionality programming that was once exclusive to information professionals and fill the need for conversation and image organization that users desire.
>
> (Alfonzo, 2014, 20)

Alfonzo suggested that hashtagging involves many aspects that can be seamlessly incorporated into the classroom, including collaboration, active engagement and innovation spurred by users taking a more active role in information sharing and creation. Hashtags can also be used for data analytics, for example via Twitter's lists of trending topics, comprising the most widely-used hashtags, keywords and conversation topics.

Alfonzo made an interesting case for the use of hashtags to teach people how to search using subject headings and keywords. Hashtags and subject headings serve the same function, in that people assign them to an information resource for identification and classification purposes. Because many searchers are far more likely to be familiar with hashtags than subject headings, the latter could be used as a filter by which to teach the concepts of authority control, controlled vocabularies, indexing, keyword searching and so forth.

A number of studies have examined the use of Twitter in scholarly communication and how tweets can extend this communication well beyond the scholarly community. Shiffman (2012) argued that scientific conferences bring together countless experts on any given topic, but are not an effective means of reaching the interested public on a large scale. In his case study of the 2011

International Congress for Conservation Biology, Shiffman found that, if used properly, Twitter and other social media technology could be a powerful tool for conservation education and outreach from scientific conferences. Ferguson et al. (2014) evaluated Twitter use during the 61st Annual Scientific Meeting at the Cardiac Society of Australia and New Zealand. The authors found that Twitter and associated conference hashtags assisted in sharing ideas and disseminating the findings and conclusions from presenters at the conference and concluded that researchers and clinicians should consider using this technology to enhance timely communication of findings. Numerous scientists actively use Twitter for public engagement and outreach. Most academic universities have their own Twitter account and most major conferences have their own hashtags (Winkless, 2013; Parsons et al., 2014; You, 2014). Hashtags associated with conferences can help promote discussion and debate and new research (Darling et al., 2013). In their examination of live tweeting at the 2013 International Congress for Conservation Biology, Bombaci et al. (2016) concluded that presenters who want their science communicated accurately and broadly through Twitter should provide Twitter-friendly summaries that incorporate relevant hashtags and usernames.

Schmidt (2016) examined the formation of relations between users and text through hashtags. Because the Twitter interface makes hashtags searchable, they connect tweets from users who have no pre-existing follower/followee relationship. Twitter has lowered the barriers for people to interact with each other and to exchange information of all kinds. Schmidt (2014) explored the notion of *personal publics*, which is the communicative space that revolves around individual accounts and structured via the follower/friend relations. In personal publics, systems select and display information according to criteria of personal relevance and users conduct these activities in a mainly conversational mode, versus the one-way mode of traditional publishing. Hashtags allow the formation of relations between users and texts. Since hashtags are unmoderated and thus not subject to formal control, Schmidt (2016) argued that the processes of suggestion, imitation and learning, as well as Twitter's trending topic functionality, can promote a shared use of certain hashtags and the creation of spontaneous and ad hoc hashtag publics. Schmidt suggested we should not dismiss these personal publics as simply the efforts of amateurs; rather, we should acknowledge the potential for inclusion and participation inherent in this new way of communicating, expressing and sharing. The notion of personal publics is worth pondering. Social tags and hashtags have the potential to enable a community-based approach to describing and sharing information resources.

As library discovery systems continue to add variety to the information resources to which they provide access, particularly in a linked data environment, where an institution's collections can range widely in scope and breadth, it may become increasingly important to tap into the knowledge and expertise of our users. This is particularly the case in the wake of shrinking budgets and the reduction in the amount of in-house original cataloguing. One way to help reduce the noise that users can produce by too many potentially inaccurate or unfocused hashtags would be to provide a system of guided tagging. Bar-Ilan et al. (2008) compared free-text tagging (also called unstructured tagging) with structured tagging, where free-text tags are assigned to predefined fields (or facets). The exercise occurred in Flickr. They used the following facets:

- general themes
- symbol
- personalities (public figures)
- description of event
- location of event
- time of event
- object type
- creator
- related links
- additional information about the image that does not match any of the predefined fields
- recommended additional fields.

The authors found that structured tagging resulted in more highly detailed descriptions, largely because the taggers made use of the event location and date and object type and creator fields. The authors concluded that free tagging does not put any limitations on the users and allows them to tag through association; on the other hand, without some guidance, users may simply forget to note important aspects of the image that could be useful for future discovery and retrieval.

Bruns and Moe (2014) presented a threefold conceptual model that examines the micro, meso and macro layers of communication in Twitter. Meso levels comprise the follower/followee networks: once an account has gained followers, tweets posted by that account will reach all its followers: this constitutes the account user's personal public. Macro levels are hashtagged exchanges: a topical hashtag in a tweet can extend the message to well beyond the user's personal public. A hashtag signals a wish to take part in a wider communicative process, potentially with anyone interested in the same topic. Topical hashtags represent the macro layer of Twitter communication, as they can connect different users to the same topic.

> Tweeting to a topical hashtag resembles a speech at a public gathering – a protest rally, an ad hoc assembly – of participants who do not necessarily know each other, but have been brought together by a shared theme, interest, or concern.   (Bruns and Moe, 2014, 18)

Micro levels involve the use of the @ symbol to highlight a Tweet to a specific user and attempt to strike a conversation with that user.

Hashtags could create macro levels of communication via the library discovery system, connecting users both within and without a particular library community to a shared topic of interest. What is fascinating here is that embedding hashtags in bibliographic records offers the potential to connect library users with outside users in Twitter, Facebook and so forth, based on common interests, and can serve to extend the scope of one's interests.

Zappavigna (2011) argued that hashtags serve as linguistic markers to provide a structured approach for gathering and analysing content. Hashtags can serve as a metadata marker for specific topics, which can serve as reference points for researchers and marketers. Zappavigna discussed the concept of *heteroglossia,* which is the co-existence of distinct varieties within a single language. Heteroglossia is 'fabricated by social actors who have woven voices of society into their discourses, contrasting these voices and the social viewpoints they stand for' (Androutsopoulos, 2011, 282). Heteroglossia focuses on the co-existence of different competing ideological points of view that are indexed by language, such as hashtags. Because hashtags can exist in different social platforms and can be republished (e.g. via retweeting) and adopted by multiple users, they serve to bring other voices in the construction of linguistic meaning. Interpersonal as well as ideational meanings could occur in a hashtag. From the perspective of library cataloguing, heteroglossia is something that we tend to fight against; in fact, we often cite this as a major drawback of an uncontrolled vocabulary (e.g. polysemy and homonymy). Zappavigna argued, however, that 'such a criticism ignores the social function of the classification which is to not only facilitate efficient relevance and recall, but to make possible what may be termed "ambient affiliation"' (Zappavigna, 2011, 800), which is the creation of ad hoc social groups or sub-communities, who explore conversations, themes and topics via a common set of hashtags.

Jones (2014) pointed to an interesting difference between hashtags and social tags. While social tags are often used to categorise data for later retrieval (Golder and Huberman, 2006), hashtags serve to draw the attention of other users to a particular message within the wider network. Jones considered hashtags to function within a networked exchange, whereby users can aggregate communication by multiple authors. Sharma posited that hashtags operate as *inline metadata*; rather than 'merely categorising content, they enable users to intensify their engagement by "organising" content and facilitating participation in conversations' (Sharma, 2013, 50). Hashtag communities emerge in emergent and malleable spaces: 'Not only are hashtags generative of ad hoc communities, they function as a means of amplifying the significance of a collection of messages and render them more readily visible and findable' (Sharma, 2013, 50). This goes back to the macro level of communication described by Bruns and Moe.

Now that we have explored the theoretical ways in which hashtags could contribute to library discovery systems, it would be useful to see such applications in practice. In this section, we will explore the impact of hashtag searches on resource discovery.

Selection of hashtags

As discussed in the previous section, the popularity, stickiness and persistence of hashtags are important criteria to consider in the exploration of the usefulness of hashtags to resource discovery. For the purpose of this small experiment, three hashtags were chosen that meet the criteria of popularity, stickiness and persistence. The first hashtag, #canpoli, was chosen because of its longstanding and popular use in Canada to discuss matters that involve politics at the federal level of government. News media outlets, politicians, political analysts and members of the public use this hashtag; as such, it serves as a form of controlled vocabulary. Further, there is consistent use of related hashtags connected with the discussion of politics and the provincial levels of government: the convention is to append the standard two-letter code for the province or territory to -poli; thus, for example, #onpoli refers to the province Ontario, #ykpoli to the Yukon Territory and so forth. The #canpoli hashtag could provide some valuable resources related to political developments, events and public engagement in Canada that might not be available via a library discovery system.

The second hashtag, #asist2016, refers to the 2016 Annual Meeting of the Association for Information Science and Technology (ASIS&T), a scholarly association that meets yearly. ASIS&T has established a convention for official hashtags for the yearly conference, namely to append the full year to the acronym for the association, hence #asist2016, #asist2015 and so forth. The #asist2016 hashtag could provide some valuable resources related to activities, events and topics associated with the 2016 conference that might not be available via a library discovery system.

The third hashtag, #solareclipse2017, refers to a very specific event that generated a great deal of excitement and coverage around the world. This hashtag could provide some valuable resources related to this solar eclipse, especially in the form of photographs and videos of the event that might not be available via a library discovery system.

Search procedures

For each hashtag, an initial search was conducted in Google to examine the scope of coverage in various social media services that use hashtags. In all cases, the first result was tied to the Twitter page related to the individual hashtag; further, the results returned links to the Instagram related page. Specific searches for the hashtag were performed in particular sites, namely, Facebook, Pinterest and YouTube, which all allow for the use of hashtags.

For each concept represented by the hashtags, a search was conducted in two public and one academic library discovery systems, as follows: Edmonton Public Library (#canpoli concept); WorldCat (#asist2016 concept); and Ottawa Public Library (#solareclipse2017 concept). These library discovery systems were chosen because they allow for the use of social tagging and because of their popularity amongst public and academic libraries across Canada. Because none of these discovery systems uses hashtags, the concepts expressed by the hashtags were searched via the most closely corresponding Library of Congress Subject Heading, as follows:

#canpoli: Canada-politics and government
#asist2016: Association for Information Science and Technology
#solareclipse: Solar eclipses

Search results

Social media services: #canpoli

The Twitter results for #canpoli provide a mixed bag of results, which one would expect, given the broad scope of this hashtag. Tweets include the opinions of members of the public about certain Members of Parliament (MPs), the Prime Minister, or specific federal government actions. There are links to opinion pieces in newspapers written about specific legislation or MPs. Of interest is the inclusion of tweets and resources that pertain to provincial developments, as hashtags such as #onpoli, #bcpoli and #nspoli are included in some tweets. This shows that (a) there is a controlled vocabulary at work, as provincial or territorial political matters are conveyed via adding the standard abbreviations for the province or territory to -poli; and (b) one hashtag can open the breadth of the results to include potentially relevant discussions pertaining to other levels of Canadian governments. This hashtag points also to the currency of this mode of communication. At the time of this search (August 2017), there were many tweets related to an anti-immigration rally in Vancouver and the corresponding thousands of people who marched to support immigration. This raises an interesting aspect of the archival potential of hashtags, as the #canpoli hashtag provides a historical account of public opinion, opinion pieces, discussions and so forth. You can see the trends of any given period via the #canpoli hashtag, especially since its use is well established.

The Instagram results for #canpoli provide links to images featuring political events, rallies, politicians and so forth. The Pinterest search was not successful, as it returned results related to cannoli; the pins did not contain the #canpoli hashtag. Unlike Instagram, Pinterest does not have a page dedicated solely to the hashtag. A limitation of Facebook is that you can see only those posts that have been marked as public, or those posted by friends you follow. Most of the posts that use the #canpoli hashtag provide links to relevant newspaper articles and videos pertaining to Canadian politics. The YouTube results were not helpful, as few of the videos retrieved from the search related to Canadian politics. Very few of the videos in the results contain the #canpoli hashtag, or any hashtag, for that matter, even though this feature is available in YouTube.

A very interesting result from the general Google result was the site Politwitter (http://politwitter.ca). The site page for #canpoli links you to sources about Canadian politics in different social media sites (each tabbed): Twitter, Facebook, Google+, News, Blogs and Hansard. The Twitter tab compiles tweets that contain the #canpoli hashtag. Further, links are provided to the official Twitter accounts of Canadian senators and Members of Parliament, federal and provincial agencies, the official political parties of Canada and the -poli hashtags of the Canadian provinces and territories. The link to this site would be a valuable addition to any library discovery system, as it provides a portal for all Twitter-related discussions related to federal and provincial governments.

Edmonton Public Library (www.epl.ca): Canada-Politics and government

The Library of Congress Subject Heading that matches #canpoli most closely is likely not intuitive to many searches, particularly as it includes both a geographic heading and a free-floating subdivision. The heading retrieves 350 items: 287 books; 20 eBooks; 17 DVDs; 1 streaming video; 14 online periodicals; and 11 DAISY (Digital Accessible Information System, which allows you to read an audiobook as you would a print book). Most of the items pertain to works about Canadian politics, including satire, memoirs and biographies. Search results may be filtered by topic, region, author, language, published date, rating and tags. Tags can be filtered by genre, tone and theme. User tags are broad in scope and contain terms such as politics, Canadian politics, electoral systems, voting systems and humour.

The addition of the #canpoli hashtag to the result screen, in the left-hand frame, with the other facets, would be very useful. Since this hashtag is well known, you can expect that many people will be familiar with it. You could restrict the links to the Politwitter site, as it is an excellent compendium for this hashtag, as we have seen. Similarly, the #_poli hashtag pertaining to Canadian provinces and territories could be added to library resources that focus on these topics.

Social media services: #asist2016

#asist2016 was the official hashtag used at the 2016 ASIS&T conference; there is a controlled vocabulary at work here, since the practice is to have the same structure for each year's conference, e.g. #asist2015; #asist2014 and so forth. ASIS&T communicates these hashtags in a variety of outlets, including the conference website and the conference programme, as well as the ASIS&T listserv, Facebook and Twitter accounts. The Twitter results varied in scope. Many tweets discuss topics mentioned in presentations. There are pictures of events, links to outside papers that support the topics discussed, blog posts discussing the conference from participants and so forth. Many of the tweets include direct links to named researchers (via @), which allows people to associate events and topics with specific researchers, as well as to follow each other.

The Google search retrieved links to individual blog posts written by academics who discussed their experiences at the conference. The Facebook results for #asist2016 include many official notes and links from the ASIS&T Facebook page, as well as commentaries, photographs and links to relevant articles from attendees of the conference. The Instagram page retrieved 40 posts of photographs posted by attendees at the conference. There were no relevant results in Pinterest or YouTube.

The Twitter and Facebook results provide very useful resources for academics interested in the ASIS&T conference. The tweets provide a historical archive of the conference that expose people who could not attend the conference, or certain sessions, to many of the discussions and themes that occurred. More importantly, perhaps, are the @ direct links to the researchers associated with the conference presentations, as this opens the door to expanded networks of communications. These tweets and links provide useful supplements to the official published conference proceedings.

WorldCat (www.worldcat.org): Association for Information Science and Technology

Since the #asist2016 hashtag pertains to the conference of the Association for Information Science and Technology, it made sense to use the authorised Library of Congress Subject Heading for this association. WorldCat was selected for this concept, as the ASIS&T conference would be more likely to appeal to researchers in academic settings. A search was conducted in the subject field of the advanced search page. The 91 results for this search (59 articles, 14 archival material, 11 books, 6 journal/magazine and 1 computer file) were not particularly useful, as they pertained mostly to published directories of various associations, among which ASIS&T was listed. The use of the author field resulted in 56 items (44 articles, 2 books, 4 journal/magazine, 1 archival material, 4 computer files, 1 website), which pertained to various ASIS&T publications, including the *Journal of the Association for Information Science & Technology, ASIS&T Bulletin,* conference proceedings and the publications of different ASIS&T special interest groups.

The conference hashtags would be a very useful addition to WorldCat, as they provide a snapshot of the various conference activities, links to scholars who presented, the musings of academics about the presentations they attended and so forth. In this case, it would be useful to link only to the Twitter page for each year's conference, as it provides the richest source of material.

Social media service: #solareclipse2017

The Twitter results for this hashtag provide links to many photographs of the eclipse by both professional and amateur photographers in different parts of the world. There are some other tweets that pertain to people's reactions and discussions, but the most notable content of this Twitter feed are the photographs.

The Instagram results provide a large variety of images of the eclipse, mostly by amateur photographers, as well as videos; this is true also for Pinterest and YouTube, where many posts included the #solareclipse2017 hashtags, which is in marked contrast to the results for the other two hashtags. The Facebook results provide many photographs, memes and personal reactions, as well as links to live streams of the eclipse from organizations such as NASA.

Ottawa Public Library (https://biblioottawalibrary.ca): Solar eclipses

An advanced search in the subject field for this heading provided 11 results (7 books, 1 eBook, 1 audiobook, 2 DVDs). Seven of the items pertain to non-fiction works about the phenomena of social eclipses, while three items pertain to works of fiction that involve solar eclipses (two novels and one film). The search filter options are the same as those in the Edmonton Public Library, since both systems use the BiblioCommons discovery layer (www.bibliocommons. com). The user tags vary in content and include, for example, the terms astronomy, eclipses, science, young adult and friendship; the latter two terms reflect the works of fiction.

The #solareclipse2017 hashtag is particularly interesting because it provides a snapshot of a very specific event in time. This hashtag could make a valuable addition to library discovery systems and could serve as an important archival tool to document events, photographs and videos of the 2017 solar eclipse and which may not be available via the library catalogue.

Conclusion

Hashtags have the potential to make positive contributions to library discovery systems; it is necessary, of course, to consider possible detractions and ways in which to mitigate them. Library discovery systems, such as WorldCat and BiblioCommons, have allowed users to add their own tags to metadata records for a number of years, so why consider hashtags? Social tags focus only on items owned by the library system; as such, they function in a similar manner as Library of Congress Subject Headings. While they serve also to describe aspects of information resources, hashtags differ from social tags in their ability to link to outside sources of information, such as Twitter, Facebook, Instagram, Pinterest and so forth. As we saw in the searches conducted for the hashtags #canpoli, #solareclipse2017 and #asist2016, hashtags can extend the resources available to users via the library discovery system.

Hashtags can allow users to connect and follow each other via their respective social media accounts should they choose to do so. This enhanced use of hashtags delves even more deeply into the concept of the catalogue as a social space (Tarulli, 2012; Tarulli and Spiteri, 2012), because hashtags do not limit this social space to the boundaries of the catalogue but can extend to social networks beyond the libraries. So, for example, if I search in the library discovery system for items pertaining to zero-waste living, I could connect to like-minded individuals via relevant hashtags. Could we do this via Google? Yes, clearly, but the idea here is to make the library discovery system more than an inventory of items owned by the library system, but a broader information portal that links library resources with those existing elsewhere. Referring back to Taylor's value-added model (Taylor, 1986), hashtags are an extension of user-generated content that can add value to the information service provided by library discovery systems.

The trending nature of hashtags can be both a blessing and a curse. On the one hand, hashtags may be more capable of reflecting new and emerging topics than, say, standard library indexing systems, such as the Library of Congress Subject Headings, which require long editorial approval processes for the creation of new subject headings, and cannot yet express the concept expressed by the #MAGA hashtag. Further, trends may be here today and gone tomorrow, so the value of some hashtags may be very short-lived. With regard to library discovery systems, the stickiness and persistence of hashtags could be important factors to consider and, possibly, to measure. For example, hashtags that are sticky and persistent, such as the hashtags #canpoli and #asist2016, could result in greater long-term exposure to library resources. Hashtags can serve as an important archival record of the various conversations, events and information sources related to specific events, as we saw with the #solareclipse2017 search.

As demonstrated by the #asist2016 search, it has become common practice for scholarly conferences, and even many public events, to have an assigned hashtag, which constitutes a form of controlled vocabulary. The hashtag provides the context for any tweets or retweets, as they are associated with the hashtag. The official hashtag thus serves as an overall collocating device to tie in all conference-related posts. Further, the conference hashtag can serve as a way to archive the conference and its communication threads. Another factor to consider is that since hashtags can reside outside Twitter, this conference thread could be diffused to an even broader audience. Conference hashtags could be very useful in an academic library catalogue, as they can link users to varied discussion threads and conversations pertaining to that conference; further, users can connect with various scholars, follow their work and so forth. Conference hashtags can serve also to connect people to conferences that occur yearly, since there is often an attempt to have a common hashtag template for a conference. The library discovery system could provide all these hashtags, for example, in the bibliographic record for the Journal of this society (*Journal of the Association for Information Science and Technology*), which would provide users with a central place to find conference information related to this association.

One can certainly understand some reluctance on the part of library staff to include hashtags in the library discovery system, as hashtags can be very uncontrolled and could also lead people to problematic external resources. A way to test the waters is to add selected hashtags, for example for conferences, events, political elections and so forth. Thus, the selection of hashtags could be restricted to only library staff, in order to minimise the noise that could be caused by irrelevant or inaccurate hashtags. This does mean an acceptance of the lack of control over the quality and relevance of outside information resources, but it is not clear that this can be avoided in a linked data environment. We can try to limit the damage, of course, but if we continue to focus too much on controlling information resources and the way in which we describe them, I think we are ignoring the reality of how people communicate today and how they look for and share information. We have already shown our willingness to relinquish control, to some extent, by incorporating tags from LibraryThing and reviews from Goodreads into library discovery systems such as WorldCat, as we cannot control the quality, accuracy, or objectivity of any of the LibraryThing and Goodreads content.

Another way to minimise the noise of hashtags would be to use structured tagging, as we explored earlier. Facets could be used to enhance the use of hashtags in library discovery systems. Facets are used extensively in many of these systems; as we saw in the searches above, results in BiblioCommons can be filtered by the following facets: content, audience, form/genre, region, author, language, published dates. These facets pertain to headings assigned by library staff. In addition, user tags are divided into the following facets: genre, tone and theme. Structured tagging is thus already in place; why not extend it also to hashtags? The use of structured tagging is an aspect that could be explored further with regard to public and academic library catalogues.

The notion of user bias in the choice of tags or hashtags could also understandably be a concern among library staff. Let us look at the concept of bias more closely. As discussed in Bade (2002), Olson (2000, 2002) and Smiraglia (2009), the provision of unbiased catalogue records, while laudable, is rarely truly attainable in practice. Decisions are made about what content to include in a catalogue record, as well as what to omit. Examples of bias include deciding which actors to include in the record for a film, based on their perceived importance or popularity. Objectivity becomes harder to defend when it comes to subject description and the assignation of a classification number. How well do the subject headings reflect the content of the item at hand? How well has the record creator understood the content of the information resource? Were subject headings assigned based only on an analysis of cursory elements, such as the title, publisher's description (which in itself could be biased), as well as the cataloguer's understanding of the subject(s)? I think we need to be careful of dismissing the contributions of our users as being that of amateurs, especially if they could, in fact, know far more about the topic than library staff. Further, hashtags could connect users to actual experts in the field. In a linked data environment, we must be prepared to surrender a degree of control, especially if we wish to link people to resources in a variety of places.

As discussed previously, hashtags, as a form of heteroglossia, can provide other voices in the library discovery system. Subject headings assigned by library staff represent one perspective and outlook that may not match that of the library users. Hashtags can thus allow for divergent views and interpretations; yes, precision of search might, and probably will, be compromised, but serendipitous discovery, as well as the creation of environments where people can form connections with like-minded people or, perhaps even more exciting, form connections with people with different perspectives, can have their own benefits. Hashtags do not create strict ties but, rather, open opportunities for new avenues of linked concepts. These avenues might not last long, but they offer people the chance to explore and follow them. So, rather than rely on library staff to make those connections, which can be a flawed process, of course, we give our users the opportunity to create their own classificatory networks around, say, a particular information need.

Hashtags can serve as an important way to link library resource discovery systems to information resources in a variety of social media services, such as Twitter, Facebook, Instagram, Pinterest and YouTube. Through the hashtags in the library metadata record, users can expand the scope of their searches to include items that relate to library resources, such as videos, images, streamed events and so forth. More rigorous and detailed studies need to be conducted to explore more clearly how hashtags would function in a library discovery system and whether the benefits do, in fact, outweigh the detractions. Many library discovery systems have incorporated a number of user-driven social features, such as ratings, reviews and tags. In an expanding linked data environment and considering their growing popularity and scope, hashtags in library discovery systems are a new frontier worthy of exploring.

References

Alfonzo, P. (2014) Using Twitter Hashtags for Information Literacy Instruction: the ubiquity of hashtags has opened the doors for the teaching of advanced searching concepts to a much wider audience than in past years, *Computers in Libraries*, 34, 19–22.

Androutsopoulos, J. (2011) From Variation to Heteroglossia in the Study of Computer-Mediated Discourse. In Thurlow, C. and Mroczek, C. (eds), *Digital Discourse: language in the new media*, Oxford University Press, 277–98.

Bade, D. (2002) *The Creation and Persistence of Misinformation in Shared Library Catalogs: language and subject knowledge in a technological era*, Graduate School of Library and Information Science, University of Illinois at Urbana Champaign.

Bar-Ilan, J., Shoham, S., Idan, A., Miller, Y. and Shachak, A. (2008) Structured Versus Unstructured Tagging: a case study, *Online Information Review*, 32, 635–47.

Bates, M. E. (2013) Of Hashtags and Descriptors, *Online Searcher*, 37 (3), 80.

Bombaci, S. P., Farr, C. M., Gallo, H. T., Mangan, A. M., Stinson, L. T., Kaushik, M. and Pejchar, L. (2016) Using Twitter to Communicate Conservation Science from a Professional Conference, *Conservation Biology*, 30, 216–25.

Bruns, A. and Moe, H. (2014) Structural Layers of Communication on Twitter. In Weller, K., Bruns, A., Burgess, J., Mahrt, M. and Puschmann, C. (eds), *Twitter and Society*, Peter Lang, 15–28.

Chang, H. C. and Iyer, H. (2012) Trends in Twitter Hashtag Applications: design features for value-added dimensions to future library catalogues, *Library Trends*, 1, 248–58.

Darling, E. S., Shiffman, D., Côté, I. M. and Drew, J. A. (2013) The Role of Twitter in the Life Cycle of a Scientific Presentation, *Ideas in Ecology and Evolution*, 6, 32–43.

Ferguson C., Inglis, S. C., Newton, P. J., Cripps, P. J., MacDonald, P. S. and Davidson, P. M. (2014) Social Media: a tool to spread information: a case study analysis of Twitter conversation at the Cardiac Society of Australia & New Zealand 61st Annual Scientific Meeting 2013, *Collegian*, 21, 89–93.

Golder, S. A. and Huberman, B. A. (2006) Usage Patterns of Collaborative Tagging Systems, *Journal of Information Science*, 32, 198–208.

Hjørland, B. (1997) *Information Seeking and Subject Representation: an activity-theoretical approach to information science*, Greenwood Press.

Jones, J. (2014) Switching in Twitter Hashtagged Exchanges, *Journal of Business and Technical Communication*, 28, 83–108.

Ma, Z., Sun, A. and Cong, G. (2013) On Predicting the Popularity of Newly Emerging Hashtags in Twitter, *Journal of the American Society for Information Science and Technology*, **64**, 1399–1410.

Naaman, M., Becker, H. and Gravano, L. (2011) Hip and Trendy: characterizing emerging trends on Twitter, *Journal of the American Society for Information Science & Technology*, **62**, 902–18.

Olson, H. A. (2000) Difference, Culture and Change: the untapped potential of LCSH, *Cataloging & Classification Quarterly*, **29**, 53–71.

Olson, H. A. (2002) *The Power to Name: locating the limits of subject representation in libraries*, Kluwer Academic.

Parsons, E. C. M., Shiffman, D. S., Darling, E. S., Spillman, N. and Wright, A. J. (2014) How Twitter Literacy Can Benefit Conservation Scientists, *Conservation Biology*, **28**, 299–301.

Pecoskie, J., Tarulli, L. and Spiteri, L. F. (2014) OPACs, Users and Readers Advisory: exploring the implication of user-generated content for readers advisory in Canadian public libraries, *Cataloging & Classification Quarterly*, **52**, 431–53.

Romero, D., M., Meeder, B. and Kleinberg, J. (2011) Differences in the Mechanics of Information Diffusion Across Topics: idioms, political hashtags and complex contagion on Twitter. In *Proceedings of the 20th International Conference on World Wide Web*, ACM, 695–704.

Schmidt, J. (2014) Twitter and the Rise of Personal Publics. In Weller, K., Bruns, A., Burgess, J., Mahrt, M. and Puschmann, C. (eds), *Twitter and Society*, Paul Lang, 3–14.

Schmidt, J. (2016) Twitter Friend Repertoires: introducing a methodology to assess patterns of information management on Twitter, *First Monday*, **21**, www.firstmonday.org/ojs/index.php/fm/article/view/6207.

Sharma, S. (2013) Black Twitter? Racial hashtags, networks and contagion, *New Formations*, **78**, 46–64.

Shiffman, D. S. (2012) Twitter as a Tool for Conservation Education and Outreach: what scientific conferences can do to promote live-tweeting, *Journal of Environmental Studies and Sciences*, **2**, 257–62.

Smiraglia, R. (2009) Bibliocentrism, Cultural Warrant and the Ethics of Resource Description: a case study, *Cataloging & Classification Quarterly*, **47**, 671–86.

Soergel, D. (1985) *Organizing Information: principles of data base and retrieval systems*, Academic Press.

Spiteri, L. F. (2012) Social Discovery Tools: extending the principle of user convenience, *Journal of Documentation*, **68**, 206–17.

Spiteri, L. F. (2016) Managing User-Generated Metadata in Discovery Systems. In

Spiteri, L. F. (ed.) *Managing Metadata in Web-Scale Discovery Systems*, Facet Publishing, 165–94.

Tarulli, L. (2012) *The Library Catalogue as a Social Space: promoting patron driven collections, online communities and enhanced reference and readers services*, Libraries Unlimited.

Tarulli, L. and Spiteri, L. F. (2012) Library Catalogues of the Future: a social space and collaborative tool? *Library Trends*, **61**, 107–181.

Taylor, R. S. (1986) *Value Added Processes in Information Systems*, Ablex.

Wikipedia (2018) *Hashtag*, https://en.wikipedia.org/wiki/Hashtag.

Winkless, L. (2013) Science and the #Hashtag, *Materials Today*, **16**, 2–3.

You, J. (2014) Who are the Science Stars of Twitter?, *Science*, **345**, 1440–1.

Zappavigna, M. (2011) Ambient Affiliation: a linguistic perspective on Twitter, *New Media and Society*, **13**, 788–806.

Chapter 6

Social information discoverability in Facebook groups: the need for linked data strategies

Laurie Bonnici and Jinxuan Ma

Information discoverability in Facebook groups

The progression of the web from a source of static information to a forum for dynamic, socially engaged, user-generated content has engendered a milieu of interaction and immediacy related to communication and information seeking. Popular online social networks (OSN) such as Twitter, Facebook, Snapchat and Instagram allow users to communicate and generate content for communication, entertainment and information seeking and sharing. Users as well as visionary developers have helped define these socially driven web tools as constructive and user-friendly.

Since its inception over a decade ago, Facebook has evolved from a communication channel exclusively for Harvard students to a worldwide forum for shared experiences in specialised groups. As Weinberger (2017) noted in *Business Insider* on 7 September 2017, Mark Zuckerberg, as a student at Harvard in 2004, created Facebook to allow students to discover information about other students. By 'friending' another student, one could discover information such as his or her class enrolment and community connections. In viral fashion, more than half of the Harvard student community joined Facebook within a month. Just two months later, students at other academic institutions such as Yale, Columbia and Stanford joined in, launching a global tech company that is now a powerful player in OSN communication and information sharing.

On 3 May 2017 – over a decade later – in a public post to the Facebook (FB) community summarising the 2017 first quarter business report, Zuckerberg, the influential FB founder, announced the company's intent to focus on building community among its more than 1.9 billion users. FB data indicates that over 100 million of its users are members of specialised community groups that have formed around significant issues, interests and concerns, such as parental support, specific illnesses and political and activist movements. Zuckerberg (2017b) described these groups as very meaningful and as an important piece of the lives of people engaged in these communities. In another public FB post – *Building Global Community* – on 16 February 2017, Zuckerberg (2017a) spoke openly regarding both humanitarian and political influences of Facebook to positively impact the human condition. In turn, he and Facebook have also become outspoken supporters of hot topics such as marriage equality, equal rights and other political and social justice issues. As Preston (2011) illustrated in a *New York Times* article on 5 February 2011, the Arab Spring movement, sparked by the Egyptian uprising in February 2011, was precipitated largely through Facebook. Political debates between FB users and revolutionary-minded FB posts often preceded mass protests on the ground. In some cases, governments used social media to engage with citizens and encourage their participation in government processes. While in other instances, governments monitored internet traffic or blocked access to websites or the entire internet. Most recently, Zuckerberg (2017a) emphasised FB's intentional support for such groups, stating 'My hope is to help more than 1 billion people join very meaningful groups to strengthen our social fabric over the next few years.'

Meanwhile, established FB groups have developed community through implicit and explicit sociocultural norms, establishing worldviews and behavioural interactions that provide social support and information that is driven by both authority and experience. Experientially generated information will be addressed in a later section on cognitive authority. User-generated content, usability and interoperability were the intended cornerstones of OSN. These system qualities would indicate the existence of an online community where users can engage with others and grant access to information and services beyond the walls of the community. However, a gap often emerges between the spoken word and human action, either intentionally or inadvertently. Due to the nature of exponential connections within the social web, input from a large membership and levels of user understanding of the system, the amount of communication and information that is promoted, stored and available to harvest in FB is vast.

Compounding the phenomenon of seemingly infinite information is the fact that mechanisms providing waypoints for discoverable information came well after the birth of FB. Hashtags, long an integral mechanism for cobbling together multitudes of posts on the same topic, have been ingrained in Twitter since 2007. Though hashtags eluded the FB community until 2013, a small group of FB users were occasionally embedding hashtags in their posts before then, perhaps driving FB developers to adopt the technology. As Warren stated in a *CNN* online tech report on 13 June 2013:

> the social network wants to make it easier for users to find content already on Facebook and functional hashtags are the first step. According to Facebook, many users already post hashtags anyway, so why not make them work? Hashtags will be both clickable and searchable.   (Warren, 2013)

However, the process was not retroactive, leaving already posted hashtags unsearchable. Thus, not only does a wealth of previously generated content remain unsearchable, but the process of diffusion and adoption among users will take time, resulting in even more unsearchable content each day.

Particularly in special topic groups, a vast amount of valuable data and opinions expressed as advice based on personal experience is lost in a sea of FB posts. Zuckerberg's FB goal to help 'more than 1 billion people join very meaningful groups to strengthen our social fabric over the next few years', gives further importance to the ability to find information and personal advice based on lived experiences within the expanse of posts.

A tale of two public Facebook groups

Groups on FB provide a virtual site that facilitates communication based on shared interests. On 30 September 2017, *Lifewire* estimated that more than 6000 FB groups exist, allowing people to come together around a common activity, cause or issue (Black, 2017). Members may use groups to organise events, express opinions, engage in discussion, post photos and share information. There are three different types of FB groups: secret, closed and public. Group type determines users' ability to access the page, post to the page and view and engage with post content.

Secret groups

Secret groups are not visible to anyone on FB except for group members. Secret groups are of little or no concern when considering linked data across environments. At this level, the group's existence is not searchable, nor is its membership list and content. The group name does not appear on a member's profile and nothing about this group is discoverable to outsiders. Exclusivity is intentional by the group administrator to keep membership, content and engagement limited to select users. Even waypoints intended to make content findable in OSN, such as hashtags, remain behind the group's privacy wall. In essence, the secretiveness indicates that the community does not want to be found, nor their content discovered for use beyond the confines of the group.

Closed groups

A closed group is a private forum that requires invitation or acceptance by a current member of the group. The ability to view content is limited to members of the group. Non-members can see that the group exists and are able to request to join. Membership is viewable by non-members, but non-members cannot view, search, or contribute content to the closed group. Much like the secret group, tags intended to make content findable in OSN remain behind the privacy wall of the group. Many of these communities hold controversial worldviews and seek the membership of like-minded individuals. Posts that fall outside the group's norms and beliefs are typically not welcome. Thus, the closed status allows group administrators to review and scrutinise those seeking membership. Membership decisions may be based on connections to current members or a brief review of the requester's FB profile to determine potential conflicts.

Public groups

Public groups are the most searchable by the general FB community. Outsiders to the group can see group members and posts. However, posting is often limited to group members. Unlike secret and closed groups, public group content is searchable by any FB user. Tags therefore render content more discoverable to both group members and outsiders. Public groups may be relevant to a limited community, who are somehow invested in the group topic. Although such groups may hold a worldview, they are typically not controversial and lend to the expression and sharing of both formal (documents and resources) and informal knowledge (experiences) that may be helpful to members. Some groups screen new membership requests by investigating connections to current members, or they may vet prospective members by requesting responses to questions that align with group interests. Two examples of public groups – the Vaccine Safety Group and the Canine Illness Group – are presented in this study, as the public forum features the greatest visibility out of the three types of FB groups and thus the greatest potential for contributing to public knowledge. The two groups share broad qualities and could thus benefit from consistently, systematically linked data to render content discoverable.

Wilson's cognitive authority theory and House's social support theory

Wilson's cognitive authority theory (Wilson, 1983) and House's social support theory (House, 1981) combine to serve as an apt lens for analysis of OSN groups and conceptualising a framework for presenting strategically linked data practice in OSN. The theories, penned well before the advent of the internet and OSN, apply particularly when content presents personal opinions and social interaction in an effort to ameliorate information deficits related to health-related, life-threatening decisions that lack formal authority. The two theories summarised below provide further insight for the proposed framework in an ensuing section.

Wilson's cognitive authority addresses a phenomenon of social perception and recognition by which a person or agent is viewed by others as a valid information source or an epistemic authority on a particular subject. The concept of cognitive authority stems from the notion that much of human knowledge comes second-hand through the observations or experiences of others rather than through one's own experiences. Only those who 'know what they are talking about' can stand out against hearsay and holding cognitive authority for others (Wilson, 1983, 13). Our belief in the reliability of information therefore hinges not so much on our evaluation of information quality, as on our perception of the person who presents the information as credible, or worthy of belief (Wilson, 1983). However, the identity and qualifications of a community member frequently are elusive in OSN, particularly for new members who are unfamiliar with the members, language and norms of the group (Bonnici, 2016).

Cognitive authority theory provides a useful theoretical lens through which to better understand the ways people seek and share information and their information assessment, particularly within a variety of contexts of health information-seeking behaviour studies (Bonnici, 2016; Ma and Stahl, 2017; McKenzie, 2003; Neal et al., 2011; Neal and McKenzie, 2011). In particular, this chapter employs cognitive authority to examine how FB group members assess group posts, with the aim of developing a better understanding of information retrieval within specific online health communities. Beyond the relevance criteria in traditional information retrieval environments, the interaction of quality and authority is considered as a central process of information retrieval that is taking place between the user and the information objects; cognitive authority, therefore, becomes 'one of the quality control components in information retrieval' (Rieh, 2002, 146). In order of prominence, diverse facets of information quality judgement are identified as good, accurate, current, useful and important; facets of cognitive authority judgement are trustworthy, credible, reliable, scholarly, official and authoritative (Rieh, 2002). Wilson recognised the challenges to cognitive authority in information seeking, underscoring the issue of trust in particular, though his work was developed when questions of authority and trustworthiness were limited to print documents. From these sources, Wilson proposed four conceptual dimensions of cognitive authority:

1 personal authority (author)
2 institutional authority (publisher forum)
3 textual type authority (document type)
4 intrinsic plausibility authority (content of text).

Recent research (Bonnici, 2016) points out the shortcomings of these concept-ual dimensions as applied to OSN, where author identity, including credentials, is often missing. This phenomenon provides a challenge to Wilson's cognitive authority outlined above. Examining users' identification of quality in content is a viable and inherently desirable strategy for library and information science researchers and practitioners, as proposed by Bonnici. However, the social nature of OSN invites consideration of informational support strategies that may raise perceptions of trust, particularly in times of high-stress information seeking. Examples include brief statements of experience, such as length of time invested in knowledge-building on the specific topic, personal experiences in context and balanced emotional expression.

Social support may be a factor in cognitive authority where it is absent in more traditional relations of authority, such as teacher-student or doctor-patient interactions. Several seminal theorists, many cited in LIS literature, have informed social support theory, including Durkheim (1951), Barnes (1954) and Cassel (1976). However, it is the more recent work of House (1981) that is relevant to OSN. House categorised social support into four types:

1 emotional (e.g. love, trust and caring)
2 instrumental (e.g. meeting material needs)
3 informational (e.g. giving advice, suggestions and information)
4 appraisal (e.g. providing affirmation, feedback, constructive criticism and social comparison).

Barnes' (1954) social support theory has been commonly adopted in health communication research when examining the effects of social relationships' structure, processes and functions on individual health behaviours and outcomes. The translation to FB groups is appropriate for an exploration of the relational dynamics and exchanges within online health social support groups. More specifically, it illuminates the ways in which group participants interact with one another to seek specific information and build a sense of community in the face of health-related problems.

Building on the concepts of cognitive authority and social support theory design structure, two highly specialised FB groups wherein an information crisis is central are considered. These groups offer information that fills an information void or challenges existing beliefs and practices. These two groups present years of cognitive authority and socially supportive content that share community-constructed knowledge across time and space to fill a void caused by conflicting opinions or a dearth of information. But the OSN world can also pose challenges for preserving these snippets of knowledge. The informality of the OSN context presents errors in spelling, punctuation and spacing, posing potential issues for search queries on FB groups.

Information retrieval and social information retrieval

One of the most fundamental elements of web activity is information retrieval (IR), an act often as simple as entering a set of terms into a search engine. Indeed, this activity and the predominant search engine have become so ubiquitous that the *Oxford English Dictionary* (2018) added the term 'Google' as a verb in 2006. IR deals with representation, storage and organization of, and access to, information as determined by satisfying user requirements (Bouadjenek, Hacid and Bouzeghoub, 2016). Insufficiently theorised in the OSN environment, IR models have been adjusted to account for social networks and user-generated information. Known as social information retrieval (SIR), this adapted model aims to provide relevant content and information to users in the domains of information retrieval, research and recommendation, covering topics such as social tagging, collaborative querying, social network analysis, subjective relevance judgments, Q&A systems and collaborative filtering. SIR encompasses social web searching, spanning social aspects such as discrepancies between search input and user-selected results; social searching, which may entail information seeking aided by social resources such as friends or online strangers; and social recommendation, which draws on the cognitive authority of a social network to aid in information seeking.

Social information retrieval is distinct from IR in its intent to consider the social aspect of OSN context. SIR research is classified by a relationship taxonomy involving three types of social relationships: symmetric, asymmetric and k-partite relationships. Symmetric relationships involve users who have equal authority, for example, friendships on FB, whereas asymmetric relationships are characterised by unilateral information dissemination (Bouadjenek, Hacid and Bouzeghoub, 2016). Such relationships are typified by one member of the OSN having authority or cognitive authority on a topic and disseminating information broadly to the audience of followers or friends, for example, followers–following on Twitter. The third relationship, k-partite relationships, refers to established multidimensional connections involving humans, content and waypoints, for example, friends, followers, post content and tags including hashtags and @ symbols (Bouadjenek, Hacid and Bouzeghoub, 2016). Although these relationships provide a basis for programming OSN systems for improved SIR, FB groups cannot be pigeon-holed into any single one of these three relationships. Rather, FB groups embody a combination of the three, complicating applications of existing SIR within the FB context.

Tagging practices in FB groups allow for user-defined information classification such as hashtags, which are valued both for their potential to improve the discoverability of online information as well as their application of natural language that mirrors users' information needs. The visible presence of tags enables users to discover information without needing to know ahead of time what to search for, as one might need to know the unique language of a given FB group in order to retrieve relevant results from within its posts.

Challenges inherent in tagging include precision and recall, as tags cannot account for synonyms, acronyms, homographs, misspelling and inconsistent abbreviations. Another noteworthy feature of tagging in OSN is its potential to create emphasis beyond the intent of information discovery. For example, a new member to the Canine Illness Group might add a tag to convey emotion over their pet's condition, such as #afraid or #confused. Furthermore, specialised language often emerges in communities that is representative of the group's worldview and beliefs (Bonnici, 2001). In this context, language refers to specialised meanings that may differ from mainstream vocabulary or usage. To encourage users aiming for discoverable term selection, folksonomies are socially generated terms and frameworks for organising and finding information. They often include linguistic attribute guidelines as examination of the elements of term choice, grammatical forms of terms, nouns and selecting the preferred form. Folksonomies informed by user-generated metatags can be strategically applied in OSN to aid users in finding multiple, widely dispersed posts (both internally and in other connected domains that address the same topic). However, adoption and diffusion rates of hashtag use in these two FB groups, combined with limitations of the FB interface, pose challenges for social information retrieval.

Data analysis of the two selected FB groups

Both groups focus on specialised topics related to life-threatening health issues. Group members typically fall into one of three roles or categories:

1 owner/administrators who established and manage the page
2 long-time members who observe and contribute to discussion
3 new members who are, frequently, experiencing an information deficit catalysed by a traumatic health-related event, where health professionals are perceived to have failed to meet the user's information needs and frequently motivate the search for information in context.

The controversial nature of one of the groups discussed here and the newness of the topic in the other mean that a lack of, or unclear, information provided by authority figures contributes to confusion in information seeking and decision making. Thus, a new member joins the group in information-seeking mode, usually under high stress, where garnering information is fuelled and constrained by the essence of time. In many cases, time sensitivity may be a major driver for seeking membership in a FB group forum.

The Vaccine Safety Group

This group focuses on the topic of childhood vaccination, a controversial issue with ramifications for public health on each side of the political divide. With more than 17,000 members, the group averages seven posts and comments per day. The group describes itself as 'the only online source, [*sic*] where people share their stories about having measles, chickenpox, mumps, whooping cough, etc.' More specifically, many of the posts focus on the risks of vaccines or injuries believed to be the result of childhood immunisations. The group description indicates an open and inviting forum where potential members are encouraged to join and share experiences that help inform others about vaccine injury. The approach of the group engages personal knowledge sharing by parents who posted accounts of vaccine injury. Group members may also ask questions about vaccines or conditions related to vaccine safety. In the events section, the group promotes anti-vaccination events that centre on vaccine information. Members share information through textual posts and images, as well as videos averaging less than one minute in length to visually and emotionally enhance their stories.

These posts may take the form of stories about vaccine injury related to specific victims, memorial posts to children believed to have died as a result of vaccine injury, advice about avoiding vaccine mandates, advice for detoxing from vaccines and more. Five documents related to the group topic are available in the files section of the site. Documents are available publicly to members and non-members in accordance with the group's goal of educating the public about vaccine injury. The group houses more than 7000 posts and comments since its inception in 2014. The proliferation of posts presents a sea of cognitive authority in which many new members might flounder while searching for information. Yet an in-depth analysis reveals patterns that indicate relevant tagging practices would increase the potential for finding relevant information.

The Canine Illness Group

Also a health-related forum, the Canine Illness Group presents information for canine owners whose pet suffers from a chronic, life-threatening illness. Long diagnosed in human medicine, this illness has only been diagnosed in veterinary medicine within the past decade. Complicating the topic further, diagnosis has been rare until recently. Not surprisingly, general veterinary practitioners have little exposure to, or experience with, treating dogs who present with the illness. In turn, the rarity of diagnosis has resulted in little research, leaving a dearth of relevant evidence-based studies in veterinary journals. Recent veterinary research has presented findings that suggest medication dosages much lower than those prescribed by pharmaceutical companies and strategies adopted from human treatment protocols. Thus, the newly published information challenges the worldview of many practicing veterinarians, who typically follow pharmaceutical dosing instructions and established treatment protocols.

Created in 2012, the Canine Illness Group now has more than 7000 members and advice is centred on recent low-dose research findings. The goal is to help educate canine owners about treatment and dealing with the side-effects of one specific disease and treatment. Although two members are veterinarians, the majority of advice originates from a group administrator with significant experience with the disease topic and the advice of numerous group members sharing their own experiences with an ill dog suffering from the disease. Members share information through images of their pets, mostly when previously healthy and at the time of diagnosis, to demonstrate the impact of the disease. A significant portion of the images are of laboratory results, sharing conditions and seeking recommendations for medication dosing.

Members also share videos, typically less than one minute in duration. Videos usually show a dog's recovery from crisis, often as an emotional expression of gratitude to the group for its support, as well as an expression of hope for those new to the illness and in crisis. Authoritative knowledge is shared in the files section and the documents are frequently pointed out in community posts, which indicates the importance of these documents to support community members' shared experiences. Seventeen of the documents are files addressing information based on authority, including abstracts of journal publications, language translations of abstracts and medicine dosing information. Only two files are personal documents of members sharing laboratory results for their pets. One file is a spreadsheet sharing information on veterinarians by location with experience of treating the disease following low-dose protocols. Members are encouraged to add their veterinarian's information to the list. The list sees an average of three newly posted cases from new members per week. Most of these posts generate high levels of interactive posts in response, probing for more information to help the member make a decision on a treatment strategy for their newly-diagnosed pet. Postings are prolific, with more than 10,000 posts available to search. Because current FB search strategies do not index or provide relevancy reviews, someone in an information crisis may be overwhelmed by the sheer number of posts. An analysis of randomly selected posts reveals a situation similar to that of the Vaccine Safety Group. Patterns discovered across community posts present potential for finding relevant information if group members employ strategic tagging strategies.

In summary, both these forums reveal high levels of interaction among members, demonstrating socially supportive relationships. The nature of posts reveals that members share personal experiences as a means of emotional support, as well as practical advice for helping members in crisis make informed decisions. In the face of politically charged information agendas and a lack of authoritative information resources, these collective personal experiences may serve as a viable basis for informing important, life-saving decisions and they hinge on the notion of cognitive authority, a central feature in much of the OSN world and especially in FB groups. Social engagement unique to OSN forums brings a proliferation of common experience and opinion to web content and their social nature provides a means of social support among group members, particularly those under high levels of stress driven by the need for time-sensitive information to inform decision making affecting the health of loved ones.

Potential group features in relation to SIR

The results of data analysis show that the in-group search engine only provides simple query search and search result filtering functions (e.g. sorting results by top or most recent posts; filtering results by resource, tagged location, or date posted). In examining the modes of information exchange among group members, symmetric relationships can rarely be identified, since information seekers and information providers commonly possess an uneven level of authoritative knowledge and cognitive authority within the group. Group interaction messages showed no apparent signs of asymmetric relationships among members, even though group administrators often publish some group guidelines or announcements or relevant source recommendations and monitor postings accordingly. Similarly, prevailing information search functions and group features provide little support for k-partite relationships, such as in the form of editing or tagging other members' posts. Therefore, it is almost impossible to implement SIR approaches in the absence of proffered system structure or tools available for current FB group members.

The preliminary findings of the absence of collaborative mechanisms employed in FB groups led to an in-depth examination of how both users and resources have been incorporated into the SIR process within the specific contexts of the two selected groups. These informed observations are framed by cognitive authority and social support theory. The findings aim to offer recommendations on FB system development for optimal user experience in deploying community-defined SIR mechanisms. Therefore, the effective use of hashtags in OSN could provide potentially life-saving information even by the non-experts who typically constitute the majority of group membership. However, information seekers would need a high level of information literacy to sort out the credible material from unreliable sources in the two forums. For the two selected groups, five sections including discussion, members, events, videos and images and files, respectively, were examined, with a focus on the discussion posts.

Group discussion area

Twenty-five original postings with comments posted between June 2017 and August 2017 were randomly selected from each of the two groups. Data analysis included the 25 original postings with up to 25 comments on each post. A total of 253 posts and comments for the Vaccine Safety Group and 232 for the Canine Illness Group were analysed. In the Vaccine Safety Group, nearly 12 (48%) original postings were linked to varying online anti-vaccine sources outside the group message, primarily by 17 group administrators; 8 (32%) were parent inquiries related to vaccine safety; the rest were shared by members who held cognitive authority (28%). Only three hashtags were employed in reviewed posts. In the Canine Illness Group, nearly 20 (80%) original postings were inquiries seeking advice or answers to questions. The nature of these posts involved inquiries about medication dosages and symptoms of illness, frequently supplemented with photographs of laboratory results to inform the group of the state of the illness. All were posted by members new to the group, having joined within one week or less before their inquiry post. No occurrences of hashtags were witnessed in analysed posts for the Canine Illness Group.

The selected group posts in both textual and graphic formats were analysed through the lens of cognitive authority and social support theories. The results of data analysis show that the majority of posts are information-based and instrumental in nature. Instrumental posts are rich in advice, where the advisor's authority is often supported by personal experiential knowledge. Emotional support is a commonly noted reaction of members in response to initial posts where a new member overtly expresses high levels of stress and confusion. These emotionally supportive expressions present mostly in the form of visual imagery, such as facial emojis indicating happiness, sadness, or anger appropriate to the topic. Immediate *thank you* responses frequently follow, demonstrating the socially supportive function of the groups. However, this type of interaction may contribute noise in a SIR task, because emotionally supportive or gratitude responses typically provide little substantial topical information related to members' information needs.

Appraisal support indicates that advice given or actions reported are collectively approved by groups. These messages are often presented through a thumbs-up emoji, much like the emotionally supportive or gratitude information. Appraisal support appears to contribute to collaborative experiential knowledge and cognitive authority building among members. Informational support is typified by primary or verifiable resources and appears less frequently than instrumental support fuelled by cognitive authority. For example, the Canine Illness Group offers pointers to veterinary journal articles, veterinarian-endorsed dosing protocols and links to websites endorsed by the group. In the Vaccine Safety Group, the collaborative experiential knowledge or evidentiary support on vaccine injury are viewed as authoritative and trustworthy sources by others. Cognitive authority, therefore, works for informational and emotional support among the members.

The richness of group posts may leave questions as to the quality of advice and content. Delving further for quality indication by information seekers in context is often desired, yet more often than not elusive. Thus, other potential FB group factors that may contribute to SIR strategies were further examined.

Members

People are what make social media social in nature. The inherent challenge in FB is that account names rarely provide any immediate indicators of authoritative knowledge or authority. For example, the majority of members of the Vaccine Safety Group are demographically disparate parents across the world. They often share diverse beliefs and goals related to childhood vaccination for religious, philosophical, economic or political reasons. One might posit that an administrator has some level of authority vested by access to moderation capabilities and some may assume that an administrator level is granted based on some level of authority on the group topic. However, making assumptions entails high risk of error. Investigation of profiles may indicate authority if the FB member self-reports in such a way, but the assumption is that rarely do FB group members choose to click on a group member's profile to investigate their background and knowledge. Thus, membership alone is problematic in identifying cognitive authority. However, in the Canine Illness Group, the use of the @MemberName format was invoked to attract the attention of one of the group administrators to encourage a response. This tactic, in addition to other indicators of cognitive authority held by this group administrator, adds evidence that the individual is viewed as holding cognitive authority among the group members. Among the posts analysed, one instance was noted where a respondent to a post stream self-identified as holding knowledge authority 'MemberName— vet here. Your labs indicate high levels of . . .'.

Events

An examination of events in the two groups revealed little fodder for cognitive authority, social support, or tagging features as framed by theoretical approaches. However, endorsement of event information through posting or linking by administrators indicates that information garnered through such events may be of substantive quality.

Videos and images

FB groups provide space for the sharing of images and videos. The results of data analysis show that the majority of visual imagery is presented in the form of photographs. Most of the photographs appear early, either in originating posts or within the third to fifth level of a cluster of posts that make up a conversation. For example, in the Canine Illness Group, an overwhelming majority of the photographs are images of laboratory results presented to garner advice about treatment. Frequently, laboratory results are accompanied by two photographs of the pet—one pre-illness and the other current—to demonstrate the impact of the disease. Responses typically provide advice on dosing (cognitive authority). Responses also include emotionally supportive comments referring to the *cuteness* of the pet accompanied by well-wishes for recovery. Informational responses reveal references to information in the files area of the FB group area. Although visually presented information in the form of images and videos is helpful to the immediate situation at hand, linking such data through tagging labels requires further research into how this data might be used.

Files

The group files could well be considered a library in that their documents provide authoritative information about treatment strategies in the Canine Illness Group. These vetted and endorsed information resources, combined with cognitive authority expressed in member posts, provide sound basis for decision making. These documents are downloadable, printable and shareable, providing potential intellectual support based on their accessible status and authoritative nature. Informational in nature, the files offer immediate and reliable sources in a sea of unsearchable cognitive authority.

In summary, the results of analysing the above group features indicate that group members often collectively accept cognitive authority in the form of collaborative experiential knowledge as an indicator of information quality and trustworthiness. Interactive and immediate emotional support in both textual and graphic forms often catalyses communication open to a wider range of members but contributes little informational value to SIR.

Indications of group search strategies to SIR

The observations do not provide sufficient evidence to justify categorising these two groups into any one of the three SIR relationships presented by Bouadjenek, Hacid and Bouzeghoub (2016). Clearly, symmetry relationships can be ruled out by the nature of information seeking versus informational and instrumental support observed in member posts. Only three posts were observed in which a general announcement was posted to the list. One was an originating post by a group administrator announcing a new article posted in the files. Only three responses were noted, all providing appraisal support through a thumbs-up response. These one-way posts are infrequent in occurrence, negating asymmetrical relationship labelling of these groups. Further, the fact that posts are neither editable nor tagged by other members precludes the categorisation of these groups as k-partite in their relationship nature.

The failure of these two groups to be categorised into one of the three SIR relationships demonstrates the challenge of SIR strategies that function within the FB group environment. Yet the nature of valuable instrumental and informational content supported by significant cognitive authority beckons for retrieval mechanisms. Observation of these two groups reveals repeated questions and redundant exchanges replicated across posts. Strategies for finding information within FB groups such as these could ameliorate anxiety in information seekers in states of high-stress information deficit. Only three hashtags focused more on self-serving and often sentimental expression than on information retrieval purposes. For instance, one hashtag composed as a highly emotional and out-of-context phrase would not be informative or valuable to (new) group members who search for relevant topical information or accumulated group resources across space and time. Therefore, suggestions for community-informed strategies for making information within groups findable will contribute to user satisfaction. Frequently, these community-based retrieval strategies are the first step in informing system designs to serve IR functions. The following section presents strategies for devising a community-informed SIR strategy for these two FB groups. The strategies offer a potential model for other FB groups.

Recommendations to enhance SIR in-context

Early online groups were deemed to have a *realness* as related to their virtual existence (Burnett and Bonnici, 2003). Groups where usernames revealed true personal identity reported less of a distinction between face-to-face and virtual engagement. The human factors in online forums have increasingly become like any other social setting in the face-to-face world. Human behaviours can significantly impact system usability. Since the inception of human virtual gatherings in online social settings, researchers have identified that the exchange of discussion regarding proper behaviours has led to guiding documents and system upgrades that allow for normalised behaviours within the online community (Burnett and Bonnici, 2003; Dibbell, 1998; Horn, 1998;

Hafner, 2001). Virtual communities have evolved and morphed with the advancement of the internet, allowing new ideas to serve the needs of communities. In light of the lack of social tagging prevalence for linked data in FB groups, the following section provides considerable solutions that would enhance SIR in context.

Tagging

For information-based FB social groups, the goal of SIR is to achieve optimal information recoverability within social dimensions that embody both distributed group members and relevant resources. A proffered structured or semi-structured social tagging system such as hashtags has the potential to enhance tagging diffusion and adoption for improved social information navigation and retrieval across group members and extended to the general public. Well recognised problematic attributes of user-generated hashtags, including acronyms, homographs, misspelling and inconsistent abbreviations, may pose barriers to their effectiveness and usefulness for SIR. An application of machine-learning approaches to generate a dataset of hashtags from the group postings and the creation of guidelines for tagging (e.g. the standardised controlled vocabulary guidelines of the National Information Standards Organization, 2005) could pave the way to folksonomy as a user-friendly and practical collaborative classification system for FB groups. It would provide a categorisation mechanism for group member profiles by information of their self-presented roles or cognitive authority, hashtags by tag attributes and members' tagging behaviours and resources by descriptive metadata and social annotation for both internal group posts and linked external sources. Such a categorisation system would provide a useful tool for distinguishing between affective or emotional aspects of group data and information-based content.

UX-informed system features

Oftentimes, human-driven factors influence systems and interface designs. User-experience (UX) data garnered from usability studies, surveys and direct observations of users active on devices and systems reveals mechanisms for system-engineered improvements. Similar to the @ and location functions available via the FB interface, an interface-embedded button within FB that generates the hashtag may encourage its use within groups. When considering such a feature in conjunction with the tagging system noted earlier, a community-centred strategy emerges. A system-provided hashtag in the FB interface with the ability for FB group administrators to prepopulate input fields with common vocabulary can aid SIR mechanisms within these unique FB forums. Further investigation of the idea among a larger FB population would inform the need for prototype development for addition to the FB interface. Subsequent tests of the prototype through human-computer interaction (HCI) methods would reveal potential for improvement to SIR in FB groups.

Simple codified guide

The description section for the two groups embodies more than a simple topic description. In an FAQ-like form, behavioural expectations are stated, mainly warning not to argue, bully, or engage in any other rude behaviours. Examples from the description areas include statements to the tenor of 'And, there is to be ABSOLUTELY NO-BASHING [sic], TRASHING, or PUTTING DOWN of any other [canine] owner or Veterinarian for ANY REASON! Complain? Yes. Have an issue? Yes. Bash? No'.

The Vaccine Safety Group advertises sanctions for such behaviours; posts containing negative expressions will be deleted. The same group offers suggestions beyond general behaviour intended to guide members regarding expected behavioural norms in the group forum: for example, 'If you have a link to a more detailed story somewhere else on the web, please link to it, but also tell a brief summary of your story in the post, so that a reader can get enough information to know they want to click your link'.

Considering that the description serves to guide expected member behaviour, it seems appropriate that this section could also include guidance for recommended strategies offered above to improve SIR. A list of recommended hashtag language would inform newcomers, as well as remind more tenured group members of strategic ways to embellish posts to increase the discoverability of useful information. Alternatively, considering the development of a system-based, administrator-defined hashtag tool, the description area could encourage members to use hashtags when posting. Strategic linking behaviours could be promoted in this description area, rendering it similar to the FAQ of earlier online communities as described by Burnett and Bonnici (2003).

Despite the best of intentions of such an FAQ-like online document, however, it must be acknowledged that few newcomers actually read these descriptions. Thus, group administrators could periodically point to and remind members of both expected and encouraged behaviours aligned with the group objective. Developing and implementing an efficient and user-friendly tagging system constitutes a potential means of advancing social information discoverability in information-based Facebook social groups. The proposed recommendations need to be validated in future user studies.

Conclusion

In summary, an examination of information-based FB groups indicates that these groups function with the intention of providing cognitive authority-empowered information. Each group's description area alludes to cognitive authority as a central goal by encouraging members to share experiences relative to the topic.

> [The Canine Illness Group] also works to educate and support the companion animal community about [xxx] disease in dogs. The goal is to foster open communication about the variety of options available to the caregiver of a dog with [xxx] disease. Members neither diagnose, treat, nor prescribe medications to other members but are encouraged to share their personal experiences and what they have learned in the course of caring for their own dogs. Any and all concerns should always be addressed directly to a trusted veterinarian. Because [xxx] disease is a life-long disease, it is imperative to find a veterinarian who will work with you.

The Vaccine Safety Group states:

> Please post ONLY stories that you have first-hand knowledge about related to the following topics: Vaccine injuries and reactions OR stories of V.P.I.'s (Vaccine preventable illnesses). Anything other than those two topics will be deleted. Conversations can be had in the threads, but let's keep the posts clean to make it easy browsing for information seekers. When telling your story, give details that would help educate someone's opinion.

A concern for information provision is explicitly stated in the Vaccine Safety Group, indicating that discoverability of information in the form of cognitive authority is a desirable outcome of the group's presence. One might assume the same for the Canine Illness Group, although its expression is related to individual information seeking rather than general discoverability of information. 'This group is a place where everyone can ask questions and ask for help no matter how small the issue may be'.

Community member behaviours in both groups, however, fail to use existing FB system strategies to make information discoverable (e.g. hashtags) and specialised language may be problematic in strategic hashtag application, further compounding the failure of linked data within and beyond the confines of these specialised groups. Another social participatory and interactive means is linking works to consolidate information relevance and currency in the process of contextualising discoverability of information across social dimensions. The notion of linking may elevate the possibility of public visibility, risking group privacy concerns in cases where group discussions are closed, or membership is subject to administrator approval. The ability to link data may be of particular interest to both closed and public FB groups, where members and potential members desire discoverability of content. Since informational support is essential for information-based FB groups, linking is proposed as a potential tool for effective SIR. Within a group, interlinking among the group members, files and content of posts over time can be used to develop a group guide to navigate member connectivity and resource connectivity. Cross-linking can connect members to relevant online sources and related media outside of the group. As a crowdsourcing effort of accessing relevant external resources, cross-linking can also be used to develop group resource lists combined with proper hashtags based on relevance, popularity, authority or information quality.

Existing strategies, such as the hashtag enhanced by information science expertise in folksonomy and information retrieval, serve to extend SIR for these types of groups. New ideas for system design provide enhanced potential for user-friendly tools that support the goal of shared and discoverable cognitive authority and aid the information seeker in high stakes crisis. These measures as applied and deployed in the FB group context encourage linked data strategies in the FB environment, integrating it within the ever-expanding body of human knowledge available via the web.

References

Barnes, J. A. (1954) Class and Committees in a Norwegian Island Parish, *Human Relations, 7*, 39–58.

Black, T. (2017) Using Facebook Groups: you can use a Facebook group like a private room, *Lifewire*, 30 September, www.lifewire.com/facebook-groups-4103720.

Burnett, G. and Bonnici, L. J. (2003) Beyond the FAQ: explicit and implicit norms in usenet newsgroups, *Library & Information Science Research*, **25**, 333–51.

Bonnici, L. J. (2001) *An Examination of Categorical Attributions through the Lens of Reference Group Theory*, Florida State University, Tallahassee, FL.

Bonnici, L. J. (2016) Subjectivity Filtering: finding cognitive authority in online social media opinion posts. In *Proceedings from the Document Academy*, **3**, 1–20, http://ideaexchange.uakron.edu/docam/vol3/iss2/13.

Bouadjenek, M. B., Hacid, H. and Bouzeghoub, M. (2016) Social Networks and
   Information Retrieval, How are They Converging? A survey, a taxonomy and an
   analysis of social information retrieval approaches and platforms, *Information
   Systems*, **56**, 1–18.

Cassel, J. (1976) The Contribution of the Social Environment to Host Resistance,
   American Journal of Epidemiology, **104**, 10–23.

Dibbell, J. (1998) My Tiny Life: crime and passion in a virtual world, *Publishers Weekly*,
   30 November, 57.

Durkheim, E. (1951) *Suicide: a study in sociology*, Free Press.

Hafner, K. (2001) *The Well: a story of love, death & real life in the seminal online
   community*, Avalon.

Horn, R. (1998) *Visual Language: global communication for the 21st century*, MacroVU.

House, J. S. (1981) *Work Stress and Social Support,* Addison-Wesley.

McKenzie, P. J. (2003) Justifying Cognitive Authority Decisions: discursive strategies of
   information seekers, *Library Quarterly*, **73**, 26–88.

Ma, J. and Stahl, L. (2017) A Multimodal Critical Discourse Analysis of Anti-
   Vaccination Information on Facebook, *Library & Information Science Research*, **39**,
   303–10.

National Information Standards Organization (2005) *Guidelines for the Construction,
   Format and Management of Monolingual Controlled Vocabularies*,
   https://groups.niso.org/apps/group_public/download.php/12591/
   z39-19-2005r2010.pdf.

Neal, D. M., Campbell, A. J., Williams, L. Y., Liu, Y. and Nussbaumer, D. (2011) 'I did
   not Realize so Many Options are Available': cognitive authority, emerging adults
   and e-mental health, *Library & Information Science Research*, **33**, 25–33.

Neal, D. M. and McKenzie, P. J. (2011) Putting the Pieces Together: endometriosis
   blogs, cognitive authority and collaborative information behavior, *Journal of the
   Medical Library Association*, **99**, 127–34.

Oxford English Dictionary (2018) 'Google',
   https://en.oxforddictionaries.com/definition/google.

Preston, J. (2011) Movement Began with Outrage and a Facebook Page that Gave it an
   Outlet, *The New York Times*, 5 February,
   www.nytimes.com/2011/02/06/world/middleeast/06face.html.

Rieh, S. Y. (2002) Judgment of Information Quality and Cognitive Authority in the
   Web, *Journal of the American Society for Information Science & Technology*, **53**,
   145–61.

Warren, C. (2013) Facebook Finally Gets #Hashtags, *CNN*, 13 June, www.cnn.com/2013/06/12/tech/social-media/facebook-hashtags/index.html.

Weinberger, M. (2017) 33 Photos of Facebook's Rise from a Harvard Dorm Room to World Domination, *Business Insider*, 7 September, www.businessinsider.com/facebook-history-photos-2016-9/#facebook-got-its-start-at-harvards-kirkland-house-dormitory-1.

Wilson, P. (1983) *Second-Hand Knowledge: an inquiry into cognitive authority*, Greenwood.

Zuckerberg, M. (2017a) Building Global Community, *Facebook*, 16 February, www.facebook.com/notes/mark-zuckerberg/building-global-community/10154544292806634/.

Zuckerberg, M. (2017b) We Just Announced our Quarterly Results and Shared an Update on our Community's Progress to Connect the World [Facebook status update], *Facebook*, 3 May, www.facebook.com/facebookcareers/posts/1938478439772174.

Chapter 7

#FandomCommunication: how online fandom utilises tagging and folksonomy

Max Dobson

Introduction

Tags are a form of linked data familiar to those of us who use the internet for social media. These pieces of metadata are usually assigned to posts on social media to help users make sense of the content (Golder and Huberman, 2006), in a way that is generally easy to understand and emulate. It is difficult to use a social media platform like Facebook, Twitter or Tumblr and not come across tagging in one form or another. Hashtags can sprout up amongst many important events or moments, like #blacklivesmatter or #yesallwomen. Generic tags that have very little indication of meaning or importance can also be added to statuses for fun, like #ThursdayThoughts. These are some of the most common uses of social tagging, but they are far from the only examples of social tagging being used in online spaces.

Although the developments leading to modern, western fandom vary according to country (Cuntz-Leng and Meintzinger, 2015), it is generally accepted that fandom as we now would recognise it largely came about in the late 1960s to early 1970s, when the original series of Star Trek (1966) was airing. Star Trek has had a varied following over the years and still attracts many kinds of viewers (Frazetti, 2011), but Star Trek was and is a byword for geek culture. The incredible devotion and love many Star Trek fans have for the series has led to conventions, collectables, and works of art. Fanfiction was a popular way for Star Trek fans to share their own interpretations of the show's characters by creating transformative works of fiction. Some of the oldest examples of modern fanfiction were created by the Star Trek fandom (Verba, 2003), and were copied and shared in person. With ease of access to the internet becoming more widespread, much of fandom now takes place in online spaces, made up of internet based communities. In spite of this massive technological shift, fanfiction and fandoms have changed very little. Put simply, fandoms today are online spaces dedicated to fans, many of whom produce content for their particular interests and share it online.

Different fandoms do have their own unique quirks, but on the whole, fandoms have embraced tagging. This has become an important practice, especially amongst fanfiction writers. Tagging within fandom suffers from many of the same problems as tagging elsewhere online, but fandoms still have a good understanding of how to use tagging, even if users do not always understand it in official terms. Given that tagging is such a widely used form of metadata, it is useful to consider how online communities might improve their tagging practices by learning from the practices of fandom.

Tagging and information needs

Tagging has been used in online communities to ensure that data is more easily findable, to varying effect. When structured in a way that can be understood by most of its users, tagging greatly improves the searchability of online data. When used effectively, it enables online communities to find relevant information quickly. This is far from the only way that tagging can be utilised. Tagging can also be used to provide further information on whatever data the user has shared, by describing the content provided. This is easier to achieve on some platforms than others. At the time of writing, Facebook and Twitter do not allow users to add tags that consist of more than one word, which greatly limits the effectiveness and accuracy users can achieve. By contrast, websites like Tumblr allow users to have long tags with spacing and limited punctuation, essentially allowing users to create tags with greater coherence.

How users can utilise tags may seem like a small thing, but there are many factors that can change their interactions. Website layout largely determines how users can interact with each other and funnels interactions down certain routes (Alaimo, 2014). Even something as simple as whether users can have spaces in their tags drastically changes the relationship users have with tags. Restrictions placed on tags can lead to users finding creative solutions to the problems posed by limitations, but this also makes it far harder for users to articulate thought or to interact with other users. In some cases, one could argue that this is the point. A blogging platform like Tumblr would obviously be better suited to a verbose use of language than Twitter, which places a strict character limit on users' posts.

Even though websites have been designed with a certain layout or idea in mind, it is important not to ignore the fact that users do not always interact with these websites in the ways in which they are expected to. There are Twitter users who post long threads of articulate arguments and there are so many short and nonsensical posts on Tumblr that it has become a well-known and expected format (Tumblr, 2017). This is not an argument in favour of changing the basic layout of Twitter and Tumblr. The creativity of internet users ensures that they will find ways of using social media and tagging that are at odds with the intended function of the website. Although Twitter recently increased the number of characters users can work with, they have still kept to a small number of characters to maintain its original theme. Restrictions can bring about interesting ways for users to interact with linked data, following Merholz's argument that internet users tend to make their own paths across the landscape of the internet, regardless of the direction they were intended to take (Merholz, 2004).

There are many other issues with tagging on social media that can limit the expression and capability of internet users. Different websites often have their own ways of implementing tagging. Some websites do not let users add spaces between words, whilst some allow users a lot of space to write phrases or sentences. Some websites prioritise the use of tags as a way of keeping track of content, whereas others seem to view tags as an optional add-on. There is not really a properly standardised method of tagging recognised across all platforms. Given the lack of a standardised system, it is hardly surprising that tagging varies wildly across platforms. This presents an issue for discussions about how valid tagging is as a form of metadata. It is more difficult for tagging to be applied or judged universally if even the basic parameters for tagging vary from platform to platform.

The problems with tagging are compounded when we try to generalise the tagging habits of internet users. Although we can identify trends in tag usage across different platforms, there is not very much consideration given to what differences may arise in various online communities. There is also an unfortunate tendency to assume, because the metadata practices of users do not provide useful information for search engines or traditional search methods, that this metadata is not useful at all. This is a dangerous misconception, as much of the information available on the internet depends upon a level of understanding and context in order to be properly appreciated. Just as we require a level of further knowledge to make a judgement about bias in academic sources, so too do we require a level of further knowledge to make judgements about whether unconventional metadata could be useful in a different context.

In any community, there has to be a certain level of communication and the exchange of ideas between its participants (McMillan and Chavis, 1986).

Different communities can have wildly contrasting needs, even before taking into consideration the different roles information technology can play in improving lives. In poorer communities, information technology can be vital in helping their members to escape poverty (Britz, 2004). This is largely because technology and access to information have become vital components for ensuring that communities can participate fully in society (Barja and Gigler, 2007). With that in mind, it is especially vital for those in less affluent areas to have access to these new technologies and to understand how to use them. One of the major problems associated with information poverty is that it directly impacts those who are socially and economically at a disadvantage far more than it impacts their wealthy counterparts (Haywood, 1995). It is possible for someone in a wealthy community to be information-poor and for someone living in poverty to be information-rich, but these positions are the exception and not the norm.

Rural communities can be greatly improved just by guaranteed access to information technology. Giving these communities access to reliable information technology means that these communities are better able to access useful services and information (Yusop et al., 2013). For example, access to online banking would eliminate the requirement for long trips in rural areas with few local amenities. Although people living in densely populated areas can often access these services, they frequently can still find amenities nearby that also fulfil their needs. Having access to online services like banking is useful, but not as necessary for those living near amenities.

In the wrong hands this access to information ceases to have the same relevance, but this does not mean there is no value to that information. It simply means the information is more effective in the right hands. The same basic premise can be extended to internet communities. The internet is full of different communities with contrasting and conflicting information needs and it is unwise to be dismissive of information simply because it does not fit personal expectations of usefulness.

The problems of 'bad' tagging

Online tagging is a useful tool for those of us who are not formally trained to use metadata. When discussing concepts important to the future of the internet and our attempts to categorise data, we so often overlook the fact that most people are not going to understand metadata the way an information professional does. This poses several issues when we then try to think about organising metadata. How are we supposed to organise a system that many of the people using it may not even understand? Can we realistically think about organising such a vast amount of knowledge in the hands of people who do not understand its capabilities? In order to better answer these questions, it is helpful to reflect upon the different advantages and disadvantages to tagging and why it is still a useful system for online communities in spite of its flaws.

Traditional search and retrieval systems are far more complex than systems that rely on social tagging. A user trying to understand how to search a more involved taxonomy would generally require at least some training. This requirement presents a barrier to anyone who has not been able to achieve this level of understanding and in turn limits the amount of people who can interact with that system. By contrast, social tagging presents users with the ability to create folksonomies. Folksonomies are generally informal vocabularies for search and retrieval, with very few, if any, obstacles in the way of user participation (Trant, 2009). In theory, as long as a user has access to the correct technology and an internet connection, they can interact with a folksonomy. In fact, it can be argued that folksonomies only thrive because of the lack of qualification required to interact with them (Mathes, 2004). This allows for greater participation than more traditional systems of indexing. It also means that folksonomies are generally easier to adapt than more traditional taxonomies.

Ease of access to folksonomies does have some significant drawbacks. Given that they lack a traditional hierarchy and formal structure, they are easily manipulated and can be vulnerable to malicious misuse (Kroski, 2005). Weinberger (2005) argued that as tagging became more widespread, it would end up losing relevance as a way of searching for data across search engines. Weinberger believed that this would be the case because users would tag overzealously and that they would also use tags that lacked relevance to the material being tagged. Weinberger was convinced that people would adopt bad tagging practices either out of ignorance or intent to mislead users and those practices would make it more difficult for tags to be used to find relevant data.

Tagging is less relevant to finding information on search engines than other factors, although these can be difficult to determine. It is also difficult for an outsider to accurately predict the factors most important to a search engine's choice of results, given that people outside companies like Google do not know exactly the logarithm for determining search results. Combined with the potential for tag spamming, a practice where irrelevant tags are used to make websites appear higher in search results, tagging is not the most useful thing for search engines to use when trying to give internet users results.

Tagging is not, however, a useless invention just because it is not useful in one particular instance. Weinberger was right that tagging would become less relevant to search engines, but he did not consider that there are many ways in which tagging is still useful to online communities. Nor did he anticipate that the inefficient methods of tagging he envisioned could become a regular part of how online communities communicate. Tagging is a convenient tool for social media in general because it is easy enough for most users to have a basic understanding of tagging without a lot of complicated instructions. It can be used to quickly draw attention to the subject of a post or an important social issue, but it can equally be a way for users to be creative and express their emotions and feelings. Tagging is also a relatively simple way for social media users to direct their followers to relevant information, by ensuring that the correct people are notified of new developments.

With all that tagging can do, it is simply unfair to write it off as a method of organization for internet users. Social tagging may not be useful to search engines, but it can be far more useful to users than many traditional forms of taxonomy and data organization systems. For one thing, using a more informal folksonomy allows users greater freedom to invent categories of their own. It means that online communities can very quickly respond to events and create appropriate metadata for their own use, without worrying about a cumbersome system. That is not to say that there is no value in formal taxonomies, or that anarchic tagging is the only system worth pursuing. There is a lot of merit to be found in conventional approaches to classification and retrieval. Merholz (2005) recognised this when discussing the issues present in trying to use tagging and newer methods of information retrieval. These systems do indeed have their places and there are plenty of instances when a more rigid system of classification works better for users and operators. However, a major issue with many such systems is that they often require a high level of understanding to operate properly.

Another interesting aspect of social tagging is that it allows internet users much more creative freedom to describe the data they are sharing with their respective social groups (Kroski, 2005). It also means that users can describe their thoughts and feelings through tagging, something which would be much harder to do under a more traditional taxonomy. To an extent it makes sense for traditional taxonomies to leave out emotional information. Most traditional information searches require search terms to be very specific and clinical. This does leave an important gap in our search capabilities, because it is entirely possible for a user to search for information based on what emotions it is likely to make them feel (Pennington, 2016).

Searching a database for academic works is unlikely to require serious emotional information. Generally, the topic of the article is more important than whatever the author or another database user felt about it. Whilst it is likely that opinions about the usefulness of the work can be important for these kinds of situations, those can be found in reviews and users can request guidance when looking for specific works. There is less value in obtaining emotional information for things like this. However, emotion and feelings are so tied to many other parts of our lives that knowing the emotions someone felt upon viewing a piece of media can be a very important piece of information in the right circumstances. In other words, what makes sense for traditional databases and searches does not necessarily make sense elsewhere.

Emotional information in tagging

Emotional information is such an important aspect of many experiences we face and yet there is very little scope for recording it in a way which is clearly visible to other users. We can interpret emotional information when users interact with media by liking posts or sharing a positive comment (Pennington, 2016). Tags can be another way for users to display their thoughts and feelings.

It can be argued that even when tagging reveals important information, there is still a lot of irrelevant information conveyed through tags (Lamere, 2008). There is truth to this, given that not everyone uses tagging to convey only the most relevant information. It is also true that we do not always appreciate that there could be hidden meaning in a post which cannot be understood out of context.

Even with the knowledge that searching for information is complicated and can depend very much on context, there is still a serious issue with trying to discuss the value of alternative indexing and research methods, given that our knowledge of the needs of specific online communities only extends so far. We know that traditional methods of retrieval work best when they give us a very narrow set of results and in a lot of cases this is exactly what the user needs. When the user has specific needs and knows exactly what those are, they generally do not require umpteen pages of search results. However, this focus on narrow recall and specificity can ignore the fact that not all those who go looking for information have the same search patterns and that traditional rationales might not hold up when applied to social media.

Traditional researching and index theory tends to prioritise specificity and precision over everything else. When the user knows what book or article it is they are searching for, it is better by far for them if they can be as unambiguous as possible to eliminate as many options as possible (Merholz, 2004; Kroski, 2005). Having a long list of possibilities is seen as a negative. This is a fair enough assumption in many cases, especially when we already know exactly what we want.

Search engines can throw up an incredible number of results and usually the majority of them will never be considered by the user. A person researching a particular topic will not want to spend extra time looking through a seemingly endless supply of potential results. Such attitudes are taken for granted and yet this way of thinking runs counter to a lot of the priorities of those in online communities.

A striking example of this can be found in the ways that fanfiction readers often search for reading material. Contrary to conventional wisdom, having an overwhelming amount of fanfiction show up on a tag search is a good thing. There is no worse feeling than having a very small selection of fanfiction to choose from. If there are fewer works to choose from, it means that the fan has to be less specific when searching through any given tag. Fanfiction is a finite resource and fanfiction writers can only create so much of it at a time. The sheer amount of work that goes into creating fanfiction means that for many smaller fandoms, there are already far fewer works than in much larger fandoms.

Even when trying to narrow down choices, a lower recall of fandom material really just means that there are fewer chances that the user will find something they will genuinely enjoy. Having a more specific list of search results is something that fans are liable to complain about if it means that they have fewer things to read. Whilst the ideal situation would be having wide recall for the very specific tropes a given fan is interested in, recall ultimately has to take priority over precision. Even in larger fandoms, search terms that are too specific or too narrow can easily leave the user with nothing to read. It is true that having an extremely large pool of search results can be overwhelming, but for fandoms it ultimately means that there is a bigger pool to dip into. There is nothing stopping fans from pausing their perusal of fan works and coming back later to search for more material.

A similar attitude could be applied to searching through posts on social media. Even if the user has a specific topic that they wish to explore, it is generally better to have a lot of content to look through, even if not all of that content is strictly relevant to the user's interests. Many social media websites understand that their users are likely to scroll through them and look at content posted by other users. Tagging precision is still important in this scenario, but not to lower potential recall. It is important because users still want to find content that is at least somewhat relevant to their interests. If a user just wants to see a lot of pictures of cute dogs, they will most likely be perfectly content to sift through a lot of semi-relevant content to get the benefits of discovering the best pictures. If a user really wants to see an adorable chihuahua wearing a top hat and tails, they may have to be extremely precise. Neither method is flawless, but both of them do have their place in information retrieval.

It is probably safe to assume that there will be times when fanfiction readers, dog lovers and other internet users have very specific needs that are most easily fulfilled with searching that values precision. There is nothing wrong with that, but we cannot ignore the fact that many website layouts essentially favour recall over precision for a good reason. Having more opportunities to discover things that are useful to us is a good thing and when so many popular websites thrive from showing us an excess of content, we need to acknowledge that there are times when traditional recall methods will not be enough.

Fandom's impact on popular culture

When dealing with questions about tagging practices within online communities, it is often useful to consider the best practices of others. In this case, this means looking for a group of people who have successfully managed to use metadata to organise their online data without formal training. There are few online communities which have made such an impressive use of tagging as those found in fandom and so this made finding an online fandom an appealing choice for study.

Choosing a fandom to use in a case study also made sense given that there has recently been a great deal of research on fandom and fan behaviour in recent academic study. Far from being a negative portrayal of fans and fandom, academic perspectives of fans have generally been quite helpful in comparison to the stereotypes used to depict fans in pop culture. In spite of this, much of the study of fans has been based on observation of fans rather than more direct engagement with them. This leaves a clear gap in research, given that fandom does have important ramifications for pop culture. In recent years modern fandom has become more visible to those who do not participate with it directly. Fandom has rallied around many important issues in our popular culture. This has taken many forms, but fandom has been especially vocal about the disturbing lack of representation of women and minorities in much of modern media.

Fans have often displayed distaste for the appalling ways in which modern media portrays women. Fandom has expressed dissatisfaction with queerbaiting, a practice which portrays two people of the same gender as though they were a couple but then refuses to acknowledge the romantic or sexual undertones. Fandom have rallied together against the horrifying 'bury your gays' trope which rears its ugly head across far too many queer storylines and leaves viewers in fear for the lives of queer characters at every turn.

Demonstrating mass distaste and hurt at these things has had an impact on media. Whilst queerbaiting is still a major issue in popular culture, there are also more creators who are willing to push at the boundaries of what is considered acceptable. The animated series *The Legend of Korra* surprised viewers and made history when the show confirmed that the titular character was bisexual, by ending the series with the protagonist holding hands with her girlfriend. The creators of *The 100* took notice when one of their storylines involved killing off Lexa, a lesbian woman, right after she had slept with her girlfriend Clarke. The resulting backlash was incredibly vocal and the show's creators were taken to task for this crass plotline, which resulted in them issuing an apology to fans. In this case the creators of the show could not make up for what they had done, but this was still an important example of the ramifications of throwing queer representation under the bus.

Other creators have tried to take positive steps to offer representation. During his podcast *The Adventure Zone* (www.maximumfun.org/shows/adventure-zone), Griffin Mcelroy killed off Hurley and Sloane, two queer characters who were in love with each other. After fans of the show explained that killing off queer characters was an overwhelmingly pervasive and upsetting trend in media, Mcelroy brought the characters back in a move that some fans dubbed 'unburying your gays'. Instead of brushing off fan concerns as some creators tend to, Mcelroy listened and adapted the story to create something truly special. This was only possible because Mcelroy was able to gather the complaints of fans via social media and learn from his mistakes.

Social media is clearly frequently used as a vehicle of both challenging and upholding culture and can be used to predict future trends or events (Zeng et al., 2010). In an interview with Billboard, Dr. Francesca Coppa argued that fandom has frequently been able to predict trends and has a long-lasting impact on the media we consume (Gaffney, 2017). Examples of fandom having reaching impact on popular culture are not difficult to find. Fans of One Direction may consider themselves vindicated for having supported the likes of Zayn Malik and Harry Styles, both of whom have received broader cultural acclaim since launching solo music careers. *Fifty Shades of Grey*, the bestselling and influential erotica novel, began its life as *Twilight* fanfiction. And who could forget *My Immortal*? This work was simultaneously loved and reviled by Harry Potter fans because of the poor quality of writing and its exact origins and purpose have been hotly debated.

These are but a few examples of how fandom has had an impact on popular culture. This does not even begin to touch on how fandoms have been used as rallying points to draw attention to a lack of positive representation of women, people of colour, queer people and other often ignored or maligned parts of society. It is absolutely true that fandom can be toxic, petty and reactionary, just like any community. Fandom still has a significant impact on the real world and on the popular imagination and for this reason it is important to consider how fandom organises itself.

Tagging in online communities

Social tagging is a very obvious feature of modern social media. Most social media applications have at least some form of tagging incorporated as part of normal use. There is a lot of scope for tagging to be used effectively by both creators and observers to make work more easily discoverable. This could be especially useful when trying to organise the metadata of other online communities that might not appreciate more complex hierarchies.

There have been many issues for those trying to update systems of organization used by online communities in order to make them fit for purpose. Hemmasi (2004) used the example of online music communities trying to get their members to participate in changing their habits and customs to ensure that it would be easier for people to find information. One of the main problems reported by Hemmasi was that the people who were using the older, uncoordinated systems of organization were reluctant to change their ways. Some of the issues with the holdouts within the community were that they did not always understand the newer system, but another major problem was that they did not see why they should expend the effort to change their practices when, as far as they were concerned, current practices were good enough. Indeed, many of the issues we have surrounding tagging metadata can be linked to a lack of common identifiers (Heery, 2004).

The practices Hemmasi observed were not good enough to meet the needs of her community. In fact, they were so poor that Hemmasi felt it necessary to discuss them in the first place. It is possible to argue that imprecise metadata does not matter in certain cases, for example on personal social media posts which are unlikely to have any future importance. There are, however, plenty of good reasons to regularly tag even mundane things. Tagging is a good way of organising content for personal use and it enables the user to find things more easily in the future. Furthermore, tagging something inaccurately can be extremely detrimental later on. Not only does insignificant tagging impede the ability of others to discover information, but it also increases the likelihood that someone else will come across the wrong kind of information. This might not seem like a particularly serious issue, but there are plenty of things we do not wish to see in our everyday lives.

Images of violence or abuse are generally unpleasant, but it is easy to forget that these can have a severe impact on those who have experienced trauma. If content is tagged incorrectly, it has a higher chance of causing a lot of unnecessary pain to a person dealing with trauma. It is also worthwhile considering that we do not necessarily know what could be upsetting to someone else. Whilst we should not avoid the things we love just because someone else might have an unfortunate reaction to them, we can still be considerate and give people a way of avoiding their triggers. In fact, it is common practice on blogging websites for bloggers to display the tags they use so that their readers can make informed choices about the content they consume. This is not done to adhere to rules or guidelines fostered by a website or company, but out of a sense of decency and politeness and it is extremely beneficial.

Developing a sense of politeness and decorum for interactions online might seem strict and authoritarian. Given that tagging can seem so chaotic and creative, it is strange to think of it being constrained by something as simple and old-fashioned as good manners. But manners can be a useful tool when trying to encourage people to behave in certain ways. We have decided that it is polite to offer our guests refreshments when they enter our homes, and so this experience is near universal. We know that some people want to avoid certain upsetting topics, so we can change our tagging habits to be accommodating. Nobody is forcing us to offer people hot drinks or to spend our time adding tags to posts and yet these things still happen.

Fandom case study

The internet is a broad church and as such it is vital to consider whether changing online behaviour is at all feasible, especially over different communities. It can be hard to guess exactly how much users understand about the different purposes and capabilities of tagging. Tags can require insider knowledge to be properly understood, so care and tact is required when trying to make judgements on the validity of a tag, or its true meaning. Such research is best done by either a member of the community, or by someone with access to an insider. This greatly influenced my decision to use the Metalocalypse fandom as a case study group, given that I had formed the necessary connections and immersed myself in that group. A survey was chosen to collect data in place of other more traditional case study methods such as interviews. This was because a survey could accrue more responses in a shorter period than interviews and also because it could collect statistical data as well as user opinions. The principles used to survey the tagging practices and knowledge of the Metalocalypse fandom could have been applied to another online community. It seemed prudent to question an online fandom community, given that fandoms tend to be encouraged to utilise tagging by fanfiction websites and blogging platforms.

If we take the responses from the survey as an example, the main obstacle in trying to alter online behaviours is a lack of user understanding. There is a lot of good which can come from internet users being better educated about their online habits. Indeed, it has been recognised that users not understanding the importance of hierarchy or precision leads to weak and inefficient systems (Kroski, 2005). Finding ways to better educate users on the importance of good tagging would go a long way to getting users to overcome issues with things like controlled vocabularies and could lead to tagging being a more stable method of data organization (Guy and Tonkin, 2006; Macgregor and McCulloch, 2013). Trant (2009) went as far as to argue that tagging could become an invaluable way of envisaging future developments, but only if user bases were able to better understand what they were doing.

The problem with trying to educate a user base is that not all users have equal opportunities to educate themselves. It is possible for users to learn about things like tagging and metadata but doing so can take up a lot of time and resources. Not all users can do this on their own and although community education incentives exist in some areas, these are not universal and they often focus on teaching the elderly basic computer functions. In no way should these services be mocked or belittled – the internet can be a great equaliser and people of all skill levels should be given the chance to interact with newer technologies. But services such as these do not tend to teach users about metadata, coding, or even how to tag things properly. Education systems often take a while to catch up to new technologies and not all education systems are primed to teach younger people about recent technology in the depth required to make significant changes to tagging practices.

Even if greater education about tagging and coding is available, this is not helpful for those who have outgrown the classroom. There is also the very real issue of the digital divide, which ensures that people do not have the same level of access to technology. Services such as public libraries are important to giving those without internet access, smartphones or computers the chance to interact with technology, but this does not level the playing field. Library technology is often out of date, slow and liable to have restrictions placed on what the users can and cannot access. Library computers can only be accessed during opening hours and they cannot be moved or taken home. It may also be difficult to get access to a computer, depending on how many the library has and whether the library has dedicated time for priority groups to use computers. There is no comparison between owning personal electronic devices and having to use public facilities to obtain internet access.

Having access to adequate technology is an important part of being digitally literate, because it means that the user can practice their skills. Even if the user is simply browsing a website, they can still see what tags are being used and in what way. When access is limited, there are fewer chances to refine their practices. Being able to alter the way people behave online has to take into account that there are barriers to entry for many people and that this will be a potential downside to any method of learning which involves observation and repetition.

Even so, learning by example is probably one of the most useful ways of learning how to navigate online spaces, given that it does not require direct instruction and can be done at the user's leisure. It is not an obvious kind of learning. Learning by observation catches the user unaware and means that they do not have to think of it like preparing for a test. This is advantageous because it avoids the pitfalls of trying to formally educate users in a classroom-type setting, exactly the kind of education many users do not want (Trant, 2009). It is exactly the kind of learning which tends to be prioritised in fandoms. Fans are rarely taught these skills explicitly. Rather, fandoms as a whole rely upon their members being able to internalise the skill of tagging by interacting with others. Even so, it would be useful for fandoms and other online communities to consider publishing short guides to point users in the right direction. This would allow users who wanted further instruction to receive it in small portions, so as to not overwhelm them.

Fandom data practices

Interestingly enough, most of the fans surveyed in the fandom case study did not understand official terms such as 'metadata' (Table 7.1 opposite). Approximately half of the participants who answered the question could not give even a simple definition of metadata. The participants overwhelmingly stated that they had never knowingly used metadata and the majority of them were not sure that they had any understanding of it (Table 7.2).

What was especially striking was that even when the respondent could offer a correct definition of metadata, they often still seemed unsure about their answers. The user base of the Metalocalypse fandom did not appear to have a great deal

Table 7.1 *Do you have any understanding of the term 'metadata'?*

		Frequency	%	Valid %	Cumulative
Valid	Yes	12	19.4	32.4	32.4
	No	15	24.2	40.5	73.0
	Unsure	10	16.1	27.0	100
	Total	37	59.7	100	
Missing	System	25	40.3		
Total		62	100		

Table 7.2 *Have you ever knowingly used metadata when creating or sharing fanworks?*

		Frequency	%	Valid %	Cumulative
Valid	Yes	3	4.8	8.8	8.8
	No	31	50.0	91.2	100
	Total	34	54.8	100	
Missing	System	25	40.3		
Total		62	100		

of knowledge about professional terms, so it was safe to assume that they probably would not have a great amount of knowledge about traditional hierarchies or systems of organization.

In spite of a lack of knowledge about traditional metadata practices, the respondents understood many of the principles of good tagging elsewhere in the study. Many of them tagged their posts and they overwhelmingly recognised that tags could have different purposes, such as to convey further information. It was especially interesting to note that a large number of fans actively read the tags on posts, suggesting that they expected to find useful information located there (Table 7.3).

They recognised that tags could be used to search for more content, but they also largely acknowledged that tags could have other purposes, such as offering nuance to the wider searchable tags. Participants seemed to understand that tags

Table 7.3 *Do you ever check what other people have said in tags on their fanfiction?*

		Frequency	%	Valid %	Cumulative
Valid	Yes	35	56.5	94.6	94.6
	No	3	3.2	5.4	100
	Total	37	59.7	100	
Missing	System	25	40.3		
Total		62	100		

could be used to convey emotional or further information, rather than just being there to act as simple search tools (Table 7.4).

Table 7.4 *Have you ever seen others use tags which expressed a further opinion on the content of a fic? e.g. 'this fic wrecked me' or 'I don't agree with the characterisation here, but it was fun'*

		Frequency	%	Valid %	Cumulative
Valid	Yes	34	54.8	91.9	91.9
	No	3	4.8	8.1	100
	Total	37	59.7	100	
Missing	System	25	40.3		
Total		62	100		

Even amongst those who did not tag consistently, there were often valid reasons for their not doing so. Personal laziness was a factor in not using systems of organization properly; however, it was motivating to see that some of the participants understood poor website design placed serious limitations on how effective their tagging could be. Poor website design acted as a deterrent to tagging, with the attitude being that if the system they were using did not work, then it was not worthwhile using it. This was further evidence that suggested that the participants were in fact aware of the tagging system even when they were not actively using it. Exposure to fandom and the practices of its members meant that they had absorbed knowledge of how the system should work. Given that fandom-oriented websites like Archive of Our Own (https:// archiveofourown.org) encourage the use of tagging to facilitate searching, fans who read or write fanfiction would be surrounded by examples of tagging practice, even if they did not use them. This meant that the participants were probably aware of how to navigate between fandom spaces simply by observing the practices of others within the fandom.

Tagging standards in fandom

The Metalocalypse fandom's apparent awareness of tagging practices posed an interesting question: if they did not understand the official terms for things but were still able to navigate fandom spaces, did they really need to know more about tagging? The short answer to this question was yes, fans should absolutely know more about tagging. It is impressive that fandom has been able to absorb basic tagging practice and organization and this represents a solid foundation that can be built upon. But without a greater understanding of tagging, fandom users are ultimately less capable of changing their tagging behaviours for the better. Hemmasi (2004) observed that complacency in the online community made it far harder for users to understand the limitations of their tagging practices and made them reluctant to change their ways. Fandom is not immune to these problems and being able to articulate issues as they arise and consider potential solutions can go a long way towards potential solutions.

Without a fuller understanding of tagging practice, users are less able to identify and solve the issues they come across. They are more likely to make mistakes and less likely to realise it when those mistakes arise. This is especially important, given that tagging systems are a very basic way of organising things, which depend greatly on accurate tags to understand what the users mean. Using tags incorrectly means that the system is clogged with useless tags and the user risks losing data or exposing another user to unwanted material by mistake.

Even as it stands, there are fans who do not always understand all the tags that have sprung up around their particular fandom. Just as with more traditional methods of organization, tagging in fandom is frequently being updated and altered. Unlike traditional systems of hierarchy, it can be far harder to track these changes over time. With a system such as the Resource Description Framework, past examples of organizational guidelines can be found relatively easily (W3C, 2017). In addition, when the system undergoes updates these are carefully documented. In comparison, tagging within fandom spaces has changed vastly within even the last decade or so, with very little documentation.

One example of how tagging in fandom has changed can be seen when trying to search fanfiction by the relationships the author has written about. This is a popular way of searching for content, because relationships between characters are so often an integral part of fanfiction. The tagging formats for relationships have undergone serious revision over time. If a fan wanted to read about Tony Stark getting into a romantic relationship with Captain America, years ago they might have tried to search for it by placing an X between the two names. This practice seems to have fallen out of fashion and it is now more common to use a slash to indicate romantic relationships between characters. However, another practice of indicating relationships in fanfiction is for fans to create nicknames for the relationship. These names can be simple mashups of the characters' names, or they can be a reference to another aspect of the characters.

If this sounds as if it has the potential to be convoluted and confusing, that is because tagging in fandom is both of these things. There can be a great many tags for the sole purpose of indicating a relationship. In a more organised, standardised system, this would be less of an issue. Fandoms are extremely lucky to have access to Archive of Our Own, which has made a lot of effort to try and work around the creativity of fandom naming. Volunteers from the archive try to stay on top of the various tags that can arise and try to ensure that the archive is run according to a set of rules and regulations that keep the archive orderly. Unlike the relatively hands-off approach to metadata employed by many other websites, Archive of Our Own takes an active interest in trying to organise tags.

Rather than take creativity away from the users of the archive, the regulations prioritise the tagging practices of users over what the archive staff might prefer the users to do. In doing so, the intention is to increase the efficiency of the archive and to help users find what they are looking for whilst maintaining the nuances provided by author tagging. This is a very interesting example of a larger online community organising its own metadata to such a degree. Not all online communities will work in exactly the same way as fandom, especially when we consider that fandoms are not monolithic. Even so, it is worth considering the way that the archive has undertaken this seemingly Herculean task and come out with a measure of success. The best aspects of a folksonomy – creativity and user freedom – have been married together with tagging oversight.

Conclusion

There are no easy answers to solving the various issues with tagging. The creativity and chaos inherent in tagging and folksonomies needs to be accounted for. Greater education of users is a necessary part of the process, but this can be incredibly difficult to realise without a better support network in place to provide it. There is scope for fandom and other online communities to teach their users how to operate and navigate in fandom spaces by enabling users to become immersed in online communities. This can be an invaluable teaching tool, but it should also be paired with better website design to maximise the potential for users to communicate effectively. Having some oversight to tagging systems, such as that present in Archive of Our Own, has paired the best aspects of folksonomy with some of the benefits of traditional hierarchy systems. Other online communities should consider the wisdom of adapting to user tagging.

Adapting to user tagging can be a daunting prospect and it does still leave significant issues. Not all users understand the tagging systems present within fandoms and this can create problems for those trying to navigate online spaces. Further instruction could be found by way of making quick, accessible guides for newcomers to fandom spaces. However, this should not lose sight of how important practising and observing other user behaviour is to folksonomies.

References and further reading

Alaimo, C. (2014) Computational Consumption: Social Media and the Construction of Digital Consumers, Doctoral Dissertation, London School of Economics, http://etheses.lse.ac.uk/975/.

Barja, G. and Gigler, B. S. (2007) The Concept of Information Poverty and How To Measure it in The Latin American Context. In Galperin, H. and Mariscal, J. (eds), *Digital Poverty: Latin American and Caribbean perspectives*, Practical Action Publishing, 11–28.

Britz, J. J. (2004) To Know or not to Know: a moral reflection on information poverty, *Journal of Information Science*, **30**, 192–204.

Cuntz-Leng, V. and Meintzinger., J. (2015) A Brief History of Fan Fiction in Germany, *Transformative Works and Cultures*, 19, http://dx.doi.org/10.3983/twc.2015.0630.

Frazetti, D. (2011) Star Trek and the Culture of Fandom, StarTrek.com, www.startrek.com/article/star-trek-and-the-culture-of-fandom.

Gaffney, A. (2017) The Business of Fandom: how teenage girls predict the future of culture, Billboard, 13 September, www.billboard.com/articles/news/lifestyle/7964650/teenage-fangirls-predict-future-success.

Golder, S. A. and Huberman, B. A. (2006) Usage Patterns of Collaborative Tagging Systems, *Journal of Information Science*, **32**, 198–208.

Gray, J. (2007) *Fandom: identities and communities in a mediated world*, NYU Press.

Guy, M. and Tonkin, E. (2006) Folksonomies: tidying up tags?, www.dlib.org/dlib/january06/guy/01guy.html.

Haywood, T. (1995) *Info-rich, Info-poor: access and exchange in the global information society*, London: Bowker SAUR.

Heery, R. (2004) Metadata Futures: Steps Toward Semantic Interoperability. In Hillman, D. I. and Westbrooks, E. L. (eds), *Metadata in Practice*, American Library Association, 257-271.

Hemmasi, H. (2004) Community-Based Content Control. In Hillman, D. I. and Westbrooks, E. L. (eds), *Metadata in Practice*, American Library Association, 191–202.

Heymann, P. (2017) *Tag Spam*, http://heymann.stanford.edu/tagspam.html.

Johnson, S. F. (2014) Fan Fiction Metadata Creation and Utilization Within Fan Fiction Archives: three primary models, *Transformative Works and Cultures*, **17**, http://dx.doi.org/10.3983/twc.2014.0578.

Kipp, M. E. I. (2006) @toread and Cool: tagging for time, task and emotion. In *SIG-CR Workshop Poster, ASIST Annual Meeting, Austin, TX, USA, 4 November 2006.*

Kipp, M. E. I. and Campbell, D. G. (2017) Patterns and Inconsistencies in Collaborative Tagging Systems: an examination of tagging practices, *Proceedings of the American Society for Information Science and Technology*, **43**, 1–18.

Kroski, E. (2005) *The Hive Mind: folksonomies and user-based tagging*, http://web20bp.com/13f1b6019/wp-content/uploads/2013/03/The-Hive-Mind-Folksonomies-2005.pdf.

Lamere, P. (2008) Social Tagging and Music Information Retrieval, *Journal of New Music Research*, **37**, 101–14.

Macgregor, G. and McCulloch, E. (2013) Collaborative Tagging as a Knowledge Organization and Resource Discovery Tool, *Library Review*, **55**, 291–300.

McMillan, D., and Chavis, D. (1986) Sense of Community: A Definition and Theory, *Journal of Community Psychology,* Volume 14.

Mahoui, M., Jones, J., Meyerhoff, A. and Toufeeq, S. A. (2011) Can User Tagging Help Health Information Seekers? In Stephanidis, C. (ed.) *Universal Access in Human-Computer Interaction. Applications and Service*, Springer, 389–97.

Mathes, A. (2004) *Folksonomies: cooperative classification and communication through shared metadata*, http://adammathes.com/academic/computer-mediated-communication/folksonomies.html.

Merholz, P. (2004) Metadata for the Masses, *Adaptive Path,* 19 October, http://adaptivepath.org/ideas/e000361.

Merholz, P. (2005) *Clay Shirky's Viewpoints are Overrated*, www.peterme.com/archives/000558.html.

Pennington, D. R. (2016) 'The Most Passionate Cover I've Seen': emotional information in fan-created U2 music videos, *Journal of Documentation,* **72**, 569–90.

Trant, J. (2009) Studying Social Tagging and Folksonomy: a review and framework, *Texas Digital Library*, **10**, 1–44.

Tumblr (2017) *Shitpost Generator*, https://shitpostgenerator.tumblr.com.

Verba, J. M. (2003) *Boldly Writing: A Trekker Fan and Zine History, 1967–1987*, Second Edition. FTL Publications.

W3C (2017) *Resource Description Framework*, https://www.w3.org/RDF.

Weinberger, D. (2005) *Tagging and Why it Matters*, https://cyber.harvard.edu/publications/2005/Tagging_and_Why_It_Matters.

Weinberger, D. (2006) *Folksonomy as Symbol*, www.hyperorg.com/blogger/2006/01/07/what-is-a-folksonomy-anyway.

Yusop, N. I., Ibrahim, H., Yusof, S. A. M., Aji, Z. M., Dahalin, Z., Ghazali, O., Saad, M. N. and Abu, M. A. (2013) Information Needs of Rural Communities, *Journal of Community Informatics*, **9**, http://ci-journal.net/index.php/ciej/article/view/586/965.

Zeng, D., Chen, H., Lusch, R. and Li, S. H. (2010) Social Media Analytics and Intelligence, *IEEE Intelligent Systems*, **25**, 13–6.

Zeng, M. L. (2008) *Metadata*, Neal-Schuman Publishers.

Chapter 8

Keys to their own voices: social tags for a dementia ontology as a human right

Diane Rasmussen Pennington

Introduction

Dementia encompasses a range of incurable brain conditions such as Alzheimer's disease, which affected 47 million people worldwide in 2015, a figure that is expected to triple by 2050. It is therefore a worldwide public health priority (World Health Organization, 2017). While the symptoms differ among individuals to some extent, the World Health Organization (WHO) defines them as follows:

- difficulties with everyday tasks
- confusion in familiar environments
- difficulty with words and numbers
- memory loss
- changes in mood and behaviour.

Caring for people living with dementia (PLWD) is a burdensome task and it tends to fall to family members, which causes them considerable stress. The WHO's Global Action Plan on the Public Health Response to Dementia 2017–2025 focuses on dementia prevention as well as on improving the lives of PLWD and their carers so that they 'live well and receive the care and support they need to fulfil their potential with dignity, respect, autonomy and equality'. The United Nations has called for dementia to be a public health priority in all countries (UN News Centre, 2015).

This chapter will first explore the uniquely challenging context of information needs and dementia. It will then use dementia as a case study to demonstrate how user-generated hashtags, or other forms of surrogate representation, could be applied in a linked data environment in order to improve access to care, resources, people and other needs.

Entities in the dementia ontology

Because just one PLWD affects and, conversely, is affected by, a range of entities, it is perhaps useful to consider some of the different entities and their unique contexts and needs individually. It is then easier to see how they intertwine within what this chapter calls a dementia ontology. An ontology is broadly defined as 'a formal representation of knowledge with rich semantic relationships between terms' (Stuart, 2016, 12). A dementia ontology, then, is a representation of knowledge with relationships between entities that are somehow related to a PLWD.

PLWD

In relation to the emphasis on person-centred care in dementia (Brooker, 2003), the PLWD should be placed at the centre of this dementia system or ontology. It is essential to view the PLWD as a *person* rather than as a *patient*, so as not to marginalise the person and their needs. Additionally, respectful language should be chosen when discussing dementia to respect the PLWD's rights and dignity; for example, do not call them 'sufferer', 'senile', or 'burden' (DEEP, 2015).

Clinical or biomedical language dominates the literature, research and care of PLWD. While evidence-based medical treatment is obviously necessary, PLWD also have a range of other needs, including socialisation, whether with family and friends or other PLWD, psychological counselling and support and assistance with managing their daily lives. Recently, new approaches have been taken to help improve the quality of life for PLWD, such as music therapy for enjoyment (Aldridge, 2000; Riley, Alm and Newell, 2008) and trained dogs for companionship and assistance with tasks of living (Swall et al., 2015). Some research has found a shorter survival time for PLWD when they have limited social networks, so interaction with others is important (Santini et al., 2015). However, since PLWD's symptoms evolve throughout the course of the condition, including demonstrable changes in general awareness (Clare et al., 2008), their needs for care, interaction and information also change constantly.

Research is obviously important for PLWD, but a human rights-based approach to dementia (Alzheimer Scotland, 2017), which is increasing in importance as a result of effective advocacy, calls for PLWD to participate in co-produced research as well as directly receive the benefits of the research. In the early stages of dementia, it might be advisable to consent to research that might take place in the future, since the ability to provide consent will change over time (Pierce, 2010).

Carers

Just as PLWD change throughout the course of the disease, the roles of carers, who are usually close family members such as the PLWD's spouse or children, also change (Berry, Apesoa-Varano and Gomez, 2015). The transitions are quite marked in the carer's context. A carer, for example, might move from occasionally checking in on the PLWD, to quitting their job in order to look after the PLWD 24 hours per day, to moving the PLWD to a care home when it becomes too much for one carer to handle, then to hospice care and then final bereavement. In most places, family members caring for the PLWD full-time are not recognised as having a job, even though they are typically exhausted and overwhelmed (Bond, Clark and Davies, 2003). This has been called role entrapment, because they cannot take breaks from their caregiving roles without potentially disastrous consequences (Lewis, 2015), such as the PLWD wandering out of the house and getting lost. Health and social care services might or might not be available, depending on a range of factors such as geographic location, socioeconomic status and stage of the condition (Robinson et al., 2014). A range of factors may determine whether a carer chooses to use the services available (Toseland et al., 2002).

Health professionals

The dementia-related responsibilities of health professionals, such as social workers and primary care physicians, can pose challenges. While highly trained in many areas of health, health professionals may not know the best ways to communicate with PLWD and their families, especially in the context of relationships (Cox and Pardasani, 2013). Since dementia is a complex condition that takes time to diagnose and there is a stigma attached to it, the diagnosis itself may cause conflict between the doctor, the PLWD and their family (Hansen et al., 2008, 1776). Additionally, physicians use a range of information sources complementarily to treat their patients, including textual, physical and social sources (Isah and Byström, 2016). These information practices are likely to provide comprehensive care, but they also add to the amount of information work physicians must do on a daily basis.

Employers and workplaces

Certain organizations and communities, such as workplaces, will feel the effects of PLWD. It is beneficial for people to stay employed in a challenging role for as long as possible because this may reduce the chances of dementia (Wilson, 2005), or even reduce symptoms after diagnosis. In the early stages of the condition, employers and work colleagues may not know how to recognise it as a potential medical issue (Lurati, 2014; McNamara, 2014) and may simply think the employee is aging or becoming forgetful. However, while cognitive changes occur in the normal ageing process, dementia is not a normal outcome of ageing. This is why colleagues of PLWD need training, including what the PLWD will need (McNamara, 2014; Pennington, 2016). Additionally, employed carers need to communicate with their employers about their challenging personal situation (Ritchie et al., 2015).

Information needs and sources within the dementia ontology

Information scientists have an opportunity to take an active role in dementia care by assisting with meeting information needs; in particular, they need to partner with other researchers or conduct complementary research, given the focus in information science 'on linking individuals with a particular information need to appropriate, specific information sources' (Erdelez, Howarth and Gibson, 2015). However, issues related to cognition, information organization and representation must also tie into these efforts, as explored later in this chapter.

From a human rights perspective, PLWD have the right to be informed about their condition and their lives (Hertogh et al., 2004). PLWD 'need information to support autonomy in making decisions and in acting on those decisions' (Clarke, Alexjuk and Gibb, 2011, 237). When provided, this information should be specific, clear, accessible and easy to understand. However, information services for PLWD and their carers, especially official sources such as physicians and related services, are limited (Corbett and Ballard, 2011). Information may also be presented in difficult clinical language, which is how much information about dementia is communicated, as mentioned previously. Despite this, in the early stages, PLWD are encouraged to take on the role of self-management, including educating themselves about the condition, but the benefit from this appears to be limited (Quinn et al., 2014). Although PLWD receive information from many sources, including their bodies, that things are changing (Yates, 2015; Polkinghorne and Chambers, 2016), it might be difficult for them to identify or to communicate what information they need, given the cognitive changes that take place as a result of the condition. Challenges with using and understanding language are frequently a symptom.

Carers also face unmet information needs. It is difficult for carers to find information and they may not know what types of information they need, or what information is available. In one study, carers who sought help about assistive technologies for dementia care had difficulty obtaining information about what technologies were available (Gibson et al., 2015). The 'self-management' role may transfer from the PLWD to their carer as the condition evolves (Quinn et al., 2014).

Additional information and education is needed to reduce the stigma and negativity in representations of dementia that exist in media messages and are held by policy makers and the general public. This can start with simple changes, such as how dementia symptoms are labelled; there are very different connotations between *cognitive change* and *cognitive decline*, for example. The general notion for the public, some policy makers and the media is that PLWD do not have their minds any longer and that they are seen as doomed and socially dead (Van Gorp and Vercruysse, 2012; Dupuis et al., 2016). Along with changing language connotations, visuals within the media can also make a difference: 'Images should be used in context. For example, when talking about someone trying to live a positive life, use an image that reflects the whole person rather than a fading face or wrinkled hands' (DEEP, 2015). While these negative messages could potentially cause PLWD and their carers to worry about an inevitable decline and a death sentence, support from their peers helps them challenge these views (Keyes et al., 2016).

Information engagement for PLWD within the dementia ontology

The opportunities with which PLWD and, quite possibly, others in the ontology, engage with information sources seem to affect their quality of life and well-being. Engagement has many definitions and is often used to define how people interact socially with digital media (O'Brien and Cairns, 2016), but it could involve any method in which people provide, receive and interact with information and social sources of information. In the context of dementia, social inclusion is important, both in the workplace, for as long as possible, and within the PLWD's local community (Robertson and Evans, 2015).

The networked environment also offers engagement opportunities for PLWD. While some might believe that PLWD would not be able to use online technologies due to cognitive functioning concerns, this is not always the case, especially in the earlier stages. Online social support for people experiencing health challenges, including mental health, has been shown to be useful for well-being and peer information sources (Yan and Tan, 2014). Online, peers facing similar medical situations work together to analyse other sources, potential treatments and apparent authorities (Neal and McKenzie, 2011; Miller, 2017). Miller analysed blog posts written by PLWD to determine where they ascribed the most authority; it rested most highly within their peer community, with PLWDs expressing a desire to collaborate in the exchange of knowledge with other PLWDs due to the importance placed on lived experience and the sense of a shared in-depth knowledge that those who do not have dementia are incapable of fully appreciating.

(Miller, 2017, ii)

This result is similar to a finding in Neal and McKenzie's (2011) study of blogs written by women living with the chronic illness endometriosis; bloggers considered other women with endometriosis to be reliable authorities. Researchers have suggested that in the future, developers could create systems that allow online consumers of health information to evaluate its quality (Zhang, Sun and Zie, 2015). Additionally, the need for PLWD to be involved in the development of systems or online sources meant for them to use is essential (Span et al., 2013), preferably in a co-design situation, in which the PLWD are actively involved in all stages of the design and development processes (Rodgers, 2017).

Surrogates, social tags and the dementia ontology

People who discuss dementia on social media apply social tags as referents to dementia-related topics and events, including hashtags, such as #dementia, #Alzheimers, #alz, #caregiver, #WorldAlzheimersDay and #MemoryWalk. When used in large numbers for searching or browsing, these tags serve as a form of user-generated, controlled vocabulary: they can link users to other posts about dementia or dementia-related events and could eventually serve more fully as linked data facilitators. How might social tags relate to a dementia ontology that would allow the multitude of different groups within the ontology to understand and connect with one another?

Because dementia varies from person to person and day to day and PLWDs' interactions with the world change over time (Vernooij-Dassen et al., 1998), it is difficult to define, with or without social tags and even with or without an ontology. Figure 8.1 opposite shows one possible branch of a dementia ontology, with the PLWD at the centre. This ontology is not highly structured, but it shows the relationships between PLWD and the different entities with which they interact. Several branches of additional ontological relationships would branch out from this starting point; for example, we would want to see the interactions between professional caregivers, health professionals, friends and family and other entities, as well as how the relationships play out between each other.

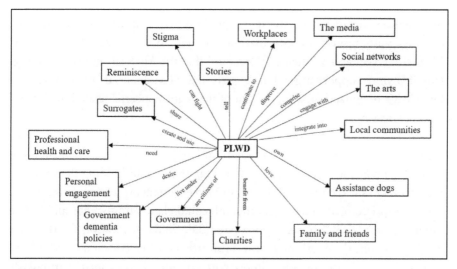

Figure 8.1 *A start of a dementia ontology, with a PLWD at the centre*

In addition to the necessity of placing the PLWD at the centre, this ontology represents the necessary integrated approach to health and social care involving formally and informally instituted entities. Information sharing takes place between and among all these entities and ultimately the PLWD benefits. For example, *the media* increases *stigma*, *stigma* can be reduced by *family and friends*, *family and friends* can influence *government dementia policies* and so on. This ontological approach can emphasise the entire system of entities that influence the experiences of PLWD. From theoretical and human rights perspectives, it reminds everyone to keep the PLWD as the focus. If this ontology were a framework for an actual linked data implementation, it would model how all sources of shared information can and should be connected. This would maximise the chances that any entity within the ontology will encounter information from any other entity when all of their information sources are semantically linked.

This chapter has already demonstrated how the different entities in a dementia ontology speak different languages. Within the domain of knowledge organization and representation, the notion of the surrogate as a language occurs frequently. In a traditional sense, the domain speaks of a surrogate as a standardised, representative metadata record that describes and refers to the actual document, such as a MARC (Machine Readable Cataloguing) record in an OPAC (online public access catalogue) for a monograph (Chan and Salaba, 2016). However, this standardised approach limits the ability of different groups to describe and retrieve items in ways that are meaningful to them. It also further marginalises already marginalised groups. This marginalisation occurs in many contexts with respect to information seeking and retrieval. For example, McTavish, Neal and Wathen (2011) found that the Medical Subject Headings (MeSH) may support a gender-neutral view of violence in its approach to knowledge organization, even in light of the many concerns related to violence against women.

What would happen if the social tags were not textual, but rather visual or sonic? In future systems, could tags be photographs, videos, or music? For example, a relaxing music clip could be a tag that would link to other relaxing music; these linked clips might help a PLWD experiencing anxiety or insomnia. A tag comprised of an infant's photograph could elicit reminiscence and link to other tags containing reminiscence potential. Some inspiration for this idea originates from the work of Lynne Howarth and her colleagues, who have explored the role of surrogate items with marginalised groups, particularly PLWD. In a general sense, Howarth explored how the surrogate can be rethought to construct space for narratives of marginalised voices, to shift the focus from consistency to commonality (Howarth and Olson, 2013). In her study of surrogates in dementia, Howarth explores whether the notion of a non-fixed surrogate can give voice to cognitively disabled PLWD by rethinking our organizational structures for surrogates and representation (Howarth, 2014) because PLWD process verbal communication and text differently (Pennington, 2016). Howarth's empirical work asked, 'when memory and/or language are impaired, how does such contextualizing and categorizing occur?' (Howarth and Hendry, 2011). In this research, non-textual or non-verbal surrogates that reminded PLWD of their life experiences, such as favourite foods or photos of their families, enhanced memory and recall. Howarth suggested future research into designing classification and categorisation systems for PLWD to help meet their information needs. Others have discussed the importance of non-textual items, such as pictures, for reminiscence therapy, memory aids and essential information such as signage in public spaces (Bate, 2014). As mentioned previously, these surrogates could become tags in future social tagging systems. At present, tags themselves are only textual, even when they describe non-textual items like photographs, but perhaps representing a photograph with a visual tag would increase the engagement of PLWD and less semantic meaning would be lost in the representation (O'Connor and Wyatt, 2004).

It is essential to consider the non-verbal and non-textual aspects of these surrogates. Typical text-based social tags can serve as search and browse tools, but they serve also as storytelling aids or commentary on social media. For example, #justforfun or #SundayMorning may not assist users too much in retrieving relevant posts, but they clearly serve a communicative function for the person who created the posts. Language can be a primary challenge for PLWD, so they may not be able to write relevant hashtags to communicate their lives, but they do have other means of communicating about their lives. Evans, Robertson and Candy (2016), for example, gave cameras to PLWD who had recently returned to the workplace after receiving their diagnosis. The photographs they took of their work environment communicated their own stories, frustrations, social connections and daily scenes, just as social tags do for many social media users. Involvement in creating art, such as acting in a play or painting a scene, can help PLWD communicate narratives as well (Dupuis et al., 2016). Clarke and Bailey's 2016 study explored how PLWD experienced life and found that they placed a strong emphasis on the roles of social and physical belongingness. The paper discussed these relationships in the context of narrative citizenship in the participants' social and physical places, which 'offers an approach that enhances individualised yet collective understandings of living with dementia' (Clarke and Bailey, 2016, 434). PLWD can communicate these understandings in many ways.

Several initiatives are in process to allow PLWD to express their experiences online in their own ways. Dementia Diaries (dementiadiaries.org), for example, 'is a UK-wide project that brings together people's diverse experiences of living with dementia as a series of audio diaries' (Dementia Diaries, n.d.). The diaries are available on the website for viewing and listening. A set of provocative videos on a Vimeo channel called *Living with Dementia* (vimeo.com/channels/1148563/188113371), supported by publicly-funded research in the UK, challenges people to rethink the perceptions and perspectives of PLWD. Miller (2017) performed a discourse analysis of blog posts written by PLWD to understand their information needs. Online artefacts such as blog posts would benefit from social tags provided by PLWD – as well as carers, health professionals, families and others involved in the dementia ontology – which truly involves everyone, because dementia is a worldwide health crisis.

Although Web platforms do not allow for a truly diverse range of social tags, at least in terms of non-textual format, they are worthy of development. The semantic web and linked data are being conceptualised and implemented in the right spirit in order to do this. This is because the semantic web is meant to 'collect Web content from diverse sources, process the information and exchange the results with other programs' (Berners-Lee, Hendler and Lassila, 2001, 34). The 'sources' could be the groups mentioned above; linked data could allow these groups to communicate and connect within their own groups, with other groups and about a series of entities. Social tags take different forms when they originate from different entities within the dementia ontology presented because various groups use differing terms for the same things. For example, #sundowning to a health practitioner could be #ConfusedAtNight to a family caregiver. Linked data has the potential to connect these tags semantically, which would result in the clinician encountering experiences of the family, while the family could then more easily find professional information about their PLWD's evening behaviour.

Linked data applications such as Google's Knowledge Graph, which retrieves and cohesively presents information from a variety of sources related to the user's search, (www.google.com/intl/bn/insidesearch/features/search/knowledge.html) do not seem to work with any type of social tags to produce unified results. Figure 8.2, for example, shows the UK's Google search results for the term *Alzheimer*. Even after incorporating the Knowledge Graph result on the right-hand side, which is a linked data application, the featured results are from (a) the news media and (b) UK third-sector organizations for ageing and health conditions. The voices of the PLWD are not necessarily present; while these sources are acting on their behalf, they may not be representative of the PLWDs' voices. If social tags from the various entities within the dementia ontology could be incorporated into Knowledge Graph's search results, this would elevate the voices of everyone involved and ultimately improve access to a broad range of

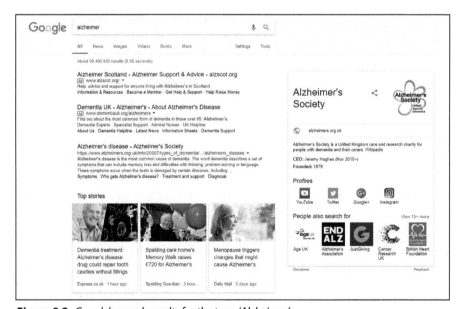

Figure 8.2 *Google's search results for the term 'Alzheimer'*

information that could result in better care and a more satisfactory quality of life for PLWDs.

Conclusion: human rights, social tags and the dementia ontology

The human-rights-based approach to dementia and dementia care reminds us that PLWD, just as anyone else with a disability, have legal protection from discrimination and abuse. 'People with dementia have the same civil and legal rights as everyone else' according to the document *Our Dementia, Our Needs* (Hare, 2016, 8). This same document states that in the UK, if PLWD 'can't understand the information provided by a health or care organization, or if you have specific communication needs, you can cite the Accessible Information Standard and ask them to make improvements' (Hare, 2016, 5). The same is true for online information description and access. PLWD must be able to describe and access online information in ways that make sense and are useful to them. This includes providing the option to add social tags that describe information in their terms.

Social tags may not always be solely presented in textual format; especially as social media platforms continue to develop technologically, we may see the ability to use a range of types of individualised user-assigned surrogates in the near future, including photos, videos, spoken words, or tactile objects such as favourite possessions serving as social tags. Because non-textual forms of information such as music and visuals tend to be more easily understandable by PLWD than written words, they should be considered as a future option for social tags that would lead to semantically-based findability. For example, if a PLWD wanted to find information about doing art projects that have the potential to improve their cognition, a tag for the topic could be an instructional video, a spoken podcast on art by another PLWD, background music for painting, or a photograph of a paintbrush. While it might seem difficult to conceptualise non-textual items serving as semantically meaningful tags, it seems likely given the ever-increasing number of multimedia objects posted on social media. Social tags may eventually also be able to serve as connectors in linked data settings, so that information sources related to dementia represent the many individuals, communities and contexts that require information about it. Web technologies should be developed that would automatically extract social tags from various sources and insert them as the predicate in the subject–predicate–object RDF (Resource Description Framework) triple store format that allows for online data interchange (RDF Working Group, 2014). While RDF requires all data to be represented as URIs, it would be a straightforward task to obtain URIs for social tags since they exist on the web. The tag-based URIs would then link together predicates and objects that would not otherwise be found due to the dispersion of different information sources and the vocabularies used by their respective groups. The ability for PLWD and others within a dementia ontology, such as carers, to describe and retrieve online information, whether for treatment options or for social connection, is a human right and therefore protected by national and international laws pertaining to disability and equality.

This chapter has reflected on the opportunities that a comprehensive dementia ontology with the PLWD at the centre, as well as the employment of social tags within a linked data framework, could provide to PLWD and those around them. This approach could bring about a broader range of information encountered to entities looking online and on social media for information and support related to dementia. This would maximise the ability of entities within the system to make more informed decisions about treatment and lifestyle options, apply scientific evidence to practice, find social and emotional support, enhance cognitive abilities and ultimately improve the quality of life of PLWD through dementia-friendly access to dementia-friendly information with the use of RDF-linked tags in multiple formats.

Consider the words of May, a PLWD who was a participant in Kotai-Ewers' (2000) study about the narratives of PLWD as told in their own words. How might appropriately implemented social tags and linked data applications have helped her?

> I just want to be at home.
> I have a right to this part of the end of my life.
> Yes, I am wringing my hands. I can't cope.
> I have a right to a life of my own.
> I am really very angry.
> I just want to be at home – and be myself.
> Do you have any ideas?

As a starting point for thinking about how May's narrative could be represented by different types of tags, Figure 8.3 following presents some visuals that might represent her feelings from various domains. Imagine each photo as a social tag that could link to related ideas and information. Does this help bring May's story to life?

I just want to be at home.

I have a right to this part of the end of my life.

Yes, I am wringing my hands. I can't cope.

I am really very angry.

Do you have any ideas?

Figure 8.3 *May's narrative represented in pictures that could also serve as linked social tags in future systems*

References and further reading

Aldridge, D. (ed.) (2000) *Music Therapy in Dementia Care: more new voices*, Jessica Kingsley.

Alzheimer Scotland (2017) *A Human Rights-Based Approach to Dementia*, www.alzscot.org/campaigning/rights_based_approach.

Bate, H. J. (2014) *Too Late to Learn to Drive: dementia, visual perception and the meaning of pictures*, Pictures to Share.

Berners-Lee, T., Hendler, J. and Lassila, O. (2001) The Semantic Web, *Scientific American*, **284**, 34–44.

Berry, B., Apesoa-Varano, E. C. and Gomez, Y. (2015) How Family Members Manage Risk Around Functional Decline: the autonomy management process in households facing dementia, *Social Science & Medicine*, **130**, 107–14.

Bond, M. J., Clark, M. S. and Davies, S. (2003) The Quality of Life of Spouse Dementia Caregivers: changes associated with yielding to formal care and widowhood, *Social Science & Medicine*, **57**, 2385–95.

Brooker, D. (2003) What Is Person-Centred Care in Dementia?, *Reviews in Clinical Gerontology*, **13**, 215–22.

Chan, L. M. and Salaba, A. (2016) *Cataloging and Classification: an introduction*, Rowman & Littlefield.

Clare, L., Rowlands, J., Bruce, E., Surr, C. and Downs, M. (2008) 'I Don't Do Like I

Used to Do': a grounded theory approach to conceptualising awareness in people with moderate to severe dementia living in long-term care, *Social Science & Medicine*, **66**, 2366–77.

Clarke, C. L. (2011) Editorial: Information and Dementia: complexity and the obvious, *International Journal of Older People Nursing*, **6**, 216.

Clarke, C. L., Alexjuk, J. and Gibb, C. E. (2011) Information in Dementia Care: sense making and a public health direction for the UK?, *International Journal of Older People Nursing*, **6**, 237–43.

Clarke, C. L. and Bailey, C. (2016) Narrative Citizenship, Resilience and Inclusion with Dementia: on the inside or on the outside of physical and social places, *Dementia*, **15**, 434–52.

Corbett, A. and Ballard, C. (2011) Information Provision Services in Dementia Care, *International Journal of Older People Nursing*, **6**, 217–26.

Cox, C. B. and Pardasani, M. (2013) Alzheimer's in the Workplace: a challenge for social work, *Journal of Gerontological Social Work*, **56**, 643–56.

DEEP (2015) *Dementia Words Matter: guidelines on language about dementia*, http://dementiavoices.org.uk/wp-content/uploads/2015/03/DEEP-Guide-Language.pdf.

Dementia Diaries (n.d.) *About the Project*, https://dementiadiaries.org/about-the-project.

Dupuis, S. L., Kontos, P., Mitchell, G., Jonas-Simpson, C. and Gray, G. (2016) Reclaiming Citizenship through the Arts, *Dementia*, **15**, 358–80.

Erdelez, S., Howarth, L. C. and Gibson, T. (2015) How Can Information Science Contribute to Alzheimer's Disease Research? In *Proceedings of the Annual Meeting of the Association for Information Science & Technology (Annual Meeting 2015)*, St. Louis, Missouri, USA, ASIS&T, https://www.asist.org/files/meetings/am15/proceedings/openpage15.html.

Evans, D., Robertson, J. and Candy, A. (2016) Use of Photovoice with People with Younger Onset Dementia, *Dementia*, **15**, 798–813.

Gibson, G., Dickinson, C., Brittain, K. and Robinson, L. (2015) The Everyday Use of Assistive Technology by People with Dementia and Their Family Carers: a qualitative study, *BMC Geriatrics*, **15**, https://doi.org/10.1186/s12877-015-0091-3.

Hansen, E. C., Hughes, C., Routley, G. and Robinson, A. L. (2008) General Practitioners' Experiences and Understandings of Diagnosing Dementia: factors impacting on early diagnosis, *Social Science & Medicine*, **67**, 1776–83.

Hare, P. (2016) *Our Dementia, Our Rights*, http://dementiawithoutwalls.org.uk/wp-content/uploads/2016/10/Our-dementia-Our-rights-booklet.pdf.

Hendry, E. and Howarth, L. C. (2013) Memory, Truth and Storytelling: evoking narrative from individuals with mild Alzheimer's Disease. In *Proceedings of the*

Annual Conference of the Canadian Association for Information Science, Victoria, British Columbia, Canada, CAIS/ACSI, http://www.cais-acsi.ca/ojs/index.php/cais/article/viewFile/833/755.

Hertogh, C. M., The, B. A. M, Miesen, B. M. and Eefsting, J. A. (2004) Truth Telling and Truthfulness in the Care for Patients with Advanced Dementia: an ethnographic study in Dutch nursing homes, *Social Science & Medicine*, **59**, 1685–93.

Howarth, L. C. (2014) Drawing Clocks Without Time: Alzheimer's, marginalization and the liberatory potential of object memoir. In *Proceedings of the Annual Conference of the Canadian Association for Information Science, St. Catharines, Ontario, Canada*, CAIS/ACSI, https://journals.library.ualberta.ca/ojs.cais-acsi.ca/index.php/cais-asci/article/view/886/799.

Howarth, L. C. and Hendry, E. (2011) Recovering Memory: sense-making and recall strategies of individuals with mild cognitive impairment. In *Proceedings of the Annual Meeting of the Association for Information Science & Technology (Annual Meeting 2011), New Orleans, Louisiana, USA*, ASIS&T, http://www.asis.org/asist2011/posters/237_FINIAL_SUBMISSION.doc.

Howarth, L. C. and Olson, H. (2013) Surrogates, Voice and Narratives from the Margins. In *Proceedings of the Annual Conference of the Canadian Association for Information Science* (CAIS/ACSI), http://www.cais-acsi.ca/ojs/index.php/cais/article/view/834/756.

Isah, E. E. and Byström, K. (2016) Physicians' Learning at Work through Everyday Access to Information, *Journal of the Association for Information Science & Technology*, **67**, 318–32.

Keyes, S. E., Clarke, C. L., Wilkinson, H., Alexjuk, E. J., Wilcockson, J., Robinson, L., Reynolds, J., McClelland, S., Corner, L. and Cattan, M. (2016) 'We're All Thrown in the Same Boat . . .': a qualitative analysis of peer support in dementia care, *Dementia*, **15**, 560–77.

Kotai-Ewers, T. (2000) Working with Words: people with dementia and the significance of narratives. In Aldridge, D. (ed.) *Music Therapy in Dementia Care*, Jessica Kingsley Publishers, 63–80.

Lewis, L. F. (2015) Caregiving for a Loved One with Dementia at the End of Life: an emergent theory of rediscovering, *American Journal of Alzheimer's Disease & Other Dementias*, **30**, 488–96.

Lurati, A. R. (2014) Recognizing Early Dementia in the Workplace: a case study, *Workplace Health & Safety*, **62**, 94–5.

McNamara, G. (2014) Dementia and the Workplace, *Occupational Health*, **66**, 27–30.

McTavish, J., Neal, D. R. and Wathen, C. N. (2011) Is What You See What You Get?

Medical subject headings and their organizing work in the violence against women research, *Knowledge Organization*, **38**, 381–97.

Miller, C. (2017). *'Don't Tell Me There Are No Answers': the information needs and preferences of people living with dementia*, University of Strathclyde.

Neal, D. R. and McKenzie, P. (2011) Putting the Pieces Together: endometriosis blogs, cognitive authority and collaborative information behavior, *Journal of the Medical Library Association*, **99**, 127–34.

O'Brien, H. and Cairns, P. (eds) (2016) *Why Engagement Matters: cross-disciplinary perspectives of user engagement in digital media*, Springer.

O'Connor, B. C. and Wyatt, R. B. (2004) *Photo Provocations: thinking in, with and about photographs*, Scarecrow Press.

Pennington, D. R. (2016) Supporting Workplace Information Needs of People with Dementia. In *SIG USE/SIG SI Symposium – Information Behavior in Workplaces, Annual Meeting of the Association for Information Science & Technology (Annual Meeting 2016), Copenhagen, Denmark*.

Pierce, R. (2010) A Changing Landscape for Advance Directives in Dementia Research, *Social Science & Medicine*, **70**, 623–30.

Polkinghorne, S. and Chambers, T. (2016) What Is Known from the Existing Literature about How People Are Informed by Their Own Bodies? *SIG USE/SIG SI Symposium – Information Behavior in Workplaces, Annual Meeting of the Association for Information Science & Technology (Annual Meeting 2016), Copenhagen, Denmark*.

Quinn, C., Anderson, D., Toms, G., Whitaker, R., Edwards, R. T., Jones, C. and Clare, L. (2014) Self-Management in Early-stage Dementia: a pilot randomised controlled trial of the efficacy and cost-effectiveness of a self-management group intervention (the SMART Study), *Trials*, **15**, https://dx.doi.org/10.1186/2F1745-6215-15-74.

RDF Working Group (2014) *RDF*, www.w3.org/RDF.

Riley, P., Alm, N. and Newell, A. (2008) An Interactive Tool to Promote Musical Creativity in People with Dementia, *Computers in Human Behavior*, **25**, 599–608.

Ritchie, L., Banks, P., Danson, M., Tolson, D. and Borrowman, F. (2015) Dementia in the Workplace: a review, *Journal of Public Mental Health*, **14**, 24–34.

Robertson, J. and Evans, D. (2015) Evaluation of a Workplace Engagement Project for People with Younger Onset Dementia, *Journal of Clinical Nursing*, **24**, 2331–39.

Robinson, C. A., Bottorff, J. L., Pesut, B., Oliffe, J. L. and Tomlinson, J. (2014) The Male Face of Caregiving: a scoping review of men caring for a person with dementia, *American Journal of Men's Health*, **8**, 409–26.

Rodgers, P. A. (2017) Co-designing with People Living with Dementia, *CoDesign: International Journal of CoCreation in Design and the Arts,* http://dx.doi.org/10.1080/15710882.2017.1282527.

Santini, Z. I., Koyanagi, A., Tyrovolas, S., Haro, J. M., Fiori, K. L., Uwakwa, R., Thiyagarajan, J. A., Webber, M., Prince, M. and Prina, A. M. (2015) Social Network Typologies and Mortality Risk among Older People in China, India and Latin America: a 10/66 Dementia Research Group population-based cohort study, *Social Science & Medicine,* **147**, 134–143.

Span, M., Hettinga, M., Vernooij-Dassen, M., Eefsting, J. and Smits, C. (2013) Involving People with Dementia in the Development of Supportive IT Applications: a systematic review, *Ageing Research Reviews,* **12**, 535–51.

Stuart, D. (2016) *Practical Ontologies for Information Professionals,* Facet Publishing.

Swall, A., Ebbeskog, B., Hagelin, C. L. and Fagerberg, I. (2015). Can Therapy Dogs Evoke Awareness of One's Past and Present Life in Persons with Alzheimer's Disease?, *International Journal of Older People Nursing,* **10**, 84–93.

Toseland, R. W., McCallion, P., Gerber, T. and Banks, S. (2002) Predictors of Health and Human Services Use by Persons with Dementia and their Family Caregivers, *Social Science & Medicine,* **55**, 1255–66.

UN News Centre (2015) *Countries Urged to Make Dementia Public Health Priority as UN Conference Opens in Geneva,* www.un.org/News/dh/pdf/english/2015/16032015.pdf.

Van Gorp, B. and Vercruysse, T. (2012) Frames and Counter-frames Giving Meaning to Dementia: a framing analysis of media content, *Social Science & Medicine,* **74**, 1274–81.

Vernooij-Dassen, M., Wester, F., Auf Den Kamp, M. and Huygen, F. (1998) The Development of a Dementia Process within the Family Context: the case of Alice, *Social Science & Medicine,* **47**, 1973–80.

Wilson, R. S. (2005) Mental Challenge in the Workplace and Risk of Dementia in Old Age: is there a connection?, *Occupational and Environmental Medicine,* **62**, 72–3.

World Health Organization (2017) *Dementia: a public health priority,* www.who.int/mental_health/neurology/dementia/infographic_dementia.pdf?ua=1.

Yan, L. and Tan, Y. (2014) Feeling Blue? Go online: an empirical study of social support among patients, *Information Systems Research,* **25**, 690–709.

Yates, C. (2015) Exploring Variation in the Ways of Experiencing Health Information Literacy: a phenomenographic study, *Library & Information Science Research,* **37**, 220–27.

Zhang, Y., Sun, Y. and Xie, B. (2015) Quality of Health Information for Consumers on the Web: a systematic review of indicators, criteria, tools and evaluation results, *Journal of the Association for Information Science & Technology*, **66**, 2071–84.

Chapter 9

Social tagging and the enterprise: an analysis of social tagging in the workplace

Sanjay Khanna

Introduction

As this book looks at how social tags can serve to link content across a variety of environments, a key environment to address is the enterprise or workplace. As people of all generations are utilising social platforms and social tagging on a regular basis to share, search and retrieve information, the impacts of tagging behaviour in the workplace open new doors as well as create a bridge to how enterprises leverage behaviours displayed by their employees outside the workplace. Enterprise social media platforms have seen increasing use during the last few years. The popularity of Facebook and other social media platforms has caused businesses to ask the question: 'Can a Facebook-like application be used to help our staff members work together?' A 2011 survey conducted by British job site Reed.co.uk found that one-third of employees used social media while at work; and of those people who logged into social networks on a daily basis, 35% claimed that they did so solely for business purposes (Holtzblatt et al., 2013). Enterprises have implemented social business or collaboration platforms that provide employees with many of the same social features and capabilities, including wikis, blogs, tagging and the ability to create user profiles.

This chapter will examine tagging in the enterprise: specifically, the approaches, advantages, challenges and effects it has on employees. We will also look at how enterprise tagging plays a role in content management and in locating expertise within an enterprise and communities of practice. The main focus of this chapter will be on content tagging, people and collaborative tagging and communities of practice.

In this chapter the term enterprise is used to refer to an organization, company or business that provides services or products to the general public locally, nationally or internationally. As defined by Allam et al. (2010), enterprise tagging, or enterprise social tagging, is a tool that offers strong potential for organizations in knowledge sharing and collaboration. Tagging in the enterprise allows for many different opportunities, including document management, collaboration and identifying subject matter experts. The enterprise must provide its employees with the means to tag content (i.e. documents, records, videos and audio) and tag people (i.e. expertise within the enterprise) through collaboration or content management platforms. This chapter will also discuss how these systems can be utilised, as well as the enterprise and employee behaviours required to enable tagging that assists in the completion of enterprise-related tasks and in saving time and effort in finding content or expertise.

Tagging content in an enterprise

Without the right type of content management processes in place, finding the right information at the right time is a challenge that many employees within enterprises experience on a daily basis. Searching for relevant files within an organization has been a source of problems for employees for a number of years and for this reason, many companies invest substantial amounts of money in searchable portals and document storage facilities (Jackson and Smith, 2011).

In order to ensure enterprise tagging can be implemented to benefit users of the content, as well as to align to objectives of the enterprise, it is important to consider a number of factors. The unstructured nature of tagging can lead to problems when items are tagged with either singular or plural versions of a tag. Spelling mistakes can cause the creation of a new but unnecessary tag with little benefit. Since users freely choose the tags, tagging can be seen as subject indexing without a controlled vocabulary. In addition, when items are tagged by multiple parties, there is a higher likelihood that different tags may be chosen in a collaborative tagging environment. This can be avoided and prevented by adding a unique identifier or a prefix, which would allow the employee to distinguish the tag from others with a few key letters, numbers or words. An example could be a generic tag for customer information data to be 'CI'. In the case where there may be confidential and non-confidential customer information, a prefix may be 'CCI' for confidential customer information data and 'NCCI' for non-confidential information. Spacing and capitalisations should also be considered. Users often do not use spaces at all within tags, to ensure optimised efficiency and effectiveness. A reason for not using spaces is that search engines generally work more efficiently with short condensed tags and after a certain length the tag may lose relevance if it is long in characters, which can increase with spaces. By using all lower-case characters, the user creates a consistency in how tags are created as well as when a user searches based on a tag. An exception to this recommendation is when using acronyms such as FBI (Federal Bureau of Investigation). Different tags may be used to express the same concept; for example, one person describes a resource with the tag *person* and another may use the tag *human* (Jackson and Smith, 2011). Content tagging in an enterprise can be divided into the following categories:

- enterprise processes
- user behaviours
- enterprise objectives and governance
- enterprise systems.

Information architecture

To create a shared content environment in an enterprise, consistent naming conventions, tags and a shared taxonomy are required to assist in creating, naming, storing, searching and retrieving content in an efficient manner. Traditional hierarchical filing systems can lead to the retrieval of irrelevant information or to none at all, even though the information exists. The study completed by Jackson and Smith (2011) focused on reducing the information overload problem in organizations by focusing on improving the filing and retrieving of electronic documents. The study showed that users employ a wide variety of different filing methods to store their files, such as storing them by content type, project, date, customer and many others. This could lead to inconsistencies in how information was searched as well as to search results that contain irrelevant information or multiple results. Results of the analysis indicated that tagging could achieve a cost-effective solution by providing a better structured filing plan that could help reduce duplication and the retrieval of irrelevant information. The study confirmed that the wide variety of different filing methods employees use to store their files could lead to problems in retrieving relevant information. The introduction of a new tagging system to store and retrieve information could lead to more consistency in how employees tag files. Ways to engage users in the new system include providing training to employees and having computer-assisted rules for creating consistent tags (Jackson and Smith, 2011). Time spent in searching for information and increased productivity are other ways in which employees can benefit from enterprise tagging. In order to ensure that employees understand how content should be tagged in the enterprise to reduce search time and the retrieval of non-related information, tags can be aligned to different enterprise processes and content inputs and outputs.

Enterprise processes

Documenting processes to complete business tasks can assist in ensuring consistency in how employees tag content, use prefixes and identify keywords for searches in different business units in an organization and can remove silos and encourage a collaborative workplace. A clear understanding of how tools and technologies are aligned to organizational policies and processes helps define the content lifecycle of the organization, i.e. how information is created, searched, retrieved, distributed and disposed of. Exploring, understanding and articulating emergent collaborative processes and practices are crucial (Ravenscroft et al., 2012). Ariouat, Andonoff and Hanachi (2016) define emergent collaborative processes as those whose definition and enactment require interactions between groups of actors using their skills and experiences towards a common goal. These processes enable users of the content to understand its purpose and how it relates to completing business tasks and to tag it accordingly. Employees can search the documented processes and understand how content should be tagged to avoid duplication of tag keywords or tagging content with a term that is relevant only to that individual or a team within a department. As the amount of content increases within an enterprise, the creation of processes to tag content is required; it is important to note that content can be tagged both by the creator of the content and by those who use it. Employees have the opportunity to use tags to provide their insights about a document they have reviewed or utilised to complete tasks. Tags need not be added at the time the document is created or even by the creator. Users can assign tags meaningful to them at any time. Tagging has great potential to overcome the 'wide gap between how employees think about the information and the way the owners of the information classify it' (Shel Holtz, as cited in Fichter, 2006).

Tagging documents with relevant and comprehensive keywords offers invaluable assistance to the readers to quickly review any document. With the ever-increasing volume and variety of documents published on the internet, the interest in developing newer and successful techniques for tagging documents is also increasing. Tagging documents with minimum words has become important for several practical applications, such as search engines, indexing of databases of research documents, comparing the similarity of documents, ontology creation and mapping and in several other stages of important applications (Singhal and Srivastava, 2014). A few examples of important applications can include customer relationship management (CRM) and enterprise resource planning (ERP) platforms. Applications such as CRM platforms can utilise tags to identify contacts and opportunities. Tags can be assigned to data in the CRM platform to prioritise contacts and opportunities based on 'sales stage.' For example, opportunities can be pre-defined in a controlled tagging list, as shown in Table 9.1, which illustrates how a controlled tagging list can create consistency to enable business opportunities to be easily looked up and monitored. Such a list, however, may deter users from creating a tag based on their experience with a specific contact as discussed further in the next section.

Table 9.1 *Examples of controlled tags*

Opportunity stage	Controlled tag
Initial meeting has been made with a contact to begin the process of selling of a service or product	New Op
Continuous meetings are taking place with a contact but the 'sale' of a service or product has not been completed	Ongoing Op
The 'sale' of a service or product has taken place and the contract has been signed	Sold Op
The 'sale' of a service or product has not taken place and the contact no longer wants to take part in discussions	Lost Op

User behaviours

As mentioned previously, content is not always tagged by the creator. In a collaborative environment, content can also be tagged by the reviewer or end-user of the content. The goal of tagging content within an enterprise needs to be defined and communicated by the enterprise leadership. This will create a level of understanding of the importance of tagging content by the creator or user of the content. Tagging by the user to show, for example, how content was used, as well as its quality and usefulness, can cause a mixed reaction within the enterprise. A level of trust and non-judgement must be created and commun-icated by the leadership of the enterprise to ensure that employees do not feel threatened by sharing content on a collaborative platform. The implementation of controlled tagging, where specific tag words are created by an initial set of users or employees, may cause other employees to feel limited in creating tags that are meaningful for them, as the selection of tags has already been pre-defined. The controlled tags are usually aligned to business processes, which can also create consistent and standardised tags. Controlled tags could inhibit employees from assigning tags because they do not perceive any benefits to themselves.

According to Raban et al. (2017), tags can be chosen from a controlled vocabulary or they can be free text assigned by the user. When free text is used, the resulting metadata can include homonyms, synonyms, spelling mistakes and errors that can lead to inappropriate connections between items and insufficient outcomes for information searches. On the other hand, with free text users can use terms they think are appropriate to describe or help recall information without the burden of selecting a category from a known taxonomy. Free text also allows for a dynamic update of the vocabulary, thus maintaining its relevance and currency. Collaborative tagging systems present new challenges to system designers because social and psychological factors may affect users' level of activity and tag choices. One factor that is particularly applicable is the principle of social proof, also known as social influence, which indicates that people model their behaviour based on others. This principle suggests that 'we view a behavior as correct in a given situation to the degree that we see others performing it' (Raban et al., 2017).

Participating in online groups often follows a power law distribution, where a minority of participants actively contribute and the majority remain receivers. In social systems, the users can act or react, post or reply. The participation ranges from complete inactivity to full activity. There are four levels of contribution (Raban et al., 2017):

1 Active\initiate – a participant who initiates discussion or interaction, acts and reacts in the interaction
2 Active\respond – a participant who responds/reacts to others and does not initiate interaction.
3 Passive\lurk – a participant who only reads others' messages. This kind of participant neither acts nor reacts.
4 Passive\inactive – a participant who is registered in a system but does not actually use it and does not even read others' messages.

Each participant in social applications belongs to one of the four levels defined above. The dilemma for individuals is to either contribute to the common good or to shirk and free-ride on the work of others. System designers prefer the users to be more on the active side and to contribute frequently to the system and the organization. This contribution may be either by duplicating existing tags (social proof) or by using new tags that will bring new information to the system. In the corporate tagging system, overall participation is expected to follow the power law distribution, with mostly passive users. In order to create tagging accountability for users, guidelines and best practices for how to tag can be created and implemented by the enterprise leadership. This will assist users to assign their own tags and ensure that these tags are aligned to processes so that the right information can be utilised in a timely manner.

Jackson and Smith (2011) developed a proof of concept, called TagDav, to enable users to tag the files they use. The system was tested at SoftwareCo, a large software organization, to examine the role of tagging, in a business context, in discovering relevant information when compared to traditional hierarchical filing systems. A five-step interpretive hybrid approach of focus groups, questionnaires and SWOT analysis was used to test the proof of concept of tagging files compared to a traditional hierarchical filing system. The study found that users employed a wide variety of different filing methods to store their files, with every participant providing a different answer: for example, storing them by content type, project, date, customer and many others. Traditional hierarchical filing systems can lead to the retrieval of irrelevant information, or to none at all, even though the information exists. The study found that tagging could provide a cost-effective solution by providing a better structured filing system that can help reduce duplication and the retrieval of irrelevant information.

Alignment to enterprise objectives and governance

Enterprises are growing at a rapid pace; this growth includes the number of employees, projects, processes and procedures. As organizations grow, new content and expertise are constantly being created. Expertise is gained from one's work and educational and personal experiences. Strategies that many enterprises are developing include capturing, storing and distributing content. To remain competitive, enterprises have implemented strategies to manage their intellectual resources and capabilities. It is important that enterprises create measures of success to monitor the effects of tagging in the organization and how tagging systems align to business objectives. Success measures and key performance indicators can show and predict what type of content is most used and to what processes that content relates. An example of this is a customer-care call centre. With the number of calls and requests that employees receive on a daily basis, it is important that individuals and teams have access to the most up-to-date information to ensure that consistent messaging on sales promotions, pricing and managing concerns is provided. By tagging these content types with keywords that are consistent and descriptive, employees can easily search and retrieve the information in a timely and efficient manner. The processes for how the content should be accessed, stored, tagged and updated should be evaluated by a governing committee consisting of leaders in the organization. Measures to track usage can be completed through the system by looking at the number of times the content has been downloaded, viewed, commented on and so forth. These measures can be aligned to such organizational measures as employee satisfaction (i.e. are you able to receive the right information when you need it?) and customer satisfaction (i.e. are you receiving consistent information from different individuals with whom you speak?).

Ravenscroft et al. (2012) identified a number of key challenges for designing tools to support informal learning processes in digitally mediated, or digitally rich, contexts. Informal learning processes are subtle and complex, so we need to actively investigate, define and design simultaneously in context, or we investigate by design. We cannot fully anticipate the behaviour of instantiated informal learning tools and any network effects without actually deploying them in a community (i.e. you cannot separate social media design from instantiated social media processes). Therefore, exploring, understanding and articulating emergent collaborative processes and practices are crucial. The adoption and use of these sorts of tools, in turn, reformulates existing communication and knowledge practices and creates new ones. This means that we need to foreground the human reality of the digital intervention, for example, how individual differences might influence levels of acceptance.

Ravenscroft et al. suggested that we cannot design and evaluate these tools in traditional ways, such as through assessing the degree to which a technological intervention is a clearly defined solution to a clearly defined problem. Similarly, ongoing evaluations are implicit in the design process itself and not conceived as separate and discrete activities. Design is inherently an ongoing and iterative process and involves an ongoing dialogue among all stakeholders.

A governing committee can engage stakeholders in ongoing dialogue on a regular basis. The governing committee can consist of stakeholders from different divisions of an enterprise, such as marketing, legal, sales and information technology. This ensures alignment and consistency of tagging conventions, information architecture, security and the content management lifecycle. A governing committee should also meet on a regular basis and assign roles and responsibilities to each of its members. Having a governing committee, and aligning processes and measures of content to enterprise goals and objectives, can ensure that the different domains of an enterprise are working toward shared overall goals. The governing committee can also evaluate systems in the enterprise and how progress can be continually made in the measures and key performance indicators.

Enterprise systems

When working with certain enterprises on implementing an enterprise collaboration platform where users are to create profiles, upload pictures and so forth, the common phrase heard is 'So this is Facebook for work?' The following section contains an introduction to enterprise systems, but this chapter will remain technology-agnostic, in that a list of the most current systems will not be provided. The goal of this section is to discuss how enterprises are moving towards creating a link between the systems used in the outside world and those used in the enterprise. As the world outside the enterprise is moving toward an informal means of communication versus the perceived formal means of communication inside the enterprise, a key challenge for contemporary enterprises is connecting and sharing knowledge that is distributed throughout the organization by linking people to each other and to knowledge content. Due to the relatively limited success of formal systems that focus on decision support, project management, expert systems and intranets, enterprises are increasingly experimenting with a variety of enterprise social media tools as potential solutions to enhance and improve knowledge coordination (Fulk and Yuan, 2013). These formal systems do not allow the enterprise to complete informal, interpersonal processes such as collaboration, content sharing and tagging. Enterprise social media (ESM) tools are enterprise-wide internet-based technologies that allow users to easily create, edit, evaluate and link to content or to other creators of content and include such applications as wikis, blogs, social tagging systems and enterprise social networking systems and align to that enterprise's goals (Fulk and Yuan, 2013).

When implementing such a system and creating the ability to tag content and people, which we will talk about in the next section, it is important that an enterprise provides a vision and a value statement for the system and its use, in order to align to the enterprise's goals. The implementation of such a system should also require a change management strategy focused on the different user segments of an organization. The implementation plan becomes a marketing campaign to provide users the understanding, knowledge of the system and its benefits and training in its use. Adoption of new social software tools is often slow and the interactions among users, changes in work practices, relationships among how different tools are used and impact on business outcomes all take time to emerge. In many cases, appropriate metrics for tying user behaviour to business value do not exist (Holztblatt et al., 2013).

When I worked with an enterprise that implemented a tagging system, success was measured by adoption, that is, how many users logged on to the system when it became available. On the first day 90% of the enterprise logged on to the system and a hearty congratulation was sent out through a mass e-mail. The adoption measure dropped the following month to 40%, however. The main reason was that users did not know how and why to use the system and perceived it as 'Facebook for work' that would just create more noise and conversation about cats and dogs and what people had for dinner. In order to increase the trust of the users a 'foot race' to complete a change management strategy and align processes to the tool needed to be completed. When I talk about a foot race, the enterprise was faced with a situation where silos were being created within the enterprise amongst users who:

- understood how to use the system and created their own processes to share information
- created groups of just people they knew and trusted and secured access to the groups
- duplicated content with inconsistent tagging and naming conventions
- just stayed clear of the system.

Implementing a change management strategy, consistent communication, aligning processes to the system and having robust measures in place to accurately address adoption might have caught this earlier. Adoption measures could have been expanded to answer the following questions:

- How many users use the system on a regular basis (i.e. return users)?
- What type of content is accessed and by how many users?
- Do users upload profiles based on their roles and responsibilities?
- What types of user groups are created?

The above section provides information on establishing a tagging system within an enterprise and how tagging relates to content management. When a system is implemented and processes are understood, not only is content readily available, but also people within the enterprise begin to use it.

Tagging people in an enterprise

The tagging system is in place and users within an enterprise can find content they require to complete enterprise tasks; they trust the content due to an understanding of how to tag content. Guidelines have been implemented by a governance committee that brings together the divisions of an enterprise and a system to store and retrieve content exists that allows for collaboration and sharing of knowledge. What comes next?

In a recent experience with an enterprise, the focus was to have users upload a photo of themselves, a résumé in a consistent format across the enterprise and create a profile based on skills and job description. The users were then provided with the guidelines to tag themselves in order to be searched by other users within the organization. A sample set of tag keywords was provided based on role, expertise and skills. Examples consisted of keywords such as *manager, developer, project management* and *account specialist*. These keywords enabled the users to tag themselves based on how they wanted to be searched within the enterprise and offered the opportunity to enter tags on areas of interest within the enterprise, namely keywords such as *finance, client relationships* and *director*. The opportunity to state, via tags, areas in which users wished to grow their career created motivation and ownership of one's own career and created new connections between users within the enterprise. There was also the opportunity to create a community based on expertise. We will discuss in detail the community-based approach, also known as communities of practice (CoP), in the next section.

The above scenario allows a user to complete self-tags; however, users can also be tagged by other users within an enterprise. A particularly explicit form of describing people is a people tagging system implemented in large organizations. In such systems, people describe themselves and their peers by the use of tags. This offers a unique opportunity to study explicit self-presentation and perception by others using real-life data. The uniqueness of people tagging, unlike tagging other online content, is that people tagging is reciprocal (Raban et al., 2017). Challenges do exist, however, with the form of people tagging, in that users may be hesitant to create a tag that may differ from existing tags based on a difference of opinion and will emulate what others are tagging in order to remain part of the crowd.

Maintaining motivation

The influence of organizational constraints and hierarchical community on tagging behaviour needs to be studied. People's tagging activity affects professional reputations and, depending on how the tags are used, (e.g. automated expertise selection), people may tailor their tagging activity so that they are called upon as experts in areas of their choosing (John and Seligmann, 2006). This challenge can be mitigated by creating a vision or value statement on why people should tag others, how it benefits enterprise goals and can assist in the learning and development of the users.

Benefits of people tagging include the development and growth of one's professional career, access to support structures, professional development and knowledge creation. In order to make the best use of the learning opportunities from personal learning networks, Cook and Pachler (2012) suggest that users need to perform the following three primary tasks:

1 Build connections by adding new people to the network so that there are resources available when a learning need arises.
2 Maintain connections by keeping in touch with relevant persons.
3 Activate connections with selected persons for the purpose of learning.

In order to motivate and increase the use of people tags, enterprises can also encourage a unit within the system to share success stories on how collaborating with others assisted in the completion of a task; for example, by completing a marketing advertisement. Let's say a commercial is to be transmitted globally; it is important to understand the commonalities of each sector of the targeted market. A user who is leading the campaign can create a post that explains the proposed approach and uses tags such as *global*, *TV ad*, *connecting cultures* and *ad experts global wanted*. Once the post is published on the enterprise systems, the tagged keywords may attract other users to read the post and understand the campaign. The platform provides a forum for the users to communicate and collaborate, as well as share ideas and content of what may work from the perspective of global unity. The result may be a commercial that will air across the targeted locations, which may lead to increased sales. Success stories such as this can be utilised to show the importance of tagging posts, people and content. On the flipside, if the marketing campaign was not successful, lessons learned can also be shared via the platform. In order for the platform to be successful, certain guidelines or principles can be provided by a governing committee overseeing the people tag element within the enterprise. Examples of guidelines may consist of statements such as 'respect your fellow users as you would expect respect yourself'; 'be thoughtful about how you respond or tag people who may not have the same skillset as you and offer words of wisdom'; and 'we are one company and represent one another in how we speak and treat each other'.

Enterprise platforms can have queries that look for tagged words that may not align with the principles or vision of the enterprise. These queries can be applied to tags for both content and people. In order to fully understand the importance of tagging users and content for collaboration and for shared interest based on skills, roles and a desire to grow one's knowledge, the next section examines communities of practice.

Communities of practice

For years, conversations around the water cooler and among special interest groups have provided a means for members of an enterprise to speak about their interests, passions and to share expertise on completing tasks associated with their roles. The bringing together of people in an enterprise based on skills, shared responsibilities and interests is referred to as communities of practice (CoP). Having CoP within enterprises connects employees to facilitate collaboration, communication and increase knowledge sharing. The use of tags expedites this coming together if implemented in a way that provides an understanding of the importance of CoP.

Brief history of CoP

The concept of CoP was introduced by Jean Lave and Etienne Wenger during their research on social theories of learning. CoP can be defined as a group of people in an enterprise who interact with each other across enterprise divisions or even across enterprise boundaries connected by a common interest or field of application (Zboralski, Salomo and Gemuenden, 2006). Enterprises have supported models of CoP in which all members of an enterprise can contribute; however, focus is now on creating CoP based on the common roles and interests of employees in order to grow the combined knowledge of their respective expertise. A necessary prerequisite for knowledge sharing is an existing network of experts and people interested in the subject organised in their CoP. CoP create activities aimed at establishing, extending and maintaining relationships between individual members and establishing informal meetings to support mutual information exchange (Zboralski, Salomo and Gemuenden, 2006). The process of sharing knowledge in CoP in the manner of an informal meeting is important in the flow of information. As employees work on given tasks, they regard CoP as places to ask questions, search for knowledge and to grow. CoP provide employees a sense of freedom to enhance existing skill sets without being judged by their colleagues. Users can use tags to ensure they are receiving information and connections to others to complete tasks and grow their knowledge. The characteristics of spontaneity and freedom from enterprise constraints link communities of practice positively to learning, knowledge flows and innovation. Evidence in support of CoP focuses on the ways innovation emerges incrementally from local adaptations of work practices within communities, in response to new problems (Swan, Scarbrough and Robertson, 2002).

Enterprise learning

Social technology within enterprises bridges the gap between individuals, removes knowledge silos and leads to improved communication and collaboration. Enterprises can use these processes to strengthen CoP and continually grow to remain competitive. With the addition of tagging content and people, users are connected in a more efficient manner based on expertise, need and alignment to enterprise tasks and objectives. Enterprises understand that by implementing processes to share knowledge through CoP and provide platforms to enable members to partake in these communities, innovative ways to conduct business and provide improved services and products to their consumers can be created. The creation of new knowledge allows enterprises the flexibility to react to a changing marketplace and stay ahead of their competitors as technological advances continue to make the world connected. There is a growing consensus that the best way to improve enterprise learning is not to simply focus on capturing, codifying and documenting knowledge of individuals, but rather to concentrate on ways through which knowledge can be shared, discussed and innovated (Mittendorf et al., 2006).

In order to close the knowledge gap between members of an enterprise, virtual CoP are being created that provide members instant access to other individuals with shared interests and common tasks. This type of virtual communication provides an increase in collaboration and innovation as more members work together to create the best results for the enterprise. This also takes into consideration input from members located globally, which provides enterprises a competitive advantage in creating global solutions, services and products. Among the chief reasons why CoP are efficient tools for knowledge generation and sharing is that most of an enterprise's competitive advantage is embedded in the intangible, tacit knowledge of its people and that competencies do not exist apart from the people who develop them (Ardichvili, Page and Wentling, 2003). Members of an enterprise also realise that the culture of enterprises strives to increase communication and collaboration and provides accessibility to connect its members. This type of culture retains members and attracts top talent.

Effects of CoP on the enterprise

CoP can drive strategy, generate new lines of business, solve problems, promote the spread of best practices, develop people's professional skills and help companies recruit and retain talent (Wenger and Snyder, 2000). For CoP to be effective and produce results they must have the support of the enterprise from a top-down perspective. Sharing knowledge and working together in a collaborative process is a very important message that can be incorporated in the overall strategy of an enterprise and aligned with information architecture to create consistent tagging, naming conventions and taxonomy. With a CoP member as a part of the primary enterprise unit, co-operation between staff and the level of trust between staff may be strengthened (Zboralski, Salomo and Gemuenden, 2006). As enterprises grow, change is often a part of this growth; whether it is with processes, teams, strategy or vision of enterprises, individuals need to fully understand the change and react accordingly. CoP can offer support to individuals on the best approach to manage the change and provide an understanding of how roles may change as well.

Due to the informal connections CoP offer, individuals can discuss openly and honestly the difficulties they are having and the best ways to cope with change. When a company reorganises into a team-based structure, employees with functional expertise may create CoP as a way to maintain connections with peers (Ardichvili, Page and Wentling, 2003). Elsewhere, people may form communities in response to changes originating outside the enterprise, such as the rise of e-commerce, or inside, such as new company strategies (Wenger and Snyder, 2000). CoP can foster trust and a sense of common purpose among individuals. Due to the informal structure of CoP and the non-mandatory process of joining them, individuals want to be a part of the team either to share or gain knowledge. CoP connect individuals for shared reasons. People in such communities decide whether they have something to contribute and whether they are likely to learn. When members of an existing community invite someone to join, they do so based on a gut sense of the prospective member's appropriateness for the group. This leads to communities creating goals based on shared expectations. Once expectations are aligned, the CoP create purpose by combining the needs of each of their members. Within CoP, existing knowledge is shared, reused, modified and transformed into new knowledge (Ardichvili, Page and Wentling, 2003). This new collaborative knowledge can be implemented to grow the individual member's knowledge as well as create solutions for the enterprise. An example can be a new marketing proposal to sell the products of an enterprise. The CoP can use the existing marketing strategies and understand what worked and what did not work from input from the members of the community and create a new approach based on the different lessons learned. When employees join communities, they establish themselves as experts, for example through gaining the formal expert status by contributing to the community, or through gaining an informal recognition through multiple postings and contributions to the community. Managers and experts feel that they have reached a stage in their lives when it is time to start giving back, by sharing their expertise and mentoring new employees through participation in the community (Kerno, 2008). The use of tags within the communities allows members to find what and who they need and allows users outside the community to create new connections and locate experts within a domain for both short-term and long-term needs.

CoP engagement

Communities offer many benefits to individuals and enterprises; when setting up communities, the barriers to their success and longevity should be considered. Communities rely on the knowledge and participation of their members; if CoP do not provide results and motivation to their members, these communities will fade away and interest in them will dissipate. Tags can be useful in that users have the opportunity to tag people and content they have utilised with keywords that have meaning to them and to the community. Enterprises need to provide support for the creation and existence of communities and instil the importance of a sharing culture in their strategic goals. These strategic goals will provide an understanding of the direction of the enterprise and the contributions required by its members. If members do not feel connected to the group's area of expertise and interest, they will not fully commit themselves to the work of the community (Wenger and Snydner, 2000).

Another barrier is knowledge hoarding, or the fear of sharing knowledge, due to the competition to stand out in an enterprise. This can stem from a fear that if individuals share knowledge they lose their individualism and find it harder to stand out in a group. This can again be eradicated by the culture of the enterprise that focuses on teamwork and rewards contributions that an individual makes in a community. Having no one assigned to lead the community once it is established can cause disengagement, as individuals do not understand the community's goal and are not motivated to take part in the community. If the knowledge gathered is not relevant, it becomes stagnant and does not get reused, modified or updated to create new knowledge; what results is a stack of knowledge that is not organised or managed. A failure of communities to provide a shared set of guidelines on how and when to tag content or people may cause users to hold back or follow what others are doing in order to fit in.

Participants in a study on knowledge sharing and communities indicated that in many cases, people are afraid that what they post may not be important, completely accurate, or relevant to a specific discussion. There was an element of a fear of losing face and of letting colleagues down and misleading them. The participants referred to their need for clearer directions for distinguishing between acceptable and unacceptable postings (Ardichvili, Page and Wentling, 2003). If guidelines do not exist on how to act in a community, rather than actively contribute, individuals will observe only and will not participate. Without the support of the enterprise, a further barrier exists in the availability of time in which to engage in the activities that are necessary for CoP to be effective (Kerno, 2008). As many individuals are busy with their everyday tasks, time to take part in a community may be limited, and so participation may not be at 100% at all times, which may lead CoP to become stagnant.

Starting and sustaining CoP

In order to start and sustain CoP, their benefits and barriers need to be understood by their creators and the enterprise leaders. Prior to starting a community, it is important to ensure that one does not already exist; if one does, the best step is to join the community and look for ways to promote it. The need for new CoP should be communicated and aligned with the enterprise's strategy and goals. In most cases, informal networks of people with the ability and the passion to develop an enterprise's core competencies already exist; the task is to identify such groups and help them come together as communities of practice (Wenger and Snyder, 2000). The use of tags can help connect users within an enterprise and lead to the creation of a community.

It is important to receive the buy-in or support of enterprise management and to demonstrate how the CoP benefit the enterprise. Managers can also assist in encouraging their colleagues and teams and leading by example. The management role shifts from one focused on command and control to that of a system builder who facilitates and brokers the development and integration of knowledge within and across communities (Swan, Scarbrough and Robertson, 2002). As enterprises and knowledge grow, it is vital that a space to create a community is enabled and that CoP have the infrastructure to support the information gathered. CoP are not viewed as a part of an enterprise that directly create financial value, therefore they are not provided with a budget. To reach their full potential, CoP need to be integrated into the business and supported in specific ways (Wenger and Snyder, 2000). Enterprises look for innovative ways to leverage the technologies that link individuals in their personal lives and implement them into the workplace. Senior executives must be prepared to invest time and money to help such communities reach their full potential; one way to strengthen communities is to provide them with official sponsors and support teams to work with internal community leaders to provide resources and co-ordination.

Communities have been in the workplace for a long time; they are an informal gathering of similar-minded individuals sharing information on how to make things better and to learn from one another's mistakes and successes. Technology has allowed us to move from the conversations during breaks and lunchtime to all the time. Using technology to communicate, collaborate and grow personally and professionally occurs amongst all generations. CoP bring individuals together to share, store, update, modify and implement their knowledge in a manner that creates measurable results for both the individuals and the enterprises. The use of tags can assist in ensuring that users receive what they need and share it with others.

Conclusion

Tagging has become a key element in how enterprises use social activity to increase knowledge sharing and collaboration and to connect employees. While we have the ability to tag pictures and articles in social platforms such as Facebook and Twitter, within an enterprise a tagging vision or value statement is necessary that aligns enterprise goals with why people should tag content and other people. Individuals will have the ability to tag what they wish, but tagging guidelines must be created and managed by a governing committee or the CoP administrators. Tagging methods and keywords should align to business processes and can be created through an enterprise information architecture. As enterprises continue to grow, it is time to create a link between social and enterprise platforms to build connections, highlight expertise and continue to grow knowledge.

References

Allam, H., Bliemel, M., Blustein, J., Spiteri, L. and Watters, C. (2010) A Conceptual Model for Dimensions Impacting Employees' Participation in Enterprise Social Tagging. In *MSM '10, Proceedings of the International Workshop on Modeling Social Media*, ACM, 1–3.

Ardichvili, A., Page, V. and Wentling, T. (2003) Motivation and Barriers to Participation in Virtual Knowledge-Sharing Communities of Practice, *Journal of Knowledge Management*, **7**, 64–77.

Ariouat, H., Andonoff, E. and Hanachi, C. (2016) Do Process-Based Systems Support Emergent, Collaborative and Flexible Processes? Comparative analysis of current systems, *Procedia Computer Science*, **96**, 511–20.

Cook, J. and Pachler, N. (2012) Online People Tagging: social (mobile) network(ing) services and work-based learning, *British Journal of Educational Technology*, **43**, 711–25.

Fichter, D. (2006) Intranet Applications for Tagging and Folksonomies, *Online*, **30**, 43–5.

Fulk, J. and Yuan, Y. C. (2013) Location, Motivation and Social Capitalization via Enterprise Social Networking, *Journal of Computer-Mediated Communication*, **19**, 20–37.

Holtzblatt, L., Drury, J. L., Weiss, D., Damianos, L. E. and Cuomo, D. (2013) Evaluating the Uses and Benefits of an Enterprise Social Media Platform, *Journal of Social Media for Organizations*, **1**, 1–21.

Jackson, T. W. and Smith, S. (2011) Retrieving Relevant Information: traditional file systems versus tagging, *Journal of Enterprise Information Management*, **25**, 79–93.

John, A. and Seligmann, D. D. (2006) Collaborative Tagging and Expertise in the Enterprise. In *Proceedings of Collaborative Web Tagging Workshop Held in Conjunction with WWW 2006*, 1–6.

Kerno, S. J. (2008) Limitations of Communities of Practice: a consideration of unresolved issues and difficulties in the approach, *Journal of Leadership & Organizational Studies*, **15**, 69–78.

Mittendorf, K., Geijsel, F., Hoeve, A., de Laat, M. and Nieuwenhuis, L. (2006) Communities of Practice as Stimulating Forces for Collective Learning, *Journal of Workplace Learning*, **18**, 298–312.

Raban, D. R., Danan, A., Ronen, I. and Guy, I. (2017) Impression Management through People Tagging in the Enterprise: implications for social media sampling and design, *Journal of Information Science*, **43**, 295–315.

Ravenscroft, A., Schmidt, A., Cook, J. and Bradley, C. (2012) Designing Social Media for Informal Learning and Knowledge Maturing in the Digital Workplace, *Journal of Computer Assisted Learning*, **28**, 235–49.

Singhal, A. and Srivastava, J. (2014) Semantic Tagging for Documents Using 'Short Text' Information. In *Fourth International Conference on Advances in Computing and Information Technology*, 337–50, IRED.

Swan, J., Scarbrough, H. and Robertson, M. (2002) The Construction of 'Communities of Practice' in the Management of Innovation, *Management Learning*, **33**, 477–96.

Wenger, E. C. and Snyder, W. M. (2000) Communities of Practice: the organization frontier, *Harvard Business Review*, January–February, 139–145.

Zboralski, K., Salomo, S. and Gemuenden, H. G. (2006) Organizational Benefits of Communities of Practice: a two-stage information processing model, *Cybernetics and Systems: an international journal*, **37**, 533–52.

Chapter 10

Use and effectiveness of social tagging recommender systems

Kishor John

Introduction

The internet is a unique medium, innovating constantly and, in turn, being shaped in accordance with the technologies, interests and needs of the time. It started with simple content, requiring facility of straightforward search; thereafter it turned into a complex network (social network) with complex content (social content) demanding complex search processes (social search). We have seen the transition from the *static* web to the *dynamic* web to the *intelligent* web. Social networking emerged with the inception of Web 2.0 and has expanded dynamically since 2003, because of both its enormous appeal to users and innovations in technology. Social tagging was immediately accepted by savvy users and gained recognition as an important feature of social networking sites and social bookmarking sites. Additionally, social tagging is a possible solution to improved searching of networked resources and enables users to use tag descriptors to label web content for the purpose of personal and shared organization of information resources (Trant, 2009). This chapter will explore the different types of traditional recommender systems, as well as those for social tagging specifically, their use and effectiveness.

History of traditional recommender systems

Recommender systems emerged during the mid-1990s (Herlocker and Konstan, 2001; Shardanand and Maes, 1995) and were collectively defined as the supporting systems that help users find information, products, or services by aggregating and analysing suggestions from other users (Frias-Martinez et al., 2006; Kim et al., 2010; Park et al., 2012). The term 'recommender' can refer also to the degree of information filtering to produce topics or content that users are interested in (O'Connor et al., 2001). A recommender system analyses user preferences, interests and behaviours and generates the potential information, service, or products needed by users (Li, Hsu and Lee, 2012). A recommender system is a technology where items such as products, movies, events and articles are recommended for users (Kordík, 2016). Burke defines a recommender system as one 'that produces individualized recommendations as output or has the effect of guiding the user in a personalized way to interesting or useful objects in a large space of possible options' (Burke, 2002a, 331).

The main goal of recommender systems is to provide timely, suitable and valuable information according to user demand. The actions in recommender systems involve data acquisition, data processing, recommendation processing and recommendation results (Li, Hsu and Lee, 2012; Resnick and Varian, 1997). 'Recommender Systems (RSs) collect information on the preferences of its users for a set of items (e.g. movies, songs, books, jokes, gadgets, applications, websites, travel destinations and e-learning material)' (Bobadilla et al., 2013, 109). The information is obtained explicitly or implicitly (Lee, Cho and Kim, 2010; Choi et al., 2012; Núñez-Valdéz et al., 2012). It can be said that every recommendation process passes through certain phases: information collection; implicit feedback; explicit feedback; learning and prediction/recommendation (Isinkaye, Folajimi and Ojokoh, 2015). 'Recommending tags can serve various purposes, such as: increasing the chances of getting a resource annotated, reminding a user what a resource is about and consolidating the vocabulary across the users' (Marinho et al., 2011, 621). 'Recommender systems are software tools and techniques providing suggestions for items to be of use to a user. The suggestions relate to various decision-making processes, such as what items to buy, what music to listen to, or what online news to read' (Ricci, Rokach and Shapira, 2015, vii). Extensive research on recommender systems emerged during the mid-1990s and has developed very quickly, strongly stimulated by the rapid development of the internet and e-commerce (Adomavicius and Tuzhilin 2005; Szlávik, Kowalczyk and Schut, 2011).

The first recommender system, Tapestry, was introduced by Goldberg et al. (1992) and was designed to recommend documents from newsgroups (Resnick et al., 1994). Since then and in response to the advances in web application, recommender systems have become an important element in facilitating expert human–computer interaction and information searches. A variety of recommender systems were developed shortly after, including Ringo for music (Shardanand and Maes, 1995), the BellCore Video Recommender for movies (Hill et al., 1995) and Jester for jokes (Goldberg et al. 2001). Web 1.0 recommender systems were used for approximation theory, information retrieval, forecasting, management science and customer relations (Fard, Nilashi and Salim, 2013). In the Web 2.0 environment, recommender systems have become an important ingredient of web applications and use. Researchers have developed many recommender systems for many domains, including entertainment, social networking sites, content-based sites (e.g. e-learning, books or articles), e-commerce, tourism and matchmaking (Lu et al., 2015; Sharma and Singh, 2016).

Functional classification of recommender systems

According to Burke (2002a), the types of recommender systems are based on:

1 the background data that the system has before the recommendation process begins
2 the input data that the user must communicate to the system in order to generate a recommendation
3 the algorithm that combines background and input data to arrive at its suggestions.

Van Meteren and Van Someren (2000) classified recommender systems into the following categories, based on the method employed for recommendations:

- content-based recommendations: the user is recommended items similar to the ones the user preferred in the past
- collaborative recommendations: the user is recommended items that people with similar tastes and preferences liked in the past
- hybrid approaches: these methods combine collaborative and content-based methods.

A number of scholars have divided recommender systems into the following categories: collaborative filtering; content-based; and context based (Chen, et al., 2008; Jain and Jain, 2016; Khurana and Parveen, 2016, Schafer, Konstan and Riedl, 2001; Su and Khoshgoftaar, 2009). Stomberg (2014) identified three types of computation models for recommender systems:

1 collaborative/social-based filters, which use ratings from thousands of users and statistical analyses to find correlations among users or items to create predictions
2 content-based filters, which use data from description or analysis of their item set and the users' ratings to create predictions

3 knowledge-based methods, which use ratings and the action history of the
   user base to learn rules that describe desired items, then use those rules to
   create predictions based on a user's explicitly stated preferences.

The major types of recommender systems are:

● collaborative filtering
● content-based
● context-based
● demographic
● knowledge-based
● hybrid.

Collaborative filtering recommender systems

Goldberg et al. (1992) coined the term 'collaborative filtering', which is used to
refer to 'the method of making automatic predictions (filtering) about the
interests of a user by collecting taste information from many users' (Wikipedia,
2018). The goal of collaborative filtering is to predict a list of suggested items or
terms to the user (i.e. the active user) based on the users who previously visited
that item or term and their votes for it. Collaborative filters may be defined as a
tool that helps people make choices based on the opinion of other people. An
example of a collaborative filtering-based system is GroupLens, which helps
people to find articles they like in the huge stream of available articles (Resnick
et al., 1994). Collaborative filtering needs an extensive database containing
exclusively the ratings of the items made by users (Bobadilla et al., 2013). In
their purest form:

> collaborative systems do not consider the content of the documents at all,
> relying exclusively on the judgement of humans as to whether the document
> is valuable. In this way, collaborative filtering attempts to recapture the
> cross-topic recommendations that are common in communities of people.
> (Sarwar et al., 2000, 2)

Miller, Konstan and Riedl (2004) argued that the main assumption of collaborative filtering is that two users rate a number of items in a similar way, or have
similar behaviours (like watching, listening and reading) and therefore will rate
or act on other items similarly.

Collaborative filtering recommender systems are typically associated with very large datasets (Schafer et al., 2007; Ekstrand et al., 2011). Collaborative filtering algorithms often require users' active participation, an easy way to represent users' interests and algorithms that can match people with similar interests (Balachandran et al., 2017)

Content-based recommender systems

Content-based recommender systems are content-oriented, implying that the content of users' interests and the content of the features of items play an essential role in the recommendation process (Sulieman, 2014). In content-based systems, the recommendations are based on items that perfectly suit users' interests; this process estimates recommendations with the help of an item's description and the user's rating of a set of items. All the information about a user, extracted either by monitoring user actions or by examining the objects the user has evaluated, is stored and utilised to customise services offered (Burke, 2002a). This user modelling approach is known as 'content-based learning', which assumes that a user's behaviour remains unchanged through time; therefore, the content of past user actions may be used to predict the desired content of their future actions (Wallace et al., 2003).

Content-based recommender systems may be divided into two types: case-based reasoning and attribute-based techniques. Case-based reasoning assumes that if users like certain items, they would probably also like similar items and would also recommend new similar items (Drachsler, Hummel and Koper, 2008). Attributes-based techniques recommend items based upon matching their attributes to the user profile.

Context-based recommender systems

Given the vast amount of information available on the web, the identification of useful information is a difficult task; to overcome this problem context-based information is used to extract features to improve search precision (Monteiro et al., 2015). Some areas of application, such as music, have explored the use of context-aware recommender systems that use contextual information such as weather, location, or time as additional input to assist in finding music relevant to the listener (Beach et al., 2010; Ricci, 2012; Wang et al., 2013). Panniello, Tuzhilin and Gorgoglione (2014) describe three steps in context-based recommendation:

1 pre-filtering: the set of items is filtered using the contextual information
   before reaching a more traditional model

2 post-filtering: output from a more traditional model is filtered based on the context before reaching the user

3 contextual modelling: the model itself uses the contextual information together with user and item data to generate recommendations.

Dynamic contextual factors change over time and are thus unstable, while static contextual factors do not change over time and remain stable (Jain and Jain, 2016). There are two kinds of context-based recommender systems: rating-based and content-based. In rating-based systems, user profiles are constructed based on items users have preferred in the past. In content-based systems, items liked by users are used as the preferred model (Jones and Pu, 2007).

Hybrid recommender systems

Hybrid systems perform the recommendation process with the help of two or more recommendation techniques to achieve better results (Abdollahpouri, Rahmani and Abdollahpouri, 2013). Hybrid recommendation systems are neither purely content-based, nor purely collaborative; instead these models seek to harness the advantages associated with each type, while also compensate for their weaknesses (Grivolla et al., 2014; Stomberg, 2014). Several researchers have attempted to combine collaborative filtering and content-based approaches in order to compensate for their respective disadvantages and gain better performance in providing recommendations. Depending on domain and data characteristics, several hybridisation techniques are possible to combine collaborative filtering and context based techniques (Sharma and Gera, 2013). Burke (2002a) devised seven hybridisation methods:

1 Weighted scores (or votes) of several recommendation techniques are combined to produce a single recommendation.

2 Switching the system between recommendation techniques depending on the current situation.

3 Mixed recommendations from several different recommenders are presented at the same time.

4 Features from different recommendation data sources are thrown together into a single recommendation algorithm.

5 Cascading one recommender refines the recommendations given by another.

6 Output from one technique is used as an input feature to another.

7 Meta-level, where the model learned by one recommender is used as input to another.

Demographic recommender systems

A demographic recommender system provides a categorisation of users based on their attributes, such as age, income level and education and makes recommendations based on the specific characteristics of demographic classes. The demographic approach does not use a user–item ratings matrix and the users get recommendations before they have rated any items, because the technique is domain-independent (Bermeo Quezada, 2015; Pazzani, 1999; Porcel, Moreno and Herrera-Viedma, 2009). Demographic filtering assumes that users with similar demographic attributes will rate items similarly (Safoury and Salah, 2013). Demographic recommender systems use prior knowledge of demographic information about the users and their opinions for the recommended items as the basis for recommendations (Prasad and Kumari, 2012). Demographic systems rely on stereotypes, because they depend on the assumption that all users belonging to a certain demographic group have similar tastes or preferences.

Knowledge-based recommender systems

Knowledge-based recommender systems compute their recommendations using case-based reasoning processes: the users provide an example similar to their aims and the system infers a profile in order to find the better matched product in the search space (Burke, 2002b). Knowledge-based systems filter and recommend items by computing the similarity among the descriptions of the items and the user profile inferred from the examples provided by the user according to their needs (Martinez et al., 2008).

> Knowledge-based recommenders do not attempt to build long-term generalizations about their users, but rather base their advice on an evaluation of the match between a user's need and the set of options available.
>
> (Burke, 2002b, 339)

Challenges of recommender systems

Sarwar et al. (2000) identified three key challenges for recommender systems: producing high-quality recommendations; performing many recommendations per second for millions of customers and products; and achieving high coverage in the face of data sparsity. Almazro et al. (2010) suggested that the key challenges to recommender systems are producing accurate recommendations, handling many recommendations efficiently and coping with the vast growth of number of participants in the system. Özgöbek, Gulla and Erdur (2014) highlighted further challenges, such as data sparsity, changing interests of users, unstructured content and accurate user profiling.

Social tagging recommender systems

Tags are created both by the authors of the tagged content and by people who reuse that content. Tags are used by people who read social media content and by machines that process it through search engines (Berendt and Hanser, 2007). Tagging is regarded as a 'sign that conveys human and machine meanings in the online communication process' (Huang and Chuang, 2009, 15). Tagging allows users to gain the benefits from effective sharing and simultaneously can organise very large amounts of information (Allam et al. 2012, 112; Golder and Huberman, 2006).

Traditional recommender systems and social tagging recommender systems follow the same pattern and principles, but both have their own attributes. Traditional recommender systems focus on the users' explicit rating data, while social tagging data has its own special characteristics and is completely different from rating data. Unlike rating data, tagging data does not contain users' explicit preference for information resources. Tagging data involves the user, the tag and the resource, while rating data only contains users and resources (Guan et al. 2010). In traditional recommender systems, the user is usually concerned only with rating resource recommendations, but in social tagging recommender systems users are interested in finding resources and tags, or even other users (Marinho et al., 2011, 620). Traditional recommender systems usually only recommend items that the user has not used, but social tagging recommender systems recommend tags that the user has already used for other resources.

Goals of social tagging recommender systems

Nunes and Marinho (2014) suggested that the goal of social tagging recommender systems is to generate personalised tag recommendations for a given target user. Social tagging recommender systems suggest tags to users that they can use to annotate sources; as such, these systems can help increase the chances of getting a resource annotated. Further, the recommender system can help consolidate tagging vocabulary across different users (Marinho et al., 2011). Recommender systems can help users to annotate their content in order to manage and retrieve their own resources and to make those resources more visible to other users by recommending tags that facilitate browsing and search (Krestel, Fankhauser and Nejdl, 2009).

Collaborative filtering social tagging recommender systems

The recommendation process is performed in three steps: first, the tool finds similar posts and extracts their tags. All the tags are then merged, building a general folksonomy that is filtered and re-ranked. The top-ranked tags are suggested to the user, who selects the most appropriate ones to attach to the post (Musto et al., 2009a). Peng et al. (2010) found that collaborative filtering is the most widely used and commercially successful approach to social tagging recommendation. Various methods have been used in collaborative filtering systems. Zhao et al. (2008) computed the similarity of two users based on the semantic distance of their tag sets on common items they had bookmarked. Tso-Sutter, Marinho and Schmidt-Thieme (2008) extended the item vectors for user profiles and user vectors for item profiles with tags and then constructed the user/item neighbourhoods based on the extended user/item profiles. Dattolo, Ferrara and Tasso (2010) suggested that tag-aware collaborative recommender systems can be applied in collaborative filtering techniques using tags to model user interests and suggested that these systems are based on the idea that users with similar interests have a similar tagging history. Dattolo, Ferrara and Tasso (2009) proposed a mechanism, called 'social ranking', which analyses the tagging similarity among users in order to produce a personalised ranking for the available resources.

Content-based social tagging recommender systems

Content-based social tagging recommender systems provide users with a list of recommended items matching their content-based profile. Content-based recommender systems analyse the user's past activities, looking for resources they have tagged (Pazzani and Billsus, 2007). The user profile is then defined describing what features are interesting for the user. Tag clustering is the primary method used in content-based systems. Tags with similar meanings are grouped into clusters: each tag is described as a vector, which counts how many times a tag is applied on each resource. The cosine similarity over two vectors defines the similarity between two tags (De Gemmis, 2008; Shepitsen et. al., 2008).

Tag-based contextual collaborative filtering

Tag-based contextual collaborative filtering (TCCF) is the combination of traditional collaborative filtering systems and social tagging systems to allow for accurate resource recommendation that takes into consideration the context of the preference (Nakamoto et al., 2007). The TCCF model adopts the following process:

1 The user evaluates a resource such as a website.
2 If the user likes a resource, they bookmark it with whatever tags are appropriate. These tags explain what the resource meant to them. These bookmarks are for later retrieval.
3 The system calculates user similarity to other users based upon their common bookmarks and tags.
4 The system then calculates the predicted scores for yet unrated resources based upon the user similarities calculated in the step before and also other users' bookmarks.
5 The system recommends new resources to the user based upon steps 3 and 4.

Personalised and not personalised tag recommender systems

Personalised tag recommender systems evaluate the tag relevance of a specific user behaviour or preferences and suggest relevant tags to the users. The systems' content-based strategies analyse the relationship between the content of a resource and the tags applied by the active user in order to predict tags for new resources (Basile et al., 2007; Musto et al., 2009b).

Not personalised tag recommender systems do not follow the conventional methods of recommender systems because these have nothing to do with users or user profiles. Suggestions are received on the basis of contents and resources used by the whole community; in other words, these systems function as public recommender systems (Baruzzo et al., 2009; Brooks and Montanez, 2006; Pudota et al., 2010).

Multimode social tagging recommender systems

Marinho et al. (2011) proposed three dimensions of tagging systems that allow for multimode recommendations; for example, finding adequate resources, tags, or users. They pointed out that recommender methods in tagging systems need to deal with common problems such as the cold start problem, where it is difficult to propose items to new users due to the sparsity of the data, or the ability to produce real-time recommendations. Liang et al. (2009) proposed collaborative filtering of items by extending the standard user–item matrix to the user–item–tag matrix. Vigneshwari and Aramudhan (2015) proposed social information retrieval based on semantic annotation and ontologies, where information is extracted from ontologies.

Challenges of social tagging recommender systems

Marinho et al. (2011) highlight a number of challenges for social tagging recommender systems. The tags should describe accurately the annotated resource. The suggested resources should be interesting and relevant. The suggestions should be traceable, such that users can easily understand why items were suggested. Data sparsity and cold-start recommendations are two major problems associated with social recommender systems. Cold start occurs when the system handles new users and new items and does not yet know the users' interests and preferences. The growth of data volume can make it difficult for social tagging recommender systems to handle the volume and complexity of the new information. The volatility of user preferences can affect the quality of the tag recommendations. Because every recommender system works differently on different datasets and uses different data-processing metrics, results are not reproducible. Further, users' information behaviour may change in accordance to the situation, which makes it difficult for the recommender systems to incorporate context information frequently (Eirinaki et al., 2018; Frolov and Oseledets, 2017).

Use and effectiveness of social tagging recommender systems

Social tagging recommender systems are a powerful mechanism that controls and maintains a correlation among users, tags and items. Each component plays an important role in making social tagging recommender systems useful and effective. Recommending tags increases 'the chances of getting a resource annotated, reminding a user what a resource is about and consolidating the vocabulary across the users' (Marinho et al., 2011, 621). Recommender systems should suggest to the user not only content, but also tags for labelling a resource. Recommenders promote a common vocabulary among users by encouraging them to use one or more suggested tags, rather than to create their own. Recommenders can reduce problems connected to the absence of both guidelines and supervised methodologies from the tagging process (Dattolo, Ferrara and Tasso, 2010; Jäschke et al., 2007). Accuracy plays an important role in finding appropriate recommendations in any system: 'the system's own confidence in its recommendations is related to accuracy and can be reflected in effectiveness' (Tintarev and Masthoff, 2011, 493). The learning rate of user preferences is also very important and the systems should respond to the changes in these preferences.

Swearingen and Sinha (2001) suggested that, from a user's perspective, an effective recommender system must inspire trust in the system; it must have a system logic that is at least somewhat transparent; it should point users towards new, not-yet-experienced items; it should provide details about recommended items, including pictures and community ratings; and finally, it should present ways to refine recommendations.

Shani and Gunawardana (2011) specified a set of important properties for recommender systems: user preference, prediction, accuracy, coverage, confidence, trust, novelty, serendipity, diversity, utility, risk, robustness, privacy, adaptivity and scalability. Caraciolo (2011) proposed two metrics for determining the usefulness and effectiveness of social tagging recommenders: precision and recall. Recall refers to the proportion of relevant results retrieved from the total corpus of relevant items, while precision refers to the number of relevant items from the results retrieved. Both the metrics have to be tested with the help of F-Score or F-measure; if the value of F-score is 1 it means the recommender system is giving its best performance, and if the value of F-score is 0, it would be considered as its worst performance.

Based on a comprehensive analysis of social tagging recommender systems, Singh (2017) outlines the following factors that impact the effectiveness of these systems:

- The system supports users to make better decisions.
- The system increases the chances of a resource being annotated.
- The system should allow users to categorise their tags differently.
- The system should recommend relevant descriptive terms.
- The system should consider the following properties: user preference, prediction, coverage, confidence, trust, novelty, serendipity, diversity, utility, risk, robustness, privacy, adaptivity and scalability.
- The system effectiveness should be measured against precision and recall algorithms.
- The system should perform real-time recommendations.
- The system should allow users to interact with it.
- The system should use a variety of techniques to offer valuable recommendations.
- The system must build trust.
- The system should work in the same manner regardless of the number of users.

Conclusion

Social applications such as Twitter and Instagram continue to grow in popularity and with them so does the number of information resources available for discovery. Social tagging recommender systems are a valuable tool for helping users successfully label resources for the purpose of sharing them with others and future retrieval. These systems can help reduce the 'noise' of irrelevant results while more content is available online. Further, recommender systems can help generate consistency in how people tag similar resources and reduce the cognitive load of tagging. Users are interested in finding not only content, but also tags and even users with similar interests. This chapter has reviewed the main types of social tagging recommender systems, as well as criteria by which their effectiveness can be measured. Future research could deal with incorporating social tagging recommender systems in the semantic web, as well as real-time dynamic social recommender systems.

References

Abdollahpouri, H., Rahmani, A. and Abdollahpouri, A. (2013) Is Always a Hybrid Recommender System Preferable to Single Techniques? *International Journal of Computer Applications*, **82**, 1–7.

Adomavicius, G. and Tuzhilin, A. (2005) Toward the Next Generation of Recommender Systems: a survey of the state-of-the-art and possible extensions, *IEEE Transactions on Knowledge and Data Engineering*, **17**, 734–49.

Allam, H., Blustein, J., Bliemel, M. and Spiteri, L. (2012) Exploring Factors Impacting Users' Attitude and Intention Towards Social Tagging Systems. In *System Science (HICSS), 2012 45th Hawaii International Conference on System Sciences*, IEEE, 3129–38.

Almazro, D., Shahatah, G., Albdulkarim, L., Kherees, M., Martinez, R. and Nzoukou, W. (2010) A survey paper on recommender systems, https://arxiv.org/abs/1006.5278

Balachandran, A., Dinesh, R., Iyyasamy, N. and Sugumaran, V. (2017) Location and Preference Based Recommendation System Using Social Network, *International Journal on Recent and Innovation Trends in Computing and Communication*, **5**, 80–3.

Baruzzo, A., Dattolo, A., Pudota, N. and Tasso, C. (2009) Recommending New Tags Using Domain-Ontologies. In *Proceedings of the 2009 IEEE/WIC/ACM International Joint Conference on Web Intelligence and Intelligent Agent Technology*, IEEE Computer Society, 409–12.

Basile, P., Gendarmi, D., Lanubile, F. and Semeraro, G. (2007) Recommending Smart Tags in a Social Bookmarking System, *Bridging the Gap between Semantic Web and Web 2.0*, **2**, 22–9.

Beach, A., Gartrell, M., Xing, X., Han, R., Lv, Q., Mishra, S. and Seada, K. (2010) Fusing Mobile, Sensor and Social Data to Fully Enable Context-Aware Computing. In *Proceedings of the Eleventh Workshop on Mobile Computing Systems and Applications*, ACM, 60–5.

Berendt, B. and Hanser, C. (2007) Tags are not Metadata, but 'Just More Content' – to Some People. In *International Conference on Weblogs and Social Media, Boulder, Colorado, March 26–27, 2007*, www.icwsm.org/papers/paper12.html.

Bermeo Quezada, F. E. (2015) *A Comparative Study of Recommender Algorithms for a Gastronomic Social Network*, Universidad Politécnica de Cataluña.

Bobadilla, J., Ortega, F., Hernando, A. and Gutiérrez, A. (2013) Recommender Systems Survey, *Knowledge-Based Systems*, **46**, 109–32.

Brooks, C. H. and Montanez, N. (2006) Improved Annotation of the Blogosphere via Autotagging and Hierarchical Clustering. In *Proceedings of the 15th international Conference on World Wide Web*, ACM, 625–32.

Burke, R. (2002a) Hybrid Recommender Systems: survey and experiments, *User Modeling and User-Adapted Interaction*, **12**, 331–70.

Burke, R. (2002b) Knowledge-Based Recommender Systems. In Kent, A. (ed.) *Encyclopedia of Library and Information Science*, Marcel Dekker, 180–200.

Caraciolo, M. (2011) Evaluating Recommender Systems – Explaining F-Score, Recall and Precision using Real Data Set from Apontador, http://aimotion.blogspot.in/2011/05/evaluating-recommender-systems.html.

Chen, L. S., Hsu, F. H., Chen, M. C. and Hsu, Y. C. (2008) Developing Recommender Systems with the Consideration of Product Profitability for Sellers, *Information Sciences*, **178**, 1032–48.

Choi, K., Yoo, D., Kim, G. and Suh, Y. (2012) A Hybrid Online-Product Recommendation System: combining implicit rating-based collaborative filtering and sequential pattern analysis, *Electronic Commerce Research and Applications*, **11**, 309–17.

Dattolo, A., Ferrara, F. and Tasso, C. (2009) Neighbor Selection and Recommendations in Social Bookmarking Tools. In *Ninth International Conference on Intelligent Systems Design and Applications, 2009*, IEEE, 267–72.

Dattolo, A., Ferrara, F. and Tasso, C. (2010) The Role of Tags for Recommendation: a survey. In *3rd Conference on Human System Interactions (HSI), 2010*, IEEE, 548–55.

De Gemmis, M., Lops, P., Semeraro, G. and Basile, P. (2008, October). Integrating tags in a semantic content-based recommender. In *Proceedings of the 2008 ACM Conference on Recommender Systems, Lausanne, Switzerland, ACM*, 163-170.

Drachsler, H., Hummel, H. G. and Koper, R. (2008) Personal Recommender Systems for Learners in Lifelong Learning Networks: the requirements, techniques and model, *International Journal of Learning Technology*, **3**, 404–23.

Eirinaki, M., Gao, J., Varlamis, I. and Tserpes, K. (2018) Recommender Systems for Large-Scale Social Networks: a review of challenges and solutions, *Future Generation Computer Systems*, **78**, 413–18.

Ekstrand, M. D., Ludwig, M., Konstan, J. A. and Riedl, J. T. (2011). Rethinking the Recommender Research Ecosystem: reproducibility, openness and lenskit. In *Proceedings of the Fifth ACM Conference on Recommender Systems*, ACM, 133–140.

Fard, K. B., Nilashi, M. and Salim, N. (2013) Recommender System Based on Semantic Similarity, *International Journal of Electrical and Computer Engineering*, **3**, 751–61.

Frias-Martinez, E., Magoulas, G., Chen, S. and Macredie, R. (2006) Automated User Modeling for Personalized Digital Libraries, *International Journal of Information Management*, **26**, 234–48.

Frolov, E. and Oseledets, I. (2017) Tensor Methods and Recommender Systems, *WIREs: Data Mining and Knowledge Discovery*, **7**, https://onlinelibrary.wiley.com/doi/abs/10.1002/widm.1201.

Goldberg, D., Nichols, D., Oki, B. M. and Terry, D. (1992) Using Collaborative Filtering to Weave an Information Tapestry, *Communications of the ACM*, **35**, 61–70.

Goldberg, K., Roeder, T., Gupta, D. and Perkins, C. (2001) Eigentaste: a constant time collaborative filtering algorithm, *Information Retrieval*, **4**, 133–51.

Golder, S. A. and Huberman, B. A. (2006) Usage Patterns of Collaborative Tagging Systems, *Journal of Information Science*, **32**, 198–208.

Grivolla, J., Badia, T., Campo, D., Sonsona, M. and Pulido, J. M. (2014) A Hybrid Recommender Combining User, Item and Interaction Data. In *2014 International Conference on Computational Science and Computational Intelligence (CSCI)*, IEEE, 297–301.

Guan, Z., Wang, C., Bu, J., Chen, C., Yang, K., Cai, D. and He, X. (2010) Document Recommendation in Social Tagging Services. In *Proceedings of the 19th International Conference on the World Wide Web (WWW 2010), Raleigh, North Carolina, USA*, ACM, 391-400.

Herlocker, J. L. and Konstan. J. A. (2001) Content-Independent Task-Focused Recommendation, *IEEE Internet Computing*, **5**, 40 7.

Hill, W., Stead, L., Rosenstein, M. and Furnas, G. (1995) Recommending and Evaluating Choices in a Virtual Community of Use. In *Proceedings of the SIGCHI Conference on Human Factors in Computing Systems*, ACM Press, 194–201.

Huang, A. W. C. and Chuang, T. R. (2009) Social Tagging, Online Communication and Peircean Semiotics: a conceptual framework, *Journal of Information Science*, **35**, 340–57.

Isinkaye, F. O., Folajimi, Y. O. and Ojokoh, B. A. (2015) Recommendation Systems: principles, methods and evaluation, *Egyptian Informatics Journal*, **16**, 261–73.

Jain, A. and Jain, V. (2016) A Literature Survey on Recommendation System Based on Sentimental Analysis, *Advanced Computational Intelligence: an international journal*, **3**, 25–36.

Jäschke, R., Marinho, L., Hotho, A., Schmidt-Thieme, L. and Stumme, G. (2007) Tag Recommendations in Folksonomies, *Knowledge Discovery in Databases: lecture notes in computer science,* **4702**, 506–514.

Jones, N. and Pu, P. (2007) User Technology Adoption Issues in Recommender Systems. In *Proceedings of the 2007 Networking and Electronic Commerce Research Conference*, ACM, 379–394.

Khurana, P. and Parveen, S. (2016). Approaches of Recommender System: a survey, *International Journal of Computer Trends and Technology,* **34**, 134–8.

Kim, J. K., Kim, H. K., Oh, H. Y. and Ryu, Y. U. (2010) A Group Recommendation System for Online Communities, *International Journal of Information Management,* **30**, 212–19.

Kordík, P. (2016) *Recommender Systems Explained*, https://medium.com/recombee-blog/recommender-systems-explained-d98e8221f468.

Krestel, R., Fankhauser, P. and Nejdl, W. (2009) Latent Dirichlet Allocation for Tag Recommendation. In *Proceedings of the Third ACM Conference on Recommender Systems*, ACM, 61–8.

Lee, S. K., Cho, Y. H. and Kim, S. H. (2010) Collaborative Filtering with Ordinal Scale-based Implicit Ratings for Mobile Music Recommendations, *Information Sciences*, **180**, 2142–55.

Li, L. H., Hsu, R. W. and Lee, F. M. (2012) *Review of Recommender Systems and their Applications*, https://pdfs.semanticscholar.org/5f4d/c82c24ad41e4d246a91bacbeeb38cf70ee50.pdf.

Liang, H., Xu, Y., Li, Y., Nayak, R. and Weng, L. T. (2009) Personalized Recommender Systems Integrating Social Tags and Item Taxonomy. In *Proceedings of the 2009 IEEE/WIC/ACM International Joint Conference on Web Intelligence and Intelligent Agent Technology*, IEEE Computer Society, 540–7.

Lu, J., Wu, D., Mao, M., Wang, W. and Zhang, G. (2015) Recommender System Application Developments: a survey, *Decision Support Systems*, **74**, 12–32.

Marinho, L. B., Nanopoulos, A., Schmidt-Thieme, L., Jäschke, R., Hotho, A., Stumme, G. and Symeonidis, P. (2011) Social Tagging Recommender Systems. In Ricci F., Rokach L., Shapira B., Kantor, P. (eds), *Recommender Systems Handbook*, Springer, 615–44.

Martinez, L., Barranco, M. J., Pérez, L. G. and Espinilla, M. (2008) A Knowledge

Based Recommender System with Multigranular Linguistic Information, *International Journal of Computational Intelligence Systems*, **1**, 225–36.

Miller, B. N., Konstan, J. A. and Riedl, J. (2004) PocketLens: toward a personal recommender system, *ACM Transactions on Information Systems*, **22**, 437–76.

Monteiro, E. J. M., Valente, F., Costa, C. and Oliveira, J. L. (2015) A Recommender System for Medical Imaging Diagnostic, *Studies in Health Technology and Informatics*, **210**, 461–3.

Musto, C., Narducci, F., De Gemmis, M., Lops, P. and Semeraro, G. (2009a) *A Tag Recommender System Exploiting User and Community Behavior*, https://pdfs.semanticscholar.org/7be3/e168e131ab0d44ebc4b5e30223e5b8c37ab0.pdf.

Musto, C., Narducci, F., De Gemmis, M., Lops, P. and Semeraro, G. (2009b) STaR: a social tag recommender system. In *Proceedings of ECML/PKDD 2009 Discovery Challenge Workshop*, ECML, 215–27.

Nakamoto, R., Nakajima, S., Miyazaki, J. and Uemura, S. (2007) Tag-Based Contextual Collaborative Filtering, *IAENG International Journal of Computer Science*, **34**, 1–6.

Nunes, I. and Marinho, L. (2014) A Personalized Geographic-Based Diffusion Model for Location Recommendations in LBSN. In *9th Latin American Web Congress (LA-WEB)*, IEEE, 59–67.

Núñez-Valdéz, E. R., Lovelle, J. M. C., Martínez, O. S., García-Díaz, V., De Pablos, P. O. and Marín, C. E. M. (2012) Implicit Feedback Techniques on Recommender Systems Applied to Electronic Books, *Computers in Human Behavior*, **28**, 1186–93.

O'Connor, M., Cosley, D., Konstan, J. A. and Riedl, J. (2001) PolyLens: a recommender system for groups of users. In *Proceedings of the Seventh European Conference on Computer-Supported Collaborative Work (ECSCW 2001), Bonn, Germany*, Springer, 199-218.

Özgöbek, Ö., Gulla, J.A. and Erdur, R. C. (2014) A Survey on Challenges and Methods in News Recommendation, *WEBIST*, **2**, 278–85.

Panniello, U., Tuzhilin, A. and Gorgoglione, M. (2014) Comparing context-aware recommender systems in terms of accuracy and diversity. *User Modeling and User-Adapted Interaction*, **24**, 35-65.

Park, D. H., Kim, H. K., Choi, I. Y. and Kim, J. K. (2012) A Literature Review and Classification of Recommender Systems Research, *Expert Systems with Applications*, **39**, 10059–72.

Pazzani, M. J. (1999) A Framework for Collaborative, Content-Based and Demographic Filtering, *Artificial Intelligence Review*, **13**, 393–408.

Pazzani, M. J. and Billsus, D. (2007) Content-Based Recommendation Systems. In Brusilovski, P., Kobsa, A. and Nejdl, W. (eds), *The Adaptive Web: methods and strategies of web personalization,* Springer, 325–41.

Peng, J., Zeng, D. D., Zhao, H. and Wang, F. Y. (2010) Collaborative Filtering in Social Tagging Systems Based on Joint Item-Tag Recommendations. In *Proceedings of the 19th ACM International Conference on Information and Knowledge Management,* ACM, 809–18.

Porcel, C., Moreno, J. M. and Herrera-Viedma, E. (2009) A Multi-Disciplinary Recommender System to Advise Research Resources in University Digital Libraries, *Expert Systems with Applications,* **36,** 12520–28.

Prasad, R. V. V. S. V. and Kumari, V. V. (2012) A Categorical Review of Recommender Systems, *International Journal of Distributed and Parallel Systems,* **3,** 1–11.

Pudota, N., Dattolo, A., Baruzzo, A., Ferrara, F. and Tasso, C. (2010) Automatic Keyphrase Extraction and Ontology Mining for Content-based Tag Recommendation, *International Journal of Intelligent Systems,* **25,** 1158–86.

Resnick, P. and Varian, H. R. (1997) Recommender System, *Communications of the ACM,* **40,** 56–8.

Resnick, P., Iacovou, N., Suchak, M., Bergstrom, P. and Riedl, J. (1994) GroupLens: an open architecture for collaborative filtering of netnews. In *Proceedings of the 1994 ACM Conference on Computer Supported Cooperative Work,* ACM, 175–86.

Ricci, F. (2012) Context-Aware Music Recommender Systems: workshop keynote abstract. In *Proceedings of the 21st International Conference on World Wide Web,* ACM, 865–6.

Ricci, F., Rokach, L. and Shapira, B. (eds) (2015) *Recommender Systems Handbook,* Springer.

Safoury, L. and Salah, A. (2013) Exploiting User Demographic Attributes for Solving Cold-start Problem in Recommender Systems, *Lecture Notes on Software Engineering,* **1,** 303–7.

Sarwar, B., Karypis, G., Konstan, J. and Riedl, J. (2000) *Application of Dimensionality Reduction in Recommender Systems – A Case Study,* Minnesota University.

Schafer, J. B., Frankowski, D., Herlocker, J. and Sen, S. (2007) Collaborative Filtering Recommender Systems. In Brusilovski, P., Kobsa, A. and Nejdl, W. (eds), *The Adaptive Web: methods and strategies of web personalization,* Springer, 291–324.

Schafer, J. B., Konstan, J. A. and Riedl, J. (2001) E-Commerce Recommendation Applications. In Kohavi, R. and Provost, F. (eds), *Applications of Data Mining to Electronic Commerce,* Springer, 115–53.

Shani, G. and Gunawardana, A. (2011) Evaluating Recommendation Systems. In Ricci, F., Rokach, L and Shapira, B. (eds), *Recommender Systems Handbook,* Springer, 257–97.

Shardanand, U. and Maes, P. (1995) Social Information Filtering: algorithms for automating 'word of mouth'. In *Proceedings of the SIGCHI Conference on Human Factors in Computing Systems*, ACM Press, 210–217.

Sharma, L. and Gera, A. (2013) A Survey of Recommendation Systems: research challenges, *International Journal of Engineering Trends and Technology*, **4**, 1989–92.

Sharma, R. and Singh, R. (2016) Evolution of Recommender Systems from Ancient Times to Modern Era: a survey, *Indian Journal of Science and Technology*, **9**, 1–12.

Shepitsen, A., Gemmell, J., Mobasher, B. and Burke, R. (2008). Personalized Recommendation in Social Tagging Systems Using Hierarchical Clustering. In *Proceedings of the 2008 ACM Conference on Recommender Systems,* ACM, 259–66.

Singh, R. (2017) A Survey on the Generation of Recommender Systems, *Information Engineering and Electronic Business*, **3**, 26–35.

Stomberg, J. C. (2014) *A Comparative Study and Evaluation of Collaborative Recommendation Systems*, Michigan Technological University.

Su, X. and Khoshgoftaar, T. M. (2009). A Survey of Collaborative Filtering Techniques, *Advances in Artificial Intelligence*, http://www.hindawi.com/journals/aai/2009/421425.

Sulieman, D. (2014). *Towards Social-Semantic Recommender Systems*, ETIS-CNRS-Université de Cergy-Pontoise.

Swearingen, K. and Sinha, R. (2001). Beyond Algorithms: an HCI perspective on recommender systems. In *ACM SIGIR 2001 Workshop on Recommender Systems*, ACM, 1–11.

Szlávik, Z., Kowalczyk, W. and Schut, M. C. (2011) Diversity Measurement of Recommender Systems under Different User Choice Models. In *ICWSM, Proceedings of the Fifth International AAAI Conference on Weblogs and Social Media*, AAAI Press, 369–76.

Tintarev, N. and Masthoff, J. (2011) Designing and Evaluating Explanations for Recommender Systems. In Ricci, F., Rokach, L and Shapira, B. (eds), *Recommender Systems Handbook*, Springer, 479–510.

Trant, J. (2009) Studying Social Tagging and Folksonomy: a review and framework, *Journal of Digital Information*, **10**, 1–44.

Tso-Sutter, K. H., Marinho, L. B. and Schmidt-Thieme, L. (2008) Tag-Aware Recommender Systems by Fusion of Collaborative Filtering Algorithms. In *Proceedings of the 2008 ACM Symposium on Applied Computing,* ACM, 1995–9.

Van Meteren, R. and Van Someren, M. (2000) Using Content-Based Filtering for Recommendation. In *Proceedings of the Machine Learning in the New Information Age: MLnet/ECML2000 workshop*, 47–56.

Vigneshwari, S. and Aramudhan, M. (2015) Social Information Retrieval Based on Semantic Annotation and Hashing upon the Multiple Ontologies, *Indian Journal of Science and Technology*, **8**, 103–7.

Wallace, M., Maglogiannis, I., Karpouzis, K., Kormentzas, G. and Kollias, S. (2003) Intelligent One-stop-shop Travel Recommendations Using an Adaptive Neural Network and Clustering of History, *Information Technology & Tourism*, **6**, 181–93.

Wang, M., Kawamura, T., Sei, Y., Nakagawa, H., Tahara, Y. and Ohsuga, A. (2013) Context-Aware Music Recommendation with Serendipity Using Semantic Relations. In *Joint International Semantic Technology Conference,* Springer, 17–32.

Wikipedia (2018) *Collaborative Filtering*, https://en.wikipedia.org/wiki/Collaborative_filtering.

Zhao, S., Du, N., Nauerz, A., Zhang, X., Yuan, Q. and Fu, R. (2008) Improved Recommendation Based on Collaborative Tagging Behaviors. In *Proceedings of the 13th International Conference on Intelligent User Interfaces,* ACM, 413–6.

Index